JOB INSECURITY AND LIFE COURSES

Sonia Bertolini, Valentina Goglio and
Dirk Hofäcker

BRISTOL
UNIVERSITY
PRESS

First published in Great Britain in 2024 by

Bristol University Press
University of Bristol
1–9 Old Park Hill
Bristol
BS2 8BB
UK
t: +44 (0)117 374 6645
e: bup-info@bristol.ac.uk

Details of international sales and distribution partners are available at bristoluniversitypress.co.uk

British Library Cataloguing in Publication Data
A catalogue record for this book is available from the British Library

ISBN 978-1-5292-0872-6 hardcover
ISBN 978-1-5292-0874-0 ePub
ISBN 978-1-5292-0873-3 ePdf

Cover design: Liam Roberts
Front cover image: devilmaya/Alamy Stock Photo
Bristol University Press uses environmentally responsible print partners.
Printed and bound in Great Britain by CPI Group (UK) Ltd, Croydon, CR0 4YY

FSC
www.fsc.org
MIX
Paper | Supporting
responsible forestry
FSC® C013604

Contents

List of Figures and Tables

Figures

Tables

Introduction

Job insecurity is the term used to describe a situation in which individuals feel themselves exposed to the risk of losing their job. It can, on the one hand, be associated with objective work conditions of greater exposure to such risk with respect to peers, for example because you have a fixed-term contract. On the other hand, it can come in the form of a feeling, a subjective perception of the individual about her/his job situation. In both cases, no matter whether objective or subjective, job insecurity influences individuals' present and future choices in life, slowing down or hampering some important transitions in the life course of individuals (such as employment entry, home-leaving or family formation). At the same time, it may influence individuals' future choices with respect to savings and retirement decisions. The relevance of studying the two dimensions of job insecurity is further supported by the fact that job security is one of the most valued features individuals rate in a job. As an example, the most recent wave of the International Social Survey Programme (ISSP) on Work Orientations show that 95 per cent of individuals in the 27 current countries of the European Union (EU27) consider security in a job to be important or very important, and the result is consistent across different age groups (ISSP, 2017).

For such reasons, this book addresses the issue of job insecurity from a holistic point of view, considering both the objective and subjective dimension and the whole life course of individuals. The interplay between the objective and subjective dimension has often been overlooked in sociology, with studies mainly focusing on one (for example, objective) or the other dimension (for example, subjective) or competing to demonstrate which of the two, objective or subjective, can have the largest influence (see Chapter 1 for a review). Analyzing the dichotomy between objective conditions and subjective perception is key to reaching an encompassing understanding of complex social phenomena that are particularly consequential for individuals' life courses, such as job insecurity (or as another example, income inequalities, Weisstanner and Armingeon, 2021). Moreover, so far most of the research has dealt with the issue of job insecurity and its consequences on the life course of individuals using quantitative methods (Blossfeld et al, 2005; Blossfeld and Hofmeister, 2006; Ebralidze, 2011; Unt et al 2021), while leaving room for further (qualitative) exploration about individuals' decision-making mechanisms and strategies of facing such types of insecurity.

Against this background, the aim of this book is to overcome an approach of simply contrasting the objective versus the subjective dimension in the phenomenon of job insecurity and to provide an encompassing analysis of determinants and associated consequences over the various life stages of individuals. This implies adopting a life-course perspective that takes into consideration the variation of both objective and subjective job insecurity at the stages of early career, mid-career employment and mature workers. Moreover, the approach taken here is based on a combination of quantitative and qualitative empirical material and methods of analysis to reach a profound and comprehensive understanding of the phenomenon.

Hence, this book intends to fill in some of the gaps left unexplored in previous research. In particular, it tries to answer the following research questions:

- How do objective and subjective job insecurity differ? To what degree do these assessments overlap? Are there inconsistencies between the two dimensions and, if so, who is affected by them?
- Since objective and subjective job insecurity are influenced by both micro and macro level factors, how does the relationship between micro variables (for example, age and gender) and macro level factors (for example, the welfare state model) unfold? And what is the relationship between objective and subjective job insecurity and macro level factors such as welfare states and labour markets?
- What are the consequence of both objective and subjective job insecurity on individuals and their life course? To what extent might the influence of job insecurity and its consequences vary across different life stages (for example, for early career, adult and older workers)?
- How do individuals cope with the different dimensions of job insecurity and how do they take decisions under such conditions of insecurity in various institutional contexts and at various stages of their life course? To what extent may the current conditions of job insecurity affect long-term decisions and opportunities, such as pensions and savings?

In order to reach such a comprehensive understanding of the phenomenon of job insecurity, the book pursues a mixed-method strategy which combines secondary quantitative data coming from both cross-sectional and longitudinal surveys (for example, EU-SILC, EQLS and OECD data) with primary qualitative data coming from semi-structured interviews and in-depth interviews. In such a complementary design, the combination of different types of data allows us to compensate for the strengths and weaknesses of each type of data and reach a more elaborated picture of the phenomenon under study (Small, 2011). Thanks to such an approach, the statistical regularities observed in the data help to reconstruct how job insecurity varies across the various welfare systems and micro level factors, while the qualitative material allows us to reconstruct the mechanisms and strategies of individuals who are making decisions in situations of insecurity. With respect to quantitative data, the book relies on a diverse set of institutional, individual, cross-sectional and longitudinal data. Indeed, institutional data from OECD are employed to depict the general picture and trends with respect to the dimension of objective job insecurity, while the subjective dimension of job insecurity is mainly explored based on the European Quality of Life Survey (EQLS), the key reference survey providing extensive and regular micro level data on that aspect, also allowing for a comparative design. Finally, micro level panel data from the European Union Statistics on Income and Living Conditions (EU-SILC) have been employed to investigate on a comparative level one of the key transitions to adulthood taken into consideration in our analysis, that is the process of young people gaining housing autonomy.

As mentioned, these quantitative sources leave unexplored the deep meanings attributed by young, adult and older workers to job insecurity, as well as their decision-making mechanisms to cope with insecurity, their attitudes and coping strategies. To reach an understanding of these spheres, the book relies on a set of 386 qualitative semi-structured interviews with young people in the age range 18 to 30 years old and residing in several European countries, representative of different welfare state models. The in-depth qualitative interviews investigate the relationship between job insecurity and the several domains of autonomy of young people, with a particular focus on the transition out of the parental home. Detailed information on the data and methods used in both the quantitative and the qualitative analyses is provided within each chapter.

The findings of the book provide an important contribution in terms of informed policy recommendations. Indeed, understanding what the mechanisms behind the perception of insecurity are helps us to understand why some policies, in particular some labour market policies, work and others do not. Moreover, the findings of the book provide new evidence on the role of policies currently enacted and recommendations for the design or reform of labour market policies, housing policies, and pension reforms.

In conclusion, addressing the theoretical and empirical dimensions, this book provides new knowledge about both objective and subjective job insecurity in Europe, and connects it with the life course of individuals and their major life-course transitions.

The book is structured in five chapters. Chapter 1 outlines the theoretical framework for the investigation of job insecurity in Europe and its consequences on the life course of individuals. The chapter refers to the seminal theoretical works and the most recent empirical investigations of the objective and subjective dimensions of job insecurity; it also considers how such phenomena may impact on some key transitions in the life course of individuals, such as gaining housing autonomy, and how a condition of job insecurity structures the decision-making processes of individuals.

The following chapters (2 to 5) are arranged in order to follow the different age stages of the life course of individuals, starting from early career workers to mid-career (Chapters 2 and 4) and older workers (Chapter 5), also considering an important life-course transitions, such as gaining housing autonomy (Chapter 3).

Chapter 2 focuses on the diffusion of both objective and subjective job insecurity across European countries for youth and young adults (18–34 years old). After a review of the status of objective and subjective job insecurity in various welfare state systems, the chapter investigates the interplay between the two dimensions of objective and subjective job insecurity, specifically exploring inconsistent profiles of individuals who are insecure in one dimension but not in the other one.

Chapter 3 focuses on the consequences of a situation of job insecurity with respect to important life course transitions and associated decision processes of individuals. By combining quantitative and qualitative data on early and mid-career workers, the chapter deepens the analysis on how individuals who experience job insecurity will transit to autonomous living from the family of origin, taking into consideration the different sets of constraints and opportunities offered by the different welfare state regimes.

Chapter 4 is devoted to the analysis of the diffusion of objective and subjective job insecurity among mid- career workers (25–50 years old) in Europe, and its determinants both at macro and micro level. The chapter also pays particular attention to the gender-specific unfolding of both dimensions in relation to the transitions that characterize the life course of women and men.

Chapter 5 focuses on the institutional and individual determinants of job insecurity among mature workers, in the age range of 50 to 64 years old. Beyond the investigation of trends in objective job insecurity among older workers and the factors which determine the subjective perception of job insecurity, this chapter also discusses how far perceived labour market insecurities impact on security prospects for older age, particularly for pension savings.

The Conclusion summarizes the main findings emerging from the analysis of such a complex and multifaceted phenomenon like job insecurity, disentangling the complexity of the relationship between the two dimensions.

Based on the qualitative and quantitative empirical material analyzed, it also includes policy recommendations that can help to more efficiently address the needs of individuals who are in different stages of their life course and therefore have different (even sometimes conflicting) interests and needs at stake.

Theoretical Background

Introduction

Various empirical studies over the past fifteen years have found a relationship between the spreading of objectively unstable work careers and different transitions into adult life. Comparative studies have shown that this effect varies between welfare state systems. A key issue to be explored and addressed in this book is how workers themselves perceive and experience instability, and how such subjective perceptions of instability interact with objective conditions, ultimately affecting individuals' representations of their economic and social situation. We argue that the subjective perception of job insecurity is very relevant, perhaps more than objective conditions, in defining the opportunities and constraints within which individuals make their work and private decisions.

The objective and subjective dimensions of job insecurity have been addressed in sociological literature by several theoretical and empirical studies, with particular attention to the variations associated with welfare regimes and labour market regulations, yet other micro level dimensions have received less attention or findings remain inconclusive. Moreover, while the effects of objective job insecurity on the transition to adult life have been extensively studied (Blossfeld et al, 2005; Blossfeld and Hofmeister, 2008; Bertolini, 2011; Ebralidze, 2011), mainly with quantitative methods, the decision-making mechanisms and strategies of young people and young adults for facing and making decisions in conditions of subjective insecurity have remained almost unexplored. Furthermore, comparatively little research has investigated how (objective and subjective) job insecurity impacts on later transitions in life, such as mid-career trajectories and transitions from work to retirement. This book aims to fill this evident gap in previous research.

The combination of quantitative and qualitative empirical data allows us to describe overall societal patterns and structures, together with a deeper comprehension of the decision-making mechanisms of individuals. Through a mixed-method approach, the book reconstructs how job insecurity varies within the different welfare systems on the one hand and, on the other hand, allows us to deepen the focus on the mechanisms and strategies implemented by individuals in situations of insecurity and in specific institutional settings (for example, under the threat of losing the job, or not being renewed in the same job, or not finding a new one in case of job loss, and so on).

Taking into account the interplay of macro and micro level factors in determining job insecurity is crucial if we are to increase the scientific understanding of such a multifaceted phenomenon. At the same time, from a policy perspective, understanding what the mechanisms behind the perception of insecurity are helps us to understand why some policies around the labour market work and others do not.

Authors like Beck (1992) have described modern society as 'risk society', in which insecurity becomes generalized across the entire population and where previously secure groups increasingly face, among others, increasing labour market risks. Other authors, in contrast (for example, Breen, 1997; Buchholz et al, 2009), have highlighted that insecurity and risks are disproportionately concentrated among specific – and in particular, weaker – labour market groups. This work aims to identify such weak groups – defined in relation to social inequality dimensions such as gender, education, and country – and describe their relative disadvantage and how it is differently declined in different institutional contexts. It asks:

- What are the social groups most exposed to the risk of job insecurity, depending on micro level characteristics?
- How does this risk vary according to the dimension of job insecurity considered (objective versus subjective insecurity, cognitive versus labour market insecurity, and so on)?
- How does this risk vary according to the institutional context in which it is included? Do institutional filters work for both the objective and subjective dimensions of job insecurity?

A second aim of this book is to investigate how and to what extent the risk of job insecurity differs across life-course phases, and affects young, mid-career and older workers in very different ways. Therefore, this work intends to expand the analysis of subjective insecurity beyond the 'traditional' focus on youth and to investigate how far it has also spread among later age groups, and what are the consequences that different generations may face.

In this respect, the research questions deal with:

- How does job insecurity affect individuals across their life course? Do different dimensions of job insecurity affect individuals in different life stages?

- To what extent do the consequences of exposure to the risk of job insecurity vary according to the life stage of individuals? How do the consequences of job insecurity vary for individuals in later life stages compared to individuals in the early life course?
- What role do the institutional contexts play in this respect?
- How do the coping strategies and decision-making mechanisms of individuals facing job insecurity vary between early and later stages of life course?

In this chapter, based on existing research, we will develop systematic hypotheses for the interplay between job insecurity and pivotal transitions in different phases of the individual life course. First, we focus on objective job insecurity, before turning to its subjective dimension. Finally, we explore on how job insecurity may impact on key life course transitions (for example, gaining housing autonomy). The hypotheses developed in this theoretical chapter will guide the empirical analyses in the subsequent chapters.

Objective job insecurity

As indicated, we will first outline the idea of objective insecurity. In doing so, we will primarily focus on individuals in a state of employment which may be considered as being uncertain. Other definitions of objective insecurity in employment are also conceivable, such as those generally excluded from employment (that is, the unemployed). From a financial or psychological perspective, the situation of these individuals may also be considered as being insecure. The focus in this book, however, rests mainly on the idea of insecurity *within* employment.

Defining objective job insecurity

The idea of insecure (or atypical) employment rests on the assumption that there is a generally secure (or typical) form of employment from which the former can be differentiated. In previous literature this kind of employment has often been described using the notion of the so called 'standard employment relationship' (see, for example, Mückenberger, 1985). This 'model' of secure employment rests on various pillars:

- First, it refers to individuals who are in a dependent contractual employment relationship with an employer; that is, their employment is regulated and secured in terms of labour law. By such regulations, employees are, for example, secured against changes in the terms of employment or unfair dismissal. Legal regulations often not only define the regulations of the employment contract itself, but also regulate specific benefits linked to employment, such as contributions to public or private insurance systems (for example, unemployment, disability or pension insurance). In this regard, they make sure that not only the employment relationship itself can be considered secure but that it also generates material security, both in present but also in future terms.

- Second, the idea behind such 'normal' employment relationships is that they are of a continuous nature. Employment contracts are not restricted to a specific pre-defined duration, but are in principle extended indefinitely, even though there are certain pre-defined options for both employers and employees to cancel the contract. At least in its initial formulation for the German labour market, standard employment relationships are also relationships with one and the same employer. Both parties, employers and employees, thus engage in a long-term bilateral relationship. This continuity is considered to be beneficial to both employers and employees. Employers can base their planning of production and personal placement, including the implementation of specific career trajectories, on such an idea of continuity. For the employee, continuous employment contracts allow for individual life planning based on foreseeable employment trajectories. Specific long-binding decisions, such as personal relationships or family formation and investment in private property or other kinds of assets are enabled by such predictable career procedures. The attractiveness of such contractual relationships may be enhanced by employer-provided benefits (for example, the provision of occupational pension schemes), a systematic pattern of promotions ('career ladders') or a standardized increase in wages or benefits depending on the tenure of an employee ('seniority wages').

- Third, the idea of a standard employment contract is often also linked to certain assumptions about working hours and wages. Normally, it is assumed that the notion of a standard employment relationship refers to full-time employment, that is, an employment of around 35–40 working hours. Standard employment relationships thus describe a 'main job' in which a sufficiently high investment is made and which generates a sufficient income for the job holder. Particularly in its classical formulation for the German labour market, standard employment contracts were considered to also generate family wages, that is a sufficient income for an entire household. As such, the standard employment contract was considered to be a main pillar of a traditional division of labour between the sexes, with men often predominantly engaged in paid employment and women often concentrating on family and household related tasks.

The idea of a standard employment relationship is often considered to refer to a specific period of time, particularly the 1960s and 1970s, that is, a period of constant economic growth and little unemployment.

Undoubtedly, such a model has increasingly become challenged in more recent decades when these conditions changed. Most prominently, the oil crises of the early and late 1970s ended a period of steady economic growth. Particularly in European countries, (long-term) unemployment became a relatively stable phenomenon that increasingly characterized national labour markets. European societies were increasingly considered to suffer from a so-called 'Eurosclerosis' (Giersch, 1985), that is, an inflexibility in labour market regulation and welfare state systems that created structural rigidities. Deregulation of labour markets was thought to be the solution to this problem that often became a heavy burden for European governments.

At the same time, an increasing degree of globalization affected national economies. Due to the rapid development of information and communication technologies, national product markets became increasingly connected, thereby facilitating market transactions on a global scale. This increasing interconnectedness enhanced not only the opportunity for cross-border trade, but also made national economies more vulnerable to economic shocks elsewhere in the world. Under these conditions, it became essential for firms to be able to react flexibly to increasingly volatile labour markets. Countries thus increasingly entered into a competition for the attractiveness of their economies, often resulting in a 'race-to-the bottom' with regard to labour market regulations and welfare state provisions. The result was an increasing spread of deregulation and liberalization of product and labour markets. (see, for example, Buchholz et al, 2009).

The described changes increasingly challenged the previously dominant standard employment relationships in multiple respects:

- First, there were changes in the nature of the contractual relationships in multiple respects. Comparative data on employment protection show that, for example, the degree of dismissal protection within European labour markets fell considerably in recent decades, thus enabling individual or collective dismissal under less restrictive conditions than before. This trend most strongly manifested in new employment relationships with previously non-employed labour market entrants, thereby introducing a generational difference in the affectedness by less protected labour contracts (OECD, 2020). In addition to the changes in bilateral employment relationships, there was also an increasing tendency to establish contracts not with individuals themselves but to involve temporary work agencies as intermediaries that could provide specifically qualified work staff on demand. While this generated increasing flexibility for production planning and staff placement on the employer's behalf, it often meant that individual workers' employment contracts became more insecure, given that their relationships with an employment agency were often less protected, of a non-permanent nature and less well paid.

In addition, employees often also had to relinquish additional employer-provided payment. The rise in temporary work and subcontracted labour thus became one form of increasingly flexibilized and more insecure working relationships.

- Another dimension of employment flexibilization relates to changes in the permanency of the employment relationship. While under the 'standard employment regime', employment relationships were of an indefinite nature, legal deregulation increasingly allowed for the flexible implementation of contracts of a limited duration. As previous employment protection often did not allow the introduction of such changes into already existing contracts, such fixed-term employment relationships were often predominantly given to young labour market entrants, who could not draw back to institutional support through collective actors (such as unions) and whose employment contracts thus could be more easily flexibilized (Blossfeld et al, 2005; Blossfeld, Hofäcker and Bertolini, 2011).

- Flexibilization of the standard employment contract also took place with regard to working time. Most prominently, the large-scale introduction of part-time working contracts also enabled firms to organize their labour more flexibly. In virtually all European countries, part-time work has become predominantly a female domain, particularly around family formation and (early) childhood years when women reduce their working time to reconcile work and family tasks, a pattern that is only rarely observed for men. When analyzing part-time work, it needs to be noted that the term encompasses a broad array of different working schedules. While international organisations such as the OECD (1997) define part-time work as work below 30 hours, national definitions often deviate from this pattern. If part-time employment includes rather high working hours (for example, around 30), it often resembles employment close to full-time work. Yet, particularly when it encompasses only low working hours and this yields only modest to low wages (marginal part-time work), it may be considered to resemble a rather uncertain work situation. An extreme case are so-called 'zero hour contracts' in which the employment contract defines a standard workload of zero working hours, but employees are expected to supply their work on demand. These types of contracts – comparable to that of temporary agency work, though on a bilateral basis – have become more widespread in recent years. The unpredictability of working hours and/or wages earned, in particular, means this work can be classified as a form of insecure and often precarious employment.

- A final form of insecurity within a work relationship may be related to the wages earned. Depending on the nation-specific labour market, tax and welfare policies, there usually is a 'natural' variation in wages earned, often dependent on an employees' educational attainment and qualification profile. However, beyond that, flexibilization and liberalization policies have also promoted the emergence of low-paid jobs or minor employment, in which wages by definition cannot exceed a predefined margin. A showcase example is the German model of so-called 'mini-jobs', in which employees can earn only a maximum of €450 per month, independent of the actual workload or respective working hours. Beyond the low level of remuneration, employees in such jobs are often also exempted from contributions to unemployment, health or care insurance (and in some cases even pension insurance). Insecurity in these jobs thus not only relates to immediate financial insecurity but may also bring about long-lasting insecurities related to insurance against basic risks in life.

In many cases, deviations from the safe, standard employment model coincide with higher levels of insecurity, at least in the short term. Previous research, however, has highlighted that 'atypical employment forms' may occasionally be ambivalent with regards to their outcomes. Fixed-term employment contracts may, for example, be detrimental, particularly when individuals remain within them or jump from one fixed-term contract to the other, and thus become 'trapped' in such employment forms. On the other hand, previous research has also highlighted that employers often use temporary employment as a kind of 'extended probation period' in which the employer can screen and evaluate prospective staff. From the individual perspective, fixed-term contracts thus may also constitute 'bridges' or 'stepping stones' into more permanent and secure forms of employment (see, for example, Scherer, 2004; Gash, 2008). Likewise, part-time employment may even be advantageous when it can be used as a temporary option to balance family and career-related tasks, particularly in early parenthood. However, it may equally turn into a form of permanent exclusion when individuals have to choose part-time work against their will, for example, when no adequate full-time jobs are available. Similarly, low paid mini-jobs may allow for life-course specific flexibility, for example when they are being used as 'top ups' to other types of employment or if they constitute an additional income through periods of qualification and training. Yet, they may be detrimental when they turn into a specific segment of employment in which individuals may become trapped.

Given this potential ambivalence, it is important to look at atypical employment forms in a differentiated way. First, it is important to look at such employment forms from a longitudinal perspective, that is, to investigate not only their immediate occurrence, but also their consequences in a trajectory-based pattern. When do such employment forms become traps and when do they enable workers to enter more secure employment?

And how far do these specific patterns differ between social groups? In the next section we look at variations of such atypical employment forms and their related consequences for individual employment insecurity, considering both individual as well as employer-based characteristics.

Second, it is important to embed these work forms in their specific national context with regard to their usage and treatment in social and labour law. In the section on variations between welfare state regimes, we relate the incidence and effects of insecure work to specific institutional constellations with regard to labour market and welfare policies, contrasting different 'employment regimes'.

Finally, and related to the former, it is important not only to investigate the objective dimension of job insecurity, but also to investigate how far atypical work forms are actually being perceived as being insecure by employees themselves. We shall turn to this investigation of subjective insecurity later in this chapter.

Variation of objective insecurity across life stages and micro level factors

Previous research has highlighted that how people are affected by insecure employment may significantly differ related to individual characteristics, that is, the properties of the respective employee him/herself. In the following, we give an overview of the factors most frequently discussed in the existing empirical literature.

One recurrent result has been the observation that affectedness by insecure employment differs significantly with regard to an individual's age and life stage.

Existing evidence concordantly supports the notion that young people in particular (aged up to their mid- or late twenties) have experienced a flexibilization of their employment relationships throughout recent decades (Blossfeld et al, 2005, Blossfeld, Hofäcker and Bertolini, 2011; Unt et al, 2021), but particularly after the EU financial crisis in 2008 (Rokicka et al, 2015; Karamessini et al, 2019a). Fixed-term employment contracts are disproportionately found among young people aged up to their mid-twenties, reaching values up to ten times that of mid-career or older workers (Hofäcker and Blossfeld, 2011; Rokicka et al, 2015). It is noteworthy that such early temporary employment is not detrimental at the individual level in all cases. Some young people still in education may, for example, use such types of jobs during vacations or as internships. At the same time, occupational training following a dual approach (combining school-based and in-firm training) is often based on temporary contracts and may act as a stepping stone for later obtaining a tenured job. However, in the majority, such jobs are involuntary, thus implying an at least transitory exclusion from secure, permanent employment.

For this reason, young people have often been termed as 'losers' of recent globalization and flexibilization processes (Blossfeld et al, 2005). There are multiple reasons for the concentration of flexible work on young people. Buchholz et al (2009: 57): have argued that young people do not yet have relevant connections to business networks or unions so that they lack the power to negotiate more stable relationships. Employers may therefore be able to flexibilize their working contracts. As an additional advantage, employers may use fixed-term employment to 'screen' younger workers with only limited wok experience before offering them more stable employment contracts.

In contrast to their younger counterparts, the employment of male workers in mid-career has been shown to be more stable. Employment contracts of these employees are usually better safeguarded by employment protection legislation, so that within this group of employees, standard employment relationships are still largely predominant (Blossfeld, Mills and Bernardi, 2006). Flexibilization of employment in this age group is still largely confined to the 'margins' of employment, that is, on low qualified workers in lower occupational classes (Buchholz et al, 2009: 58).

The employment situation appears to be markedly different for mid-career women. Even though women's employment has almost constantly risen in European societies, they still exhibit persistent labour market disadvantages in comparison to men. Beyond the widely debated 'gender wage gap', women are also more often found in insecure, atypical forms of employment. This holds particularly for part-time employment which represents a significant share of women's employment (30 per cent, Eurostat, 2020; see also Chapter 4), while it makes up only a marginal share among men (8 per cent, Eurostat, 2020). Often, mothers' employment hours are being significantly reduced throughout early motherhood when the youngest child is still at primary school; yet their hours often remain significantly lower than those of men thereafter (see Chapter 4). Even though gender differences are often not as pronounced, women are also found more often in temporary work (OECD, 2014). The overrepresentation of women in atypical forms of employment often not only increases financial and employment insecurity in the short run; as atypical forms of employment are often also connected to insufficient contributions into social security systems, they may even extend into later life phases, for example, when accrued pension contributions are too low to allow for a decent standard of living in old age, a phenomenon often referred to as the 'gender pension gap' (Betti et al, 2015).

While young employees and women are often particularly affected by less secure and flexible work forms, older workers traditionally have enjoyed higher stability and lower levels of insecurity in their careers. With regard to their employment relationship, they often enjoy comparatively strong levels of employment protection, given their longer tenure. In some countries, seniority wages that increase with firm tenure often also imply higher material security than that of younger employees. Nevertheless, labour market pressures through globalization and flexibilization have also affected older workers, whose safe employment relationships and high labour costs often stood in stark contrast to necessary flexibilization demands (Blossfeld, Buchholz and Hofäcker, 2006; Blossfeld, Buchholz and Kurz, 2011). In response to this apparent contradiction, many countries offered redundant older workers financially attractive opportunities for an early exit from employment (Ebbinghaus, 2006; Hofäcker, 2010). Flexibilization of older workers' employment thus initially meant the cessation of their employment relationship under socially acceptable conditions. With the rising awareness of demographic ageing and its expected implications for the capacity to finance pensions systems, however, such early retirement systems became increasingly unpopular: nowadays, many governments have shifted their policy focus to promoting longer working lives and employment up to or even beyond retirement age (Hofäcker, Hess and König, 2016). Such 'active ageing policies' were often coupled with reductions in (early) retirement benefits that made a premature exit from employment less attractive. Particularly for older workers at the margins of the labour market, the increased necessity to work longer has often also meant that they need to remain employed for financial reasons and are thus more likely to accept even atypical types of employment such as mini-jobs or temporary employment. A sizeable number of older employees also use part-time work schemes as 'bridges' out of employment into retirement (Doeringer 1990; Lippke, Strack and Staudinger Lippke, Strack and Sackreuther 2015).

The life phases described here represent one major individual dimension alongside which different degrees of objective employment security can be differentiated. Accordingly, the book is organized according to these life phases. Yet, previous research has also highlighted that there are numerous other micro level dimensions which mediate the degree to which individuals are being exposed to employment insecurity.

Most prominently, previous research has referred to the role of human capital resources in mediating objective employment insecurity. Educational attainment is one major individual characteristic that influences the exposure to employment insecurity. Following works by, for example, Buchholz et al (2009) or Breen (1997), it has been argued that it is particularly those with lower educational background and less transferrable and often manual qualifications, towards whom insecurities arising from globalization and flexibilization have been channelled. Similar claims may be made with regard to the occupational status. Empirical evidence shows that uncertain employment is mostly concentrated on lower qualified employees with simple (non-transferable) manual skills. In contrast, those with high educational attainment, and respectively more transferable occupational skills, are in a better position to negotiate better and more stable work contracts.

The previous discussion of employment flexibilization in mid-career already highlighted the significance of gender differences in the exposure to insecure employment in this phase of the life course. While mid-career men are more often found in rather stable full-time employment, flexible and more uncertain types of employment are often concentrated on women. As shown previously, this holds particularly for part-time work, which remains a strongly feminized work form. Yet, women are also more often found in other flexible work forms, such as fixed-term employment or marginal employment/mini-jobs. This unequal distribution of insecure work forms according to gender is often attributed to persistent gender norms and gender-specific labour market discrimination that assigns women the main responsibility for unpaid household and care tasks. In the absence of sufficient institutional support structures (for example, through work–family reconciliation policies, which we discuss later), this 'double burden' often leads to women reducing their work engagement and thus to being more likely to accept non-standard working contracts (see, for example, Blossfeld and Hofmeister, 2006).

In order to assess the importance of insecure work forms for an individual, it is important not only to consider the person him/herself, but also their embeddedness in a specific household context. This appears to be most obvious for single person households where there is no other household member that could compensate for, for example, limited tenure or lower earnings. Particularly when there are additional care responsibilities for minor children, as it is often the case for single parents, insecure employment may thus be connected with severe financial and/or material insecurity. In contrast, living with a partner in a joint household may provide the opportunity to balance out insecurity of employment for one partner with safe employment of the other. This is, for example, the case in many one-and-a-half earner households in which part-time employment of the (often female) spouse is compensated by full-time employment of the (often male) main earner. Yet, if both partners are affected by insecure employment, such compensation mechanisms cannot operate; in such households it can be assumed that employment insecurities accumulate and may even reinforce one another.

For similar reasons, it seems also important to consider wider family support, particularly for younger individuals. Not only the partner but also parents or the larger family can compensate for the financial risks arising from insecure employment. This may be the case through material support, for example, the provision of free housing or direct monetary transfers. Support can also be provided in the form of services, notably when parents take care of their grandchildren and thus preserve their working children from child-care related costs. While such 'intergenerational transfers' may often operate top-down, that is, from parents to children, they may also need to be considered in the opposite direction, for example, when children support parents in providing family-related care.

Variation across welfare state regimes
The idea of institutional filters

It is not only micro level factors that influence the likelihood of individuals being negatively affected by insecure employment forms. Previous research (for example, Blossfeld et al, 2005 has highlighted that, by setting the contextual political framework conditions, 'institutional filters' at the national level can mediate the ways in which employment insecurity occurs and how it impacts on individuals.

There are various institutions that may be important in this respect:

- For young people in particular, education systems and systems of vocational training shape the ways in which employees are able to enter into safe standard employment contracts. It has been shown that highly standardized education and training systems in which the degrees attained have a strong signalling function for employers (Allmendinger, 1989) are able to promote an entry into employment. This holds particularly for the so called 'dual systems' of countries like Germany, in which theoretical learning in centralized schools is combined with practical on-the-job training in firms (Blossfeld and Stockmannn, 1999). In such systems, a smooth entry of qualified young people from education to employment is being promoted. While uncertain employment may occur, it more often constitutes only a transitory phase of 'probation' before entering into more standard employment contracts. In contrast, in countries with less standardized education systems, signalling effects are clearly weaker and do not provide sufficient information about the qualifications and skills of young labour market entrants. Under these conditions, employers may be more inclined to offer less binding, flexible employment contracts. Such a hiring policy may become particularly detrimental to employees when they are not able to leave such work forms, but become permanently trapped within them. Notably, the overall design of education and training systems may not only be important for young people but also for their older counterparts. If education is generally restricted to early parts of the career and not refreshed thereafter, mid-career and particularly older workers skills and qualifications are more likely to be devalued in times of swift technological change, thus increasing their risk of marginalization in the labour market. In contrast, in systems relying more on a lifelong learning approach, in which further education and training is provided largely irrespective of age, such relative labour market disadvantages according to age will be less likely (Blossfeld, Buchholz and Hofäcker, 2006). The selectivity of uncertain employment according to individual characteristics may furthermore depend on the degree of stratification within educational systems, that is, the degree to which there is a hierarchical ordering in degrees and certificates obtained (Allmendinger, 1989). Educational systems that are highly stratified hierarchically are more likely to promote education-based social inequalities in uncertain employment, given that such employment is concentrated on those in lower skill levels while those at higher skill levels remain comparatively protected.

- Another institutional feature which may influence the incidence and social inequalities in uncertain employment is the degree of labour market regulation. Some countries, particularly those in Central and Southern Europe, are known to have highly regulated labour markets in which standard employment is highly protected through legal measures against individual or collective dismissal, and in which stricter restrictions apply with regard to the renewal of non-permanent contracts respecting their number of successive contracts with the same employer (OECD, 2020). Strong labour market regulation has been shown to promote ambiguous results: On the one hand, those in safe and permanent employment are strongly protected against undue job loss and enjoy high levels of labour market security. On the other hand, those in non-permanent employment often face higher unemployment risks, given the restrictions on non-permanent work. At the same time, employers often shy away from offering these employees a permanent contract, given the strong protection of such jobs. High labour market regulation thus frequently has promoted the emergence of a so-called 'insider-outsider' labour market (Lindbeck and Snower, 1988; Saint-Paul, 1996), where highly protected labour market insiders in secure employment stand face to face with highly flexibilized, uncertain labour market outsiders. In less regulated labour markets, most typically represented by the liberal countries of the Anglo-Saxon world, such insider-outsider structures hardly exist. Given low levels of protection against dismissal, even permanent employment contracts are objectively insecure given that they can be terminated at short notice. At the same time, however, there are also few entry barriers for finding new employment. In such 'hire-and-fire' labour markets, the high levels of objective insecurity are counterbalanced by high re-employment chances, thus restricting the degree to which objective insecurity may translate into subjective insecurity (this is discussed later in this chapter).

- Finally, the design of welfare state support policies may influence the objective risks associated with non-standard employment (Esping-Andersen 1990). Generous welfare state support as reflected, for example, in high overall replacement rates of public transfers (support in cash) may mediate the immediate material consequences on atypical employment, for example, by avoiding poverty and low-income situations. Mediating effects can also be assumed for public support in kind, for example, by providing cost-free or inexpensive public services such as family care which may help individuals with care responsibilities to avoid precarious marginal employment forms. The latter example already highlights the importance of work-family reconciliation policies in not only restricting the overall degree of (material) inequalities but also in reducing gender inequalities.

Institutional packages: education, labour market and welfare state structures

Institutional filters, however, do not exert their influence in an isolated way. Instead, the different filters just outlined may complement or even reinforce one another in nation-specific contexts. The influence of institutions thus needs to be considered following a logic of 'institutional packages' rather than that of single institutions. In the following, we will differentiate various types of such packages as reflected in the ideas of specific 'regimes' (Esping-Andersen, 1990; Buchholz et al, 2009).

Conservative countries

The group of so-called conservative regimes incorporates Central European countries such as Germany, France or the Netherlands. In most of these countries, job-relevant education takes place rather early in the life course, that is, within the school systems, at universities or in vocational training systems. Education throughout the life course is often of lesser importance, reflected in continued education and training rates significantly declining with age. Stratification in the educational system tends to be rather high. The organization of occupational training differs between the countries and is often based on a strong school-based component. The German-speaking countries (Austria, Germany and Switzerland) in particular combine this school-based component with practice-oriented training in firms; the so-called 'dual training' system.

Labour markets in conservative countries are rather regulated, with medium to high levels of dismissal protection. Such modes of employment regulation tend to constitute rather segmented labour markets, in which the employment insiders are comparatively well-protected against labour market risks and a flexibilization of their employment relationships. At the same time, there exists a group of labour market outsiders, found more often in atypical work forms, who face considerable difficulties entering the 'core labour market' with its predominantly 'normal' employment relationships.

Welfare state provisions in conservative countries tend to be rather generous in terms of replacement rates, meaning that, on average, individuals in these countries are often rather well-protected against basic life risks. However, these provisions are strongly linked to previous contributions, which are mostly generated through paid employment. Both the eligibility to welfare state benefits as well as the degree of benefit generosity thus appears to be unevenly distributed within these societies. By means of family policy, most conservative countries have long promoted a male breadwinner/female part-time earner model, fostering a rather traditional distribution of work between the sexes, with an increased focus on work-family reconciliation measures only in more recent years. France represents a notable exception to this pattern with a long tradition of well-developed early childcare provision.

What do these institutional patterns imply for objective employment insecurity in conservative countries? Persistent insider-outsider structures within the labour market have promoted the emergence of a flexibilized segment at the margins of the labour market (Buchholz, 2008). Previous research has shown that such 'selective flexibilization' has particularly affected young people whose employment contracts were disproportionately flexibilized, reflected in their above-average rates in fixed-term employment. At the same time, women – particularly in their family phase – had to reduce their working time due to lack of reconciliation support measures. Within both groups, it has been difficult – particularly for lower qualified employees – to escape their marginal and insecure labour market position. Particularly for this group, we can expect high levels of long-term employment insecurity. Older employees in conservative countries have long benefitted from high levels of job security embedded in their long-term contracts. However, their educational deficits (due to the lack of lifelong learning) have increased labour market pressures on them that were initially answered by sending lower skilled workers in particular into early retirement (Blossfeld, Buchholz and Hofäcker, 2006). However, the recent trend of 'active ageing' has increasingly closed this opportunity and increasingly expects these employees to prolong their work careers (Hofäcker, Hess and König, 2016). There are increasing signs that such continued employment is often involuntary and connected to unfavourable employment conditions (Hess, 2018; Hofäcker, Hess and König, 2019). Taken together, we can thus expect that levels of objective insecurity are moderately high in conservative countries, and particularly pronounced among younger and increasingly older employees, as well as for women.

Southern European countries

Southern European countries display several similarities to conservative countries with regard to their institutional patterns, but also notable differences. Educational systems in the South of Europe appear to be weakly stratified, and vocational differentiation is often less developed, implying an often less smooth and slower entry into the labour market (Reyneri, 2017; Bertolini, Hofäcker and Torrioni, 2018; Gangl, 2001). This situation is exacerbated by traditionally highly regulated labour markets with dismissal protection even surpassing that of conservative countries. As a consequence, employers often shy away from offering young people permanent contracts, so that both unemployment as well as flexible, unsafe employment – particularly fixed-term employment – are particularly widespread among youth (Klijzing, 2005). Such employment insecurity is often coupled with material insecurity given that access to social benefits in Southern European countries is linked to previous (full-time) employment, which effectively excludes many young people from social protection (Ferrera, 1996). Instead, the family often serves as a compensational provider of welfare through either housing or material support (Naldini, 2003). It is this particular combination of institutional features that have delayed individual autonomy for youth in many Southern European countries, reflected in late home-leaving and the postponement or even foregoing of family transitions (Bertolini et al, 2021). While employment risks disproportionately have been directed towards youth, the situation of older people in Southern Europe has remained comparatively protected. Due to age-specific clientelism (Ferrera, 1996), pension provisions for older people are relatively safeguarded and wage replacement rates are among the highest in Europe (OECD, 2021d: 145). Employment flexibilization in late career is a rather marginal phenomenon (Blossfeld, Buchholz and Hofäcker, 2006). In addition to these age-graded differences, there are also strong gender-based cleavages, given the traditionally strong reliance on a male breadwinner model and high levels of welfare state familialism. The lack of adequate family policy support for work-family reconciliation, as well as the low prevalence of part-time solutions, have often pushed women to decide between family and employment. Barbieri's description of Italy as 'no country for young men (and women)' (Barbieri, 2011) may thus serve as an adequate description for Southern Europe as a whole: objective employment insecurity is generally high and only weakly buffered through welfare transfers. This holds especially for young people and women who find it particularly hard to enter safe employment.

Liberal countries

Liberal countries, most typically represented by Anglo-Saxon countries such as the US or the UK, in many respects make up a polar opposite to conservative welfare states (see, for example, Buchholz et al, 2009). Education systems in these countries exhibit a high degree of stratification; yet, relevant qualifications are often not obtained in centralized educational institutions, but are acquired through job-specific training in firms. This predominance of 'on-the-job-training' promotes smooth entries into one firm's internal labour market and a frequent upgrading of skills to firm-related demands, but rather restricts mobility between different firms. The degree of employment protection in such countries is often minimal, leading to the frequent description of these countries as exhibiting 'hire-and-fire' labour markets in which the risk of job loss is high but where new jobs are also easier to access. Notably through these flexible labour markets, liberal countries have kept unemployment at a modest level. Atypical, flexible forms of work (such as fixed-term employment) are of relatively low importance, given the comparatively high flexibility of the labour market as such. The role of the welfare state in such countries is residual, often only guaranteeing security against basic life risks, while additional, status-maintaining security is dependent on additional investment into private insurance.

The overall level of insecurity in these countries thus is high, given that there are high levels of employment insecurity and only marginal welfare state protection. Unlike in conservative or Southern European countries, there are no particular age- or gender-specific cleavages in the exposure to objective employment risks. However, human capital – as reflected in educational attainment or occupational class – clearly structures the individual's ability to buffer risks through private insurance.

Social-democratic countries

While in liberal countries, the state assumes a rather residual role in preventing only against basic life risks, it is of central importance in social-democratic countries, reflected by Scandinavian countries such as Norway, Sweden or Denmark. In these countries, educational systems are largely standardized while exhibiting only a modest degree of stratification (Allmendinger, 1989). An outstanding feature that sets the 'Scandinavian model' aside from other countries is the strong reliance on lifelong learning (Rubenson, 2006). State institutions promote continued education and training throughout the life course, reflected in a low age gradient in Continuing Education and Training (CET) participation. Older workers' employability in Scandinavian countries thus has been actively promoted, so that they have been less subject to displacement, early retirement or a flexibilization of their work (Blossfeld, Buchholz and Hofäcker, 2006). Scandinavian labour markets formally show levels of regulations comparable to those of Central European countries. Yet, the state assumes a much more central role; both in its more central role as an employer but also through its strong investment into active labour market policies (Buchholz et al, 2009). Given that the financial feasibility of the strong Scandinavian welfare state is dependent on high tax and social revenues, state policies put a strong emphasis on reintegrating the unemployed into the labour market through customized support policies. Welfare state provision is comparatively generous and universally available to all individuals through citizenship status. Family policies in Scandinavian policies are particularly pronounced and guarantee both high levels of material support but also already provide for work-family reconciliation when children are younger. As a result, women's employment rates, also in the early family phase, are higher than in the remainder of Europe (Hofäcker, 2006). The aim is to keep both spouses in close to full-time employment and to avoid, where possible, the emergence of atypical employment forms.

Taken together, the Scandinavian system should allow only low levels of employment insecurity: Even in case of possible job loss, the generous welfare state and active reintegration policies reduce long-term labour market risks. Due to the universal nature of education, labour market and welfare state policies, social cleavages in these countries will be modest, with only few gender- and age-based differences.

Post-socialist countries

Post-socialist countries normally refers to a group of countries from Central and Eastern Europe, including the Baltic area which gained national independence before or shortly after the fall of the Iron Curtain in the 1990s. Welfare state scholars have intensively debated the question of whether these countries can be considered as a welfare state type of their own (as done by Buchholz et al, 2009) or whether they should be differentiated into further regime clusters (Fenger, 2007; Bohle and Greskovits, 2012). One common denominator among these countries is that they were confronted with a 'shock transformation' from a planned economy to a globalized market economy within only a few years. For many of these countries, this was connected with the emergence of massive job losses and high levels of unemployment. Welfare state measures during these times remained largely restricted to buffering the severe labour market consequences of the transformation so that other areas (pensions, social insurance, (continued) education) remained underfunded. This holds also for family policies, which were initially based on comprehensive childcare support, although this has been substantially reduced in recent years.

Even though a number of these countries have been able to stabilize their economies in more recent years, the level of labour market insecurity has remained high. At the same time, rudimentary welfare provisions often were not able to adequately buffer these insecurities, suggesting that objective labour market insecurity in these countries may be among the highest in Europe. Given that the repercussions of the economic transformation did affect large parts of the economy, it can be assumed that there will be no major variations in employment insecurity across social groups.

Table 1.1 summarizes the results of the previous discussion of micro and macro level factors and their projected hypothetical influence on the emergence of objective insecurity.

Subjective insecurity

Defining subjective job insecurity

Subjective job insecurity deviates from the objective measures in multiple respects, even though its definition varies across existing literature. Subjective job insecurity is often defined as a 'subjectively experienced anticipation of a fundamental and involuntary event related to job loss' (Sverke, Hellgren and Näswall, 2002: 243). Others' definitions in psychological literature share the idea that job insecurity is a subjective phenomenon based on individual perception (De Witte, 2010; Richter, 2011). Moreover, the subjective dimension of job insecurity concerns not only the anticipation of job loss as such, but also the anticipation of losing important aspects of the job (Greenhalgh and Rosenblatt, 1984). Similarly, it is also related to the perceived difficulty of finding a first job or of finding a new job after a period of unemployment.

Sociological research has identified several components of the subjective dimension of job insecurity (Näswall and De Witte, 2003; Anderson and Pontusson, 2007; Chung and Mau, 2014). The cognitive part refers to the subjective worry perceived by an individual about losing his/her current job in the near future. The other components deal with the perception of the consequences of losing one's job, differentiating between income insecurity and labour market insecurity. The former derives from the loss of economic resources that follows the cessation of a work relationship; the latter refers to the subjectively perceived probability of finding a new job with similar characteristics in the case of involuntary job loss. All these single dimensions (cognitive, labour market and income insecurity) influence the overall 'worry or anxiety about losing one's job' (Anderson and Pontusson, 2007: 4), also defined as affective job insecurity. The latter is a broader conceptualization of job insecurity which encompasses both the perceived threat to one's current job and the consequences associated with this event (see Figure 1.1).

Table 1.1: Determinants of objective job insecurity

	Objective job insecurity	
Macro level: single institutional factors	Education systems:	(–)
	Standardization of certificates	(–)
	Dual organization of training Importance of lifelong learning	(–)
	Active labour market policies	(–)
	Generosity of welfare state and unemployment benefits	(–)
	Dismissal protection and labour market segmentation	(+)
Macro level: institutional regimes	Conservative	Level of insecurity: moderate Main dimensions of inequality: age, gender, education
	Southern European	Level of insecurity: high Main dimensions of inequality: age, gender, education
	Liberal	Level of insecurity: low Main dimensions of inequality: human capital
	Social-democratic	Level of insecurity: low Main dimensions of inequality: generally low, migrants versus national citizens
	Post-socialist	Level of insecurity: high Main dimensions of inequality: generally low
Micro level	Contract (temporary)	(+)
	Part-time	(+/–)
	Age	Young employees: high Mid-career men: low Mid-career women: high Older employees: dependent on institutional design
	Gender (female)	(–)
	Education	(–)
	Partner/family resources	(–)

Source: own elaboration.

Figure 1.1: Dimensions of subjective insecurity

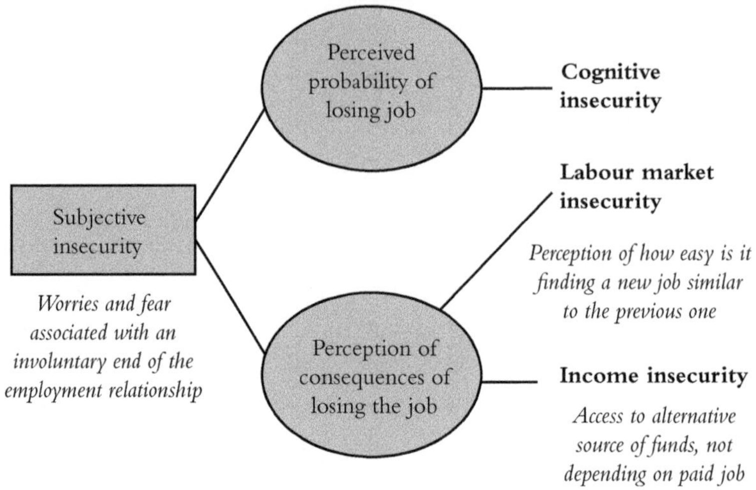

Source: own elaboration on Abbiati (2012) from Anderson and Pontusson (2007).

All these dimensions are sensitive to the institutional context and macro level indicators can affect the perception of job insecurity. With respect to income insecurity, the presence or absence of generous subsidies, and therefore of passive labour policies, plays an important role in mitigating individuals' perception. Similarly, labour market insecurity can vary as a function of the macro-economic situation of the labour market: in contexts where there is a low level of unemployment or institutions guarantee a high level of active labour policies, such as helping to find another job, this type of subjective job insecurity will likely be lower. As far as cognitive insecurity is concerned, the level of employment protection regulation determined at institutional level can affect the extent to which individuals perceive their job to be secure, together with information about the type of contract at micro level. Therefore, both the local labour market conditions and the institutional context play a strong role on the perception of job insecurity and on the individuals' representations that ultimately affect their choices. Particularly important for the impact on the transition to adult life is the perception of job instability by young people (Inanc, 2012; Gallie, 2017).

Recent research has also shown an additional dimension of job insecurity, 'job status insecurity', which addresses the perceived fear of losing valued features of the job, thus emphasizing the qualitative aspects of job rather than job tenure only (Gallie et al, 2016). This type of perceived job insecurity is based on the perception that some key determinants of the intrinsic quality of a job – such as personal treatment by one's superiors, the ability to use one's skills, the degree of task discretion, interest and own initiative, as well as the level of pay – are somewhat under threat. This type of job insecurity, focusing on the qualitative characteristics of the job, has received comparatively less attention in research than job tenure insecurity, but where it was investigated, it has been shown to have negative effects on employees' wellbeing, with the effect increasing over time. However, the limited availability of comparative data on detailed measures of job quality has made it a difficult field of research and the dimension of job tenure is still dominant in comparative scholarship on subjective job insecurity.

Another step further in the conceptualization of job insecurity is the one proposed by Chung and van Oorschot (2010) and Dixon, Fullerton and Robertson (2013) who focus on perceived employment (in)security. In Chung and van Oorschot (2010), this concept is declined with a positive connotation – security – and aims to encompass both the short-term probability of keeping a particular job or employment contract and the longer-term perspective of maintaining a secure and continuous employment career, which may also imply changing job and employer but nonetheless assures a certain stability of income and professional relationships. Dixon and colleagues (2013) focus on the negative side – insecurity – and conceive employment insecurity as the combination of both cognitive insecurity (the perception of job loss) and labour market insecurity (the likelihood of finding a similar new job). Ultimately, the empirical application of the concept in both studies is tightly rooted in the same concepts of cognitive and labour market insecurity outlined by Anderson and Pontusson (2007) and presented earlier. Indeed, the analyses of Chung and van Oorschot (2010) relies on the question 'How likely is it that during the next 12 months you will be unemployed and looking for work for at least four consecutive weeks?', which is the combination of cognitive insecurity (an individual estimate of losing the current job and consequently being unemployed) and labour market insecurity (the perception of the probability of finding a new similar job in around one month). Similarly, Dixon and colleagues (2013) use an additive index of cognitive and labour market insecurity.

Variation of subjective job insecurity across life stages and micro level factors

In the following, we will outline which factors have been identified in previous literature as impacting on subjectively perceived insecurity. As in the previous part, we will first look at individual-level characteristics that may influence subjective insecurity, including socio-demographic and job characteristics. Subsequently, we turn to factors at the societal macro level. Again, a systematic overview of determinants concludes this section.

Demographic characteristics

As for objective insecurity, the age of workers has been identified as a key determinant of subjective insecurity perceptions. However, existing literature has been ambiguous with regard to which age range is related to higher or lower levels of perceived job insecurity (Abbiati, 2012). According to Erlinghagen (2008), workers beyond the age of 40 are more affected by job insecurity than younger workers. In contrast, findings from Fullerton and Wallace (2007) investigating US workers' perception of job insecurity found a non-linear relationship with age, showing that such perception increases particularly among mid-career workers. Consistent with this result, Kiersztyn (2017) shows that young workers may be less affected by subjective job insecurity due to their relatively shorter job experience compared to adult workers. Indeed, while young workers in temporary positions are more likely to be exposed to cognitive insecurity compared to workers of the same age in permanent positions, they are also more optimistic compared to older workers about their prospects of a career even if they are in a temporary job. In other words, young workers in temporary positions have lower chances of experiencing labour market insecurity. Given that they are still in the initial stages of their career, a temporary job may be seen as an entry point leading to permanent positions ('stepping stones'; see Scherer, 2004). Young workers may also accept a lower prestige attributed to their initial job in view of future upgrades. Finally, they are less likely to have family responsibilities compared to their adult counterparts. However, under specific macro level contexts, such as in Southern European countries, young workers may be more likely to end up being trapped in temporary positions. While they enjoy lower levels of job protection, they have fragmented careers with more frequent periods of unemployment, and lower chances of accessing passive and active labour market policies (Barbieri and Scherer, 2009). Therefore, so far there is no consensus on which age groups are particularly hit by job insecurity. Yet, focusing on the distinction between young workers and adult workers is particularly relevant if we consider that early job insecurity has negative consequences on subsequent stages of transition to adulthood.

Other individual level characteristics identified as associated with job insecurity are related to gender, to the level of qualification of the individual as well as to her family composition. With respect to cognitive insecurity, female workers were found to be affected similarly to men. At the same time, they felt less insecure about the risk of losing their current job, but tended to be more sceptical about their prospective job opportunities in case of job loss (labour market insecurity) (Anderson and Pontusson, 2007; Erlinghagen, 2008; Kiersztyn, 2017). Consistently, Chung and van Oorschot (2010) found that women were more likely than men to perceive employment insecurity (that is, the risk of losing their job and being unemployed for at least four weeks).

Investment in human capital – particularly higher levels of (tertiary) education, but also participation in continued training – tend to protect employees from the perception of job insecurity. Results show that such investments lower the perception of cognitive and labour market insecurity (Erlinghagen, 2008; Kiersztyn, 2017) as well as employment insecurity (Chung and van Oorschot, 2010).

As far as the household composition is considered, having a partner reduces the perception of job insecurity – in particular if the partner is employed (Chung and van Oorschot, 2010). Conversely, if the partner is employed in an insecure position, this tends to increase cognitive insecurity (Kiersztyn, 2017). Overall, the availability of adequate income tends to be a major factor in reducing the perception of various forms of job insecurity (Erlinghagen 2008), while the presence of children leads to non-significant results or even lowers job insecurity. Such unexpected results may be the outcome of selective mechanisms by which insecure workers tend not to have children (Chung and van Oorschot, 2010).

Job characteristics

The type of employment contract is often used as a proxy of objective insecurity (Chung and van Oorschot, 2011; Chung and Mau, 2014: 306; see also the first section of this chapter on objective job insecurity). At the same time, it is considered a key determinant of subjective job insecurity as well. Due to the nature of their contract, temporary employees are more likely to experience fear of job loss compared to employees with open-ended contracts. This finding is supported by several studies identifying temporary employment as promoting a rise in perceived (cognitive) job insecurity (Erlinghagen, 2008; Chung and Oorschot, 2010; Kuroki, 2012). Given that temporary employees are not as well integrated and less likely to cover core positions within an organization, their chances of being dismissed during reorganizations are higher (Chung and Mau, 2014). However, a temporary contract is 'far from being the only source of job insecurity' (Gallie, 2017: 235): among those employees reporting high job insecurity, less than a third are employed with a temporary contract.

Further studies have pointed to the significance of part-time work. Fullerton, Dixon and McCollum (2020) found no unequivocally negative association between part-time work and subjective job insecurity. The influence of part-time work rather varied according to the type of insecurity at individual level and differed with the institutional treatment of part-time work at national level. Working part-time increased the perception of cognitive job insecurity (but not of labour market or affective job insecurity) particularly for men, but not for women, unless part–time work was perceived as an involuntary choice. If it was perceived as being involuntary, it increased the perception of cognitive job insecurity for both women and men. At country level, the strength of the association between the rate of part-time employment and job insecurity varied according to the level of the employment regulation and the degree of gender segregation of part-time work: job insecurity tends to augment in case of segregation.

Beyond the type of contract, Lambert et al (2019) extend the analysis by also including the role of shifting scheduling practices on perceived job insecurity. In their study on US workers, the authors investigate to what extent their perception of job (in)security and economic insecurity varies as a function of the variation in their working hours. In the US labour market, scheduling practices by employer aimed at keeping labour flexible are widespread and tend to involve to a greater extent low-skilled workers, young people and those belonging to a minority. These practices have been on the rise since the Great Recession of 2008, resulting in an increase in the changing number and timing of working hours for hourly workers. This trend has impacted negatively on the perception of job security and the predictability of workers' immediate futures. In particular, the practice of non-regular schedules and the lack of advance notice (for example, for jobs 'on call') have adversely affected the perception of job security, especially when it was associated with fluctuating weekly work hours.

Having a safe position and being well-integrated into an organization tend to be associated with lower levels of perceived job insecurity. Longer job tenure is generally associated with lower cognitive insecurity for temporary workers who may exploit their job experience on the labour market when searching for a new job. At the same time, particularly for regular workers (Kiersztyn, 2017) and for workers with long years of job tenure (Erlinghagen, 2008), the long-term investment into one's job may increase perceived labour market insecurity. Finally, having influence on the decisions of the company, working longer hours than regular employees (>48 hours per week), having a supervisory role and receiving employment-sponsored training were shown to reduce employment insecurity (Chung and van Oorschot, 2010).

Variations across welfare state regimes

Previous research has shown that subjective job insecurity depends not only on the objective contractual condition of the worker or other micro level factors, but also on macro factors such as welfare state systems (Anderson and Pontusson, 2007; Chung and van Oorschot, 2011; Dixon, Fullerton and Robertson, 2013; Hipp, 2016), cultural variables (Erlinghagen, 2008) and the interrelation between those individual level contractual conditions (for example, part-time work, temporary contracts) and its macro level regulation (Hipp, 2016; Fullerton, Dixon and McCollum, 2020). As Chung and Mau have highlighted 'a coupling between institutions and subjective insecurity does not only exist, it is manifold and complex' (Chung and Mau, 2014: 304).

Institutional characteristics

Existing research shows that not only objective but also subjective job insecurity are influenced by labour market institutions, as well as by the generosity of welfare state and unemployment benefits (Anderson and Pontusson, 2007; Chung and van Oorschot, 2011; Dixon et al, 2013; Hipp, 2016; Kalleberg and Vallas, 2017; Kalleberg, 2018). In particular, the presence of generous subsidies in case of job loss (passive labour market policies) plays an important role in reducing perceived income insecurity. At the same time, where unemployment is low and institutions provide support in finding another job (active labour market policies), the level of labour market insecurity can be expected to be lower.

Further studies investigating the relationship between objective and subjective job insecurity have shown that welfare regimes with high labour market protection increase perceived job security for permanent labour market 'insiders' since they increase dismissal costs (Gebel and Giesecke, 2016). However, the gap in perceived job security between permanent and temporary employees significantly increases with strong job security provisions and strict regulations on temporary contracts (Balz, 2017), highlighting the previously described cleavage between labour market 'insiders' and 'outsiders' (see the first section of this chapter). Some studies even demonstrate a negative association between dismissal protection and perceived job security (Bockermann, 2004; Clark and Postel-Vinay, 2009; Chung and van Oorschot, 2011) particularly for those who are not employed on permanent contracts (Hipp, 2016).

In her comparative research, Hipp (2016) added further evidence on the mechanisms by which welfare state protection affected subjective insecurity perceptions, showing that the level of unemployment protection sheltered workers from the worry of losing their job and increasing the confidence of finding a new one. Dismissal protection itself (associated Employment Protection Legislation, EPL) did not protect workers from the fear of losing their job. Instead, stringent regulation against the dismissal of workers in temporary positions was observed to be beneficial in countries with high shares of temporary workers (for example, Spain and Portugal). This finding underlined that the institutional configuration is complementary to the effectiveness of policies.

Institutional packages: welfare regimes and cultural norms

While the afore-mentioned studies focused on the impact of specific institutional characteristics, Erlinghangen (2008) could not identify 'any typical regime clusters that could be linked up to different welfare state' regarding the diffusion of subjective job insecurity, but instead underlined the necessity to take into account both specific cultural and institutional aspects in examining perceived job insecurity. However, other authors found more systematic association with macro level regimes. For example, according to Green (2009), job insecurity is relatively low in the Nordic economies given their low unemployment rates. In contrast, job insecurity was especially high in the transitional economies of Eastern Europe (Bohle and Greskovits, 2012). Linking labour market policies, welfare state systems and labour market regulation, Ebralidze (2011) identified two mechanisms for reducing subjective job insecurity and one for potentially increasing it. She highlighted that, compared to other welfare state models, both the Danish and the Anglo-American system reproduce a low level of subjective job insecurity, although the mechanisms underlying this result are different. In Denmark, low job protection is offset by a high probability of re-employment guaranteed by strong active labour policies (contributing to reduce labour market insecurity) and a low risk of income loss due to generous unemployment benefits (reducing income insecurity). In contrast, in the US, the very low level of job protection is compensated by a high likelihood of re-employment, although this occurs at the cost of a high level of job and territorial mobility. In contrast, job insecurity is particularly high among young people in Southern European countries, even though the percentage of unstable work is not so high compared to the rest of Europe (Ebralizde, 2011).

Table 1.2 briefly summarizes the main macro and micro level factors and the direction of their relationship with perceived job insecurity.

Literature on the mechanism of perception in general highlights that people's perception is particularly influenced by most recent changes. In this sense, market and institutional changes can have a strong impact on the subjective dimension of job insecurity. People tend to compare their previous situation with their current one, taking into account recent dynamics of the economy (particularly after the economic crisis of 2008) and associated with reforms in welfare state and labour market policies (for example, related to employment protection legislation or expenditure in active labour market policies) (Lübke and Erlinghagen, 2014). Most recent reforms in these areas could have an even stronger impact on the perception of job insecurity, compared to the real objective situation. Chung and van Oorschot (2011) found that policies oriented at securing employment and income are more effective in reducing employment insecurity than policies

Table 1.2: Summary of factors affecting job insecurity

	Subjective job insecurity	
Macro level	Active labour market policies	(-)
	Generosity of welfare state and unemployment benefits	(-)
	Dismissal protection and labour market segmentation	(+)
	Deunionization, financialization of economy, globalization, digital revolution	(+)
	Cultural variables and tradition (what is considered as 'normal')	(+/-)
Micro level	Contract (temporary)	(+)
	Part-time	(+/-)
	Age	(+/-)
	Gender (female)	(+/-)
	Education	(-)
	Partner	(-)
	Adequate income	(-)

Source: own elaboration.

Table 1.3: Variations of subjective job insecurity

	High subjective JI		
Models: *Low subjective JI* ----------------------x-------------------- *Low subjective JI*			
(E.g. Danish)			(E.g. US)
Factors: Low segmentation	High segmentation		Very low segmentation
Low dismissal protection	High dismissal protection		Very low dismissal protection
High passive and active LMP	Low passive and active LMP		Low passive and active LMP
High social protection	Low social protection		Low social protection
Low labour mobility	Low labour mobility		High labour market mobility

Note: JI = job insecurity; LMP = labour market participation
Source: own elaboration on previous studies.

oriented at securing a particular job (Table 1.3). Nonetheless, in the particular period after the Great Recession of 2008, market forces (such as the average employment rate and the strength with which the financial crisis hit the country) seem to matter most and institutional factors lost significance, leading to a situation in which 'differences in economic and labour market conditions between countries better explain why workers feel insecure about their employment, than the differences in employment and income policies' (Chung and van Oorschot, 2011: 287).

The authors also acknowledge that the role of market forces may have been amplified by the particular period of the Great Recession and its media coverage. With respect to institutional changes, scholars furthermore pointed out that 'structural forces converged to erode the Fordist employment regime' (Kalleberg and Vallas, 2017): such forces – including deunionization, financialization of the economy, globalization, and the digital revolution – had an impact on the perception of job insecurity depending on how structured the 'Fordist employment regime' was in the previous period.

The perception of job insecurity is also influenced by a country's dominant labour market culture. Respondents in countries in which the dominant model is a stable job exhibit higher levels of job insecurity compared to others. Research on Italy, for example, showed that the existence of a strong preference for stable work makes the condition of being a temporary worker less satisfactory and that being an atypical worker is very often involuntary rather than a matter of choice (Bertolini, 2012). Other research highlights that individuals living under similar institutional conditions may evaluate job insecurity also according to their individual norms of what is perceived as 'normal' in a given environment (Ebralizde, 2011). Against this background, the question of when and how atypical employment contracts were introduced in the respective national context can play a central role. In Southern European countries such as Italy, a very rapid introduction of temporary employment combined with very low and targeted social protection, may differently affect the life of young people than in other countries where such changes have been slower or accompanied by higher levels of social protection. A study by the Italian North West Observatory (Barbera et al, 2007) showed that 41 per cent of Italians perceived job insecurity as one of the greatest threats to their existence. Moreover, the introduction of unstable work forms produced a strong division of the Italian labour market into 'outsiders' and 'insiders' (Regini, 2000): permanent workers often enjoyed a high level of protection both when working and when not working (for example, through state unemployment funds, sick leave arrangements and so on) while there was only a low level of social protection for fixed-term workers (for example, no unemployment benefits between one contract and another).

Coping strategies and decision-making mechanisms under conditions of insecurity

In order to study the effects of objective job insecurity on specific transitions such as that of leaving the parental home (see Chapter 3), it is crucial to investigate the perception of insecurity and the consequences it has on individuals' decisions, as well as the various strategies individuals use to cope and to react to the combination of objective and perceived job insecurity.

Coping strategies

Some recent studies have started to consider the psychological consequences of job insecurity and the strategies that people use to cope with them, using the classic distinction between problem-focused and emotional-focused coping strategies (Folkman and Lazarus, 1985; Baranowska-Rataj et al, 2015). This research approach is aimed at understanding the possible moderating effect of coping strategies in the relationship between job insecurity and different outcomes (Richter, 2011).

Coping is considered as a dynamic process characterized by a set of cognitive, emotional and behavioural strategies implemented by people to deal with a problematic situation (Lazarus and Folkman, 1987). A fundamental distinction in the literature is between problem-focused and emotion-focused coping: the first one is related to the strategies used to deal directly with the problem in order to resolve it; the second one is related to the strategies used to deal with negative emotions associated with the problematic situation (Folkman and Lazarus 1985).

Although some scholars suggest that problem-focused coping may be more beneficial in buffering negative consequences of job insecurity, recent studies did not find this buffering effect (Richter, 2011). This could be related to the fact that people generally use different coping strategies in different situations: coping preferences are mostly contextual and related to a specific type of problem (Grimaldi et al, 2009).

Detecting general coping strategies, therefore, may not be the best way to understand how individuals specifically cope with job insecurity, or to investigate the potential buffering role of coping in the relationship between job insecurity and different outcomes (Richter, 2011). Therefore, it is necessary to investigate, through qualitative studies, specific strategies that people put in place to cope with job insecurity, identifying specific behaviours and their perceived consequences. Particular attention may be dedicated to those behaviours aimed at reducing insecurity, for example, searching for a new job, enhancing personal employability, promoting personal career, and so on.

The role of emotion-focused strategies should also be investigated. According to some hypotheses, emotion-focused strategies may be useful in the case of job insecurity, as in other cases in which the source of the stressor was not clearly identified. Existing research evidence in this regard is ambiguous. It will be important to identify which emotion-focused strategies are able to reduce the negative effects of job insecurity and which ones will increase these effects (distinguishing between short- and long-term).

Decisional mechanisms

Some studies show four strategies used by young adults to cope with insecurity (Mills et al, 2005; Blossfeld et al, 2012): (1) They increasingly postponed decisions requiring a long-term commitment; the youth phase became more and more a sort of a 'moratorium', and transitions to gainful employment often took a chaotic course. (2) They increasingly switched to alternative roles instead of employment (for example, they spent longer in the education system instead of letting themselves be defined as 'unemployed'). (3) They increasingly formed more flexible forms of partnership (for example, consensual unions) that permitted an adaptation to rising insecurity without having to make long-term commitments (Nazio and Blossfeld, 2003; Nazio, 2008). (4) Particularly in the family-oriented welfare states of Central and Southern Europe, they developed gender-specific strategies to deal with insecurity: men were increasingly less able to guarantee any long-term income security as the 'breadwinner' for a household, often leading to a delay in family formation. In contrast, many unqualified women who 'had nothing to lose' reacted to the growing insecurity on the labour market by turning to the security of the family and the traditional roles of mother and housewife (as a strategy to reduce insecurity). Conversely, the tendency for highly qualified women to have children in increasingly uncertain labour markets depended on whether they could protect their careers by making both the family and career compatible.

What has been less studied are the strategies (and the coping strategy) that explain this behaviour and how they vary according to the institutional context. It is very important for future research to take into account these strategies because they can help to explain the links between the different levels of analysis – micro, meso and macro – and the mechanisms that produce social inequalities.

Social scientists agree that under conditions of job insecurity, it is impossible to take optimal decisions on the life course. What individual decisional mechanisms and coping strategies can be observed? One is the mechanism of suspension of the decision in conditions of high insecurity. In other words, the individual tends to slip towards a short-term decision-making horizon; 'self-binding' decisions become problematic and, therefore, it becomes rational to postpone decisions regarding transitions to adulthood, because the information search process takes time (Blossfeld et al, 2005). Qualitative research can help to identify some unexpected effects of atypical contracts. Temporary workers find it difficult or impossible to plan their own working career, and consequently their private life, in the long term when dealing with fixed-term labour contracts. Having to suspend decisions due to their work, because no one knows what will happen at the end of the contract, may lead to a similar attitude in other spheres of family life and create significant problems with the reconciliation of the two spheres, especially when the individual is thirty years old or more, when he/she has already formed a new family or aspires to form it.

However, when individuals are forced to choose, what other strategies are there that they may develop? One strategy is that of the maximization of minimum where individuals prepare themselves for the worst situation and choose the best option among the worst. For example, 'if the worst scenario for the future is losing my job, then I do not leave parental home'. Risk-adverse people like this strategy (Jansen, 2011; Bertolini, 2012). With respect to risk aversion among temporary workers, Di Mauro and Musumeci (2011) investigated and compared temporary workers' attitudes toward risk with those of permanent (and guaranteed) workers and found that the first (in particular, women in temporary jobs) were more risk-adverse than the second.

Another strategy, the affordability norm (Oppenheimer, 1994; Jansen, 2011) consists in making the transition when you have access to sufficient and adequate economic resources to sustain a certain standard of living. When the threshold is reached, the individual stops her/his search for the best alternative. In this case, the young man/woman chooses to leave the parental home when he/she considers he/she has sufficient financial resources to do so; these resources may come from work or from the welfare state system. If the decision involves a long-term commitment, however, not only will the current conditions count but also the future economic perspective, therefore having a stable job or being able to count on a high probability of re-employment.

A third strategy consists in a mechanism reducing the insecurity 'to bind themselves to courses of action that are largely independent of future states of the world' (Friedman, 1994: 382). This mechanism reduces the insecurity that is caused by the work sphere, by choosing to make an early and definitive transition to adult life within the familial sphere. In this way, the individual ensures her-/himself a certain degree of security at least in the family sphere ('I will get married or have a child even if I'm a temporary worker'), as opposed to the insecurity that he/she is forced to experience in the work sphere. The expected result is that the young adult anticipates a transition to a couple or family life as an effect on (more precisely, regardless of) his/her job insecurity;

In the spill-over effect, the individual transfers the anxiety that comes from job insecurity to other areas of family life. The expected result is that, as a consequence of job insecurity, the young adult could postpone decisions, and then transitions, or anticipate them.

Finally, individuals may make a strategic use of time: in this framework women tend to either have children early in order to free time for paid work or have them very late. By contrast, men tend to postpone this kind of choice. The expected result is that, as a consequence of job insecurity, the young adult could postpone decisions, and then transitions, or anticipate them.

These mechanisms have been applied to the explanation of some of the results of research on the impact of the contractual form on the decision to leave the family home. For example, in Italy, an interesting result (Bertolini, 2012) is that the impact of the contractual form on the decision to leave the parental home is not significant among low-educated women, while it is significant for medium- or high-educated women. Therefore, the impact of gender and the strategy that is adopted by individuals varies depending on their educational level. Women with a low level of education, who are also those that mostly leave home for marriage, apply the mechanism of reduction of insecurity. They reduce the job insecurity by leaving the parental home and getting married: 'I'm getting married even though I have an unstable job'. This is facilitated by the fact that in Italian society gender relations are still traditional, and therefore is a socially shared 'norm' that the goal for a woman is to get married by a certain age (to avoid being called an «old maid»). In fact, we know that in terms of the approval of the involvement of women in the non-domestic sphere, the change in Italy seems to have been slow and not homogeneous (Solera, 2009).

Highly educated women, instead, investing more in the working career, apply a mix of two strategies: one is that of maximizing the minimums and the other the affordability norm, both leading them, similarly to men, to postpone the transition.

2

Objective and Subjective Job Insecurity in Europe

This chapter first provides an overview of the diffusion of the various dimensions of objective and subjective job insecurity across European countries for young and adult workers.

The analysis presented in this chapter is comparative across European member states and is based on data from several sources, including all 28 member states across relevant years (UK included). As regards objective job insecurity, cross-sectional data from OECD and Eurostat are employed, while for subjective job insecurity the source of data used is the European Quality of Life Survey (EQLS, 2012, 2016).

One of the aims of this section is to investigate whether the institutional filters of the welfare state regime still play a role in mediating the perception of job insecurity, according to the literature on the filtering role of the different welfare states (Blossfeld et al, 2005; Blossfeld, Buchholz, Hofäcker and Kolb, 2011) and the variety of capitalism (Hall and Soskice, 2001).

Second, the analysis identifies micro level patterns associated with individual characteristics, with particular attention to age, separating young workers in the age range 18–34 from adult workers (35–54).

Data for objective insecurity are presented for youth and young adults; data for subjective job insecurity compare young and young adults with adults.

Finally, a last section is devoted to the interrelationship between objective and subjective job insecurity, analyzing inconsistent profiles, namely individuals who fall out of the automatic match between objective and subjective job insecurity. These findings contribute to a better understanding of the overall (and multidimensional) concept of job insecurity. Moreover, identifying which groups – particularly if young workers – are mainly affected by this mismatch has important consequences in terms of policy implications, in particular regarding the chances of young people taking the next steps into adulthood.

Objective and subjective job insecurity in Europe for young and adult workers

Overview of objective job insecurity for young people (18–34) across welfare state regimes

In line with standard definitions, the age bracket used in this book to identify young people is 15–24 years. For the sake of the analysis of a multidimensional concept like job insecurity, and due to the cross-country comparison that involves different labour market and welfare regimes (associated with different timings of entering the labour market), this chapter extends the age range of interest to include young adults as well, namely individuals in the age range 25–34.

Young people are well-known to be particularly affected by labour market insecurity; they are often even considered as the 'losers' in recent globalization and flexibilization processes (Blossfeld et al, 2005; Blossfeld, Buchholz, Hofäcker and Kolb, 2011). Their comparatively disadvantageous position within the labour market stems from the fact that they possess fewer linkages to relevant labour market actors (such as unions) that could protect their employment contracts. The process of flexibilization in some countries has been a process of segmentation, in which young people as new entrants without experience often cover the external positions. The flexibilization needs of employers thus often have been shifted onto young people.

Such a situation also holds true for the group of young adults (aged 25–34), who keep facing difficulties in labour market integration and the persistence of disadvantages in reaching stable working positions, especially in countries where temporary jobs at early stages tend to represent traps rather than stepping stones (Barbieri and Scherer, 2005, 2009).

In addition, youth are facing a demographic disadvantage, given that job positions across the period studied are occupied by large 'baby boomer' cohorts (i.e. individuals born in the period 1946–1964). Furthermore, economic crises, most recently the financial crisis in 2008, have harmed young people's job prospects. The COVID-19 pandemic exacerbated the situation: during periods of lockdown restrictions in most countries it was not allowed to fire workers but, as young people were working in fixed-term positions, they were losing their jobs simply because their contracts had not been renewed.

The focus of the first paragraph is on the problems young people face in European labour markets that were discussed in the literature (Blossfeld et al, 2005; Rokicka et al, 2015), that is, youth unemployment and non-permanent/temporary contracts. Other flexible work forms – such as self-employment or part-time employment – are not particularly widespread among youth (see also Chapter 5).

If we look at some indicators of labour market attachment of young people in the last ten years, we can have an idea of the weakness of their position. In virtually all countries considered, youth unemployment is higher than unemployment among other age groups (see Table 2.1). Further analyses of NEET rates (not in education, employment or training) (OECD, 2021c) suggest that, in addition, a sizeable proportion of youth is inactive in this way.

Youth unemployment (15–24) appears to follow a cyclical pattern, particularly regarding the financial crisis in 2008, after which youth unemployment rates rose in most countries. In most, rates had declined after 2012, but once again increased since 2019 with the pandemic period.

The magnitude of youth unemployment shows clear variations across welfare regimes (see Figure 2.1). This is particularly so in Southern European countries, with unemployment rates of 20 to 30 per cent before the 2008 crisis and a strong increase after it, even rising to over 50 per cent in Greece and Spain. In fact, in these countries the process of segmentation had been particularly strong in the phase of recession since the fixed-term contracts of youth had not been renewed.

Lowest values of youth unemployment are observed in the employment-maintaining regimes of social-democratic and liberal countries. In the latter, they temporarily rose during the financial crisis, while they behaved less cyclically in the former.

The liberal countries have the more cyclical trend. Mainly due to a very flexible labour market, in which the differences between open-ended and fixed-term contracts in terms of protection are few and very low, young people appear to be the first in line for losing their job in periods of economic crisis.

Conservative and social-democratic countries appear better able to protect their young workers from unemployment, even in the time of recession.

In Conservative countries, unemployment has remained equally low with only little cyclical variations. Particularly in the German-speaking countries (Austria, Germany and Switzerland), even if regulation is very similar to the welfare regimes in Southern European countries and flexibilization has been based on labour market segmentation, a combination of the 'dual training' system with active labour market policies has maintained comparatively low unemployment rates among its youth (see Chapter 1).

In the social-democratic countries, the generous welfare state and active reintegration policies reduce long-term labour market risks (see Chapter 1). This appears to protect young people from unemployment, even in the period of financial and economic crisis.

Eastern European countries initially suffered from youth unemployment, particularly after the system transformation following independence from the Russian Federation in the 1990s, reflected in high values in

Figure 2.1: Unemployment rate, youth aged 15–24, 2000–20

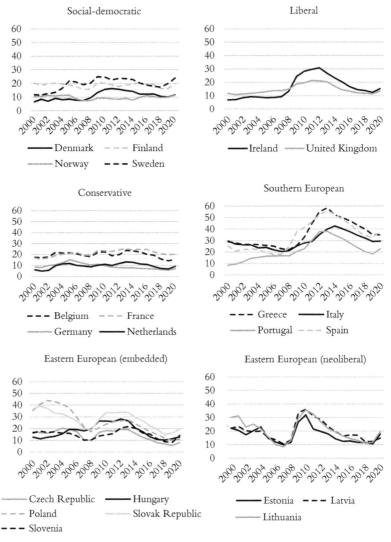

Source: OECD, 2021a.

the early 2000s. After a second peak around the financial crisis, they have normalized.

The trend is very similar for young adults (25–29 and 30–34). Table 2.1 shows that unemployment is still low (near or under 10 per cent) in liberal, conservative and social-democratic countries, but high in Southern European countries, in particular in Greece and Spain. In all Eastern European countries, the situation is improved from 2010–20 after the

Table 2.1: Unemployment rate, young adults aged 25–29 and 30–34, 2010–20

	25–29 years		30–34 years	
	2010	2020	2010	2020
Social-democratic				
Denmark	11.2	10.2	7.1	5.5
Finland	9.2	8.6	6.3	6.7
Norway	5.3	5.7	3.7	4.8
Sweden	10.0	9.5	6.5	7.7
Liberal				
Ireland	17.5	7.8	12.7	5.3
United Kingdom	8.2	3.7★	6.8	2.8★
Conservative				
Belgium	11.6	7.8	8.1	5.9
France	11.8	11.4	8.6	8.2
Germany	8.4	5.2	7.3	4.5
Netherlands	4.5	4.0	3.7	3.1
Southern European				
Greece	19.7	27.2	14.1	19.3
Italy	14.8	17.1	9.9	11.6
Portugal	14.6	11	11.4	7.5
Spain	24.7	22.9	19.2	16.8
Eastern European (embedded)				
Czech Republic	9.4	3.9	6.2	3.6
Hungary	14.2	6.1	10.5	3.8
Poland	12	4.8	7.9	2.9
Slovakia	16.7	8.6	12.7	6.4
Slovenia	13	6.8	7.3	5.6
Eastern European (neoliberal)				
Estonia	17.7	8	13.5	6.4
Latvia	21.2	12.1	15.9	6.8
Lithuania	20.8	8.8	15.5	7.4

Note: ★Data substituted from prior year.

Source: Eurostat (2021c).

transition to new regimes, and percentages are low at 10 per cent. This indicator is important, because with the labour market reform the majority of youth enter the labour market via unstable job forms; this indicator shows whether these become a route to more stable participation for young adults after they mature and gain more experience or whether precariousness becomes a vicious circle for them. Data show an influence of welfare state regimes.

If we look at single countries for people 30–34, Norway, Sweden, Greece and Italy have a worsening situation from 2010–20.

Generally, long-term unemployment is particularly prevalent in countries where overall unemployment is high (see Tables 2.2 and 2.3). It has been particularly persistent in Southern Europe but is of little or no importance in employment-maintaining regimes (social-democratic, liberal). It is high in conservative countries, despite only modest overall unemployment rates. This can likely be attributed to insider-outsider labour market structures. Eastern European countries had high long-term unemployment initially after the system transformation, but have recovered remarkably since then.

Long-term unemployment also follows a largely cyclical pattern, with highest values around the 2008 financial crisis and a marked decline more recently.

Fixed-term employment per youth 15–24 (Table 2.4) shows some cyclical variations with a high point in the early- to mid-2010s and a decline more recently. In general, it is most prevalent in countries with an insider-outsider labour market (Conservative/ Southern European countries): the process of labour market flexibilization meant workers with these contracts were assumed to be new labour market entrants, as adults still work under permanent contracts. Greece and Italy had a lower percentage in 2000 because they introduced atypical job forms into their labour market later. Greece now has a lower level of fixed-term employment because it has a very high level of youth unemployment. Fixed-term employment plays only a minor role in liberal countries with flexible labour markets, particularly the UK. There is no unique pattern in social-democratic and Eastern European countries, where fixed-term rates vary extensively, pointing to country-specific factors. In particular, among social-democratic countries, it is useless by country with less protection for permanent contracts, like Denmark and Norway. Among Eastern European countries, fixed-term contracts are more used in Poland and Slovenia which have more segmented labour markets.

For young adults, the percentage of fixed-term employment is still high for Southern European countries only, at around 40 per cent, while it is around 20 per cent for conservative countries and for Poland and Slovenia. For all the others, it is under 10 per cent (Table 2.5).

Table 2.2: Share of long-term unemployment, youth aged 15–24, 2000–20, 5-year intervals

	2000	2005	2010	2015	2020
Social-democratic					
Denmark	2.1	4.5	6.4	8.0	na
Finland	8.8	6.1	7.7	8.0	3.0
Norway	3.1	5.6	11.0	10.3	10.3
Sweden	8.9	6.9	6.4	4.4	1.8
Liberal					
Ireland	19.9	22.1	42.0	38.5	na
United Kingdom	12.3	12.6	23.6	21.9	13.3
Conservative					
Belgium	29.7	27.2	30.1	35.7	21.7
France	20.6	23.8	30.1	27.3	21.5
Germany	23.5	31.8	26.8	22.5	20.7★
Netherlands	na	17.7	11.6	18.7	8.5
Southern European					
Greece	50.2	45.1	35.4	56.1	54.8
Italy	57.5	45.3	44.5	55.7	44.1
Portugal	21.2	31.5	30.2	30.9	na
Spain	29.3	13.4	29.2	35.0	17.3
Eastern European (embedded)					
Czech Republic	37.8	38.5	30.2	30.9	16.6
Hungary	37.8	35.8	39.9	27.2	22.5
Poland	28.0	38.4	15.5	29.2	15.1
Slovakia	43.1	56.6	50.2	51.2	36.8
Slovenia	42.4	37.0	33.8	35.8	25.0
Eastern European (neoliberal)					
Estonia	26.3	34.7	37.1	15.5	5.9
Latvia	43.4	22.2	33.1	27.1	12.8
Lithuania	43.1	21.3	30.3	16.4	9.8

Note: ★Data substituted from prior year.

Source: OECD, 2021a.

Table 2.3: Share of long-term unemployment, young adults aged 25–29, 2012–20

	2012	2020
Social-democratic		
Denmark	2.2	1.5
Finland	1.2	1
Norway	0.6	na
Sweden	1.4	0.9
Liberal		
Ireland	10.7	na
United Kingdom	3.0	0.8
Conservative		
Belgium	na	na
France	4.0	3.5
Germany	2.1	0.9
Netherlands	1.3	0.7
Southern European		
Greece	23.4	15.7
Italy	9.1	7.3
Portugal	8.2	2.8
Spain	12.4	5.2
Eastern European (embedded)		
Czech Republic	na	na
Hungary	5.8	1.4
Poland	5	0.8
Slovakia	11.3	3.4
Slovenia	6.5	2.2
Eastern European (neoliberal)		
Estonia	5.4	na
Latvia	6.4	3.3
Lithuania	5.7	1.6

Source: Eurostat (2021b).

Table 2.4: Share of fixed-term employment, youth aged 15–24, 2000–20, 5-year intervals

	2000	2005	2010	2015	2020
Social-democratic					
Denmark	27.4	26.9	21.1	22.7	33.8
Finland	45.6	44.2	43.1	41.9	40.3
Norway	28.5	27.8	27.3	25.0	26.4
Sweden	49.5	55.3	56.8	55.9	53.8
Liberal					
Ireland	15.9	11.6	30.1	32.7	34.9
United Kingdom	14.2	12.3	13.8	15.0	13.9
Conservative					
Belgium	30.8	32.1	30.4	36.6	48.3
France	55.1	49.6	55.1	59.6	55.8
Germany	52.4	58.2	57.2	53.6	50.9
Netherlands	35.5	41.7	48.3	53.4	50.3
Southern European					
Greece	29.5	26.1	30.2	33.3	22.3
Italy	26.6	36.9	46.8	57.1	58.9
Portugal	41.4	46.2	56.4	67.5	56.0
Spain	68.3	66.3	58.4	70.4	66.4
Eastern European (CEE or embedded Eastern European)					
Czech Republic	19.6	18.3	22.5	31.0	25.1
Hungary	13.9	17.2	25.0	24.1	12.1
Poland	35.5*	66.5	64.5	72.7	54.7
Slovakia	10.5	12.8	17.1	29.1	21.4
Slovenia	46.3	62.5	69.6	75.5	55.9
Eastern European (Baltic or neoliberal Eastern European)					
Estonia	6.4	8.5	12.3	11.4	11.3
Latvia	10.9	17.8	13.3	10.9	5.6
Lithuania	9.4	13.1	7.6	6.5	7.0

Note: * Data substituted from subsequent year.

Source: OECD, 2021a.

Table 2.5: Share of fixed-term employment, young adults aged 25–29, 2012–20

	2012	2020
Social-democratic		
Denmark	15.6	19.7
Finland	25.6	23.4
Norway	13.0	11.4
Sweden	24.9	21.3
Liberal		
Ireland	12.4	11.1
United Kingdom	5.9	4.4
Conservative		
Belgium	12.8	16.4
France	22.8	21.7
Germany	22.0	17.7
Netherlands	26.2	23.3
Southern European		
Greece	16.3	16.1
Italy	29.4	37.2
Portugal	37.8	35.9
Spain	38.8	44.2
Eastern European (embedded)		
Czech Republic	na	na
Hungary	12.2	6.9
Poland	40.5	28.2
Slovakia	8.3	8.0
Slovenia	35.2	22.3
Eastern European (neoliberal)		
Estonia	3.2	2.9
Latvia	4.3	na
Lithuania	na	1.2

Source: Eurostat (2021d).

Subjective job insecurity across welfare state regimes

As introduced in Chapter 1, the perception of one's own insecurity is as relevant, if not even more relevant, as the objective condition experienced by individuals in the labour market. For this reason, this section presents an overview of the distribution of the subjective dimension of job insecurity in European countries. Building on Anderson and Pontusson's (2007) definition of subjective job insecurity, which entails several sub-dimensions, the descriptive statistics of this section deal with both a) cognitive insecurity (that is, the perceived risk of losing one's own job in the next 6 months) and b) perceived insecurity in the labour market (that is, the fear of not finding a similar job in case of job loss). Moreover, the intersection between the two sub-dimensions is also considered, that is, individuals who see it as likely they will lose their job in the next 6 months (cognitive job insecurity) and at the same time also think they will be unlikely to find a new job, with a similar salary, in case of job loss (perceived insecurity of the labour market). The figures presented in this chapter are based on the most recent wave of the European Quality of Life Survey (EQLS). Due to the small sample size, the European countries included in the survey have been grouped into country clusters, following the traditional scheme of welfare state regimes (Esping-Andersen, 1990; Ferrera, 1996; Bohle and Greskovits, 2012).

Cognitive job insecurity in European countries

Aggregate data for cognitive job insecurity show a wave-like trend for all country groups (Figure 2.2), recording in 2012 a substantial increase of employed individuals (considering both young and adult in the age range 18–54) who think that job loss in the next six months may be very or quite likely, and a subsequent decrease in the following wave of 2016, returning to percentages similar to those recorded ten years earlier (2007). This result may be interpreted as the tail of the big shock provoked by the 2008 financial crisis, and its serious consequences on the labour market in terms of job dismissals (Chung and Oorschot, 2010). [Two] exceptions are the countries of the conservative cluster, where values remained almost stable over time, and the post-socialist neoliberal countries (shortened in the acronym PSNL, corresponding to the Baltic countries), where, given the very high rates recorded in 2003, there has been a significant decrease in cognitive job insecurity over time. However, despite the decreasing trend, figures for cognitive job insecurity remain above the average in all waves (>10 per cent) for countries in the post-socialist and Southern European clusters. Scandinavian countries, despite showing below average values in all waves, recorded a significant increase in 2012.

Figure 2.2: Percentage of cognitive job insecurity, age group 18–54

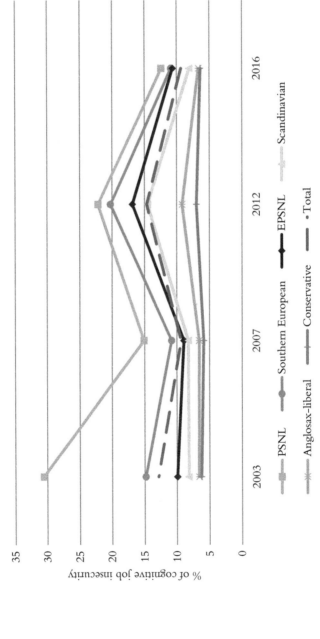

Note: % of employed individuals. Original question: how likely or unlikely do you think it is that you might lose your job in the next 6 months? Very +, Rather likely = 1.

Source: own elaboration on EQLS data.

Figure 2.3 and Table 2.6 show that, within this general trend, young workers systematically perceive higher levels of cognitive job insecurity (the solid line) in all country clusters, indicating that new entrants and early career workers perceived their jobs more at risk compared to their mature peers. The only exception are adult workers in post-socialist neoliberal countries, who show higher percentages of cognitive job insecurity in all waves. Consistent with the interpretation of 2012 figures as the tail of the consequences of the 2008 financial crisis, greater cognitive job insecurity for adult workers (compared to younger peers) is observable in the Anglo-Saxon countries and in Southern European countries, but only for the 2012 wave (see Table 2.6).

Perceived insecurity in the labour market

As far as the second type of job insecurity is considered – that is, the fear of not finding a similar job in case of job loss, data in the EQLS survey are only available for the two latest waves, 2012–16. The general trend depicts a decreasing pattern for all country groups in the period considered (Figure 2.4 and Table 2.7), but much higher percentages of perceived job insecurity compared to the previous type of subjective insecurity. Indeed, values recorded in 2012 show that more than half of the working population in Southern European, Anglo-Saxon and post-socialist neoliberal countries thought that it would be very or rather unlikely to find a job with similar salary in case of job loss. While these figures decreased for all groups in the following wave (with the exception of the conservative countries, where values remained stable), this percentage remained above 50 per cent for Southern European workers, while the less worried are employees in Scandinavian countries, where less than 30 per cent think they will have difficulties in finding a new job. Figure 2.5 and Table 2.7 show that that adult workers are systematically more worried about re-employment opportunties than their younger peers.

Cognitive and labour market insecurity

Finally, figures for the combination of the two types of subjective job insecurity are shown in Figure 2.6. Overall, the share of individuals who perceive their job as insecure (likely to be at risk in the next six months) *and* are also afraid of not finding a similar one is relatively limited (starts at much lower levels than the figures of cognitive and labour market job insecurity) and show a steep decrease between the two waves, particularly for workers in the post-socialist neoliberal, Southern European and Anglo-Saxon countries. The figures for 2012 indicate a clear differentiation between three groups: the Scandinavian and conservative cluster with the lowest percentages (2 per cent) of individuals who fear that their job is at risk and they will also have difficulties in finding a new one; Anglo-Saxon and embedded post-socialist

Figure 2.3: Percentage of cognitive job insecurity, young (aged 18–34) and adult (aged 35–54) workers

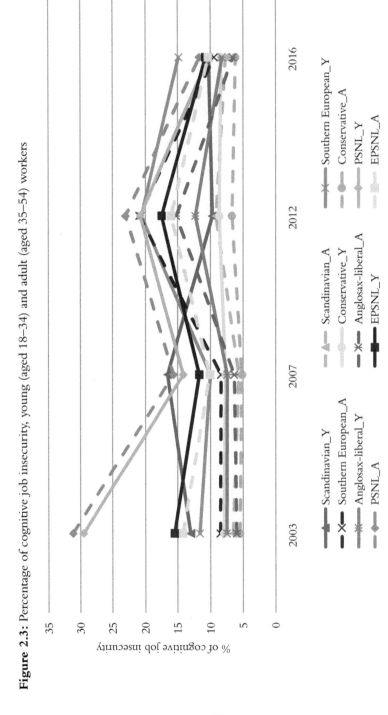

Note: the solid line is for young adults (18–34), the dotted line is for adult workers (35–54).

Source: own elaboration on EQLS data.

Table 2.6: Percentage of cognitive job insecurity by age group

Country clusters		2003	2007	2012	2016
Scandinavian	young	13.01	16.52	9.7	10.31
	adult	6.54	5.65	9.16	7.68
	Δ (Y–A)	6.47	10.87	0.54	2.63
Southern European	young	11.64	10.0	20.61	14.84
	adult	8.51	8.38	20.9	9.45
	Δ (Y–A)	3.13	1.62	-0.29	5.39
Conservative	young	7.94	7.69	8.65	8.38
	adult	5.5	5.18	6.69	6.15
	Δ (Y–A)	2.44	2.51	1.96	2.23
Anglosax-liberal	young	7.5	7.44	12.31	8.22
	adult	5.98	6.36	15.18	6.57
	Δ (Y–A)	1.52	1.08	-2.87	1.65
PSNL	young	29.52	14.1	20.79	10.29
	adult	31.17	15.61	23.02	11.71
	Δ (Y–A)	-1.65	-1.51	-2.23	-1.42
EPSNL	young	15.44	11.73	17.44	10.78
	adult	14.2	10.12	15.99	10.38
	Δ (Y–A)	1.24	1.61	1.45	0.4

Source: own elaboration on EQLS data.

neoliberal (EPSNL) countries in an intermediate position (between 8–10 per cent); and post-socialist neoliberal and Southern European countries as those with the highest perception of workers suffering from both types of subjective job insecurity (13 per cent). The steep decrease experienced in 2016 significantly lowered the percentage of workers concerned with these two types of job insecurity but the pattern of distribution among the European countries remained the same, with post-socialist neoliberal and Southern European countries scoring higher (6 per cent) than all the other European countries.

Given the generally low percentage of workers who declare both types of job insecurity, the comparison by age does not highlight substantial gaps between young adults and adult workers (Figure 2.7). Overall, adult workers tended to be more interested by the combination of both types of job insecurity in 2012, but in 2016 a slightly greater level of concern (+2 percentage points) remained observable for adult workers in post-socialist neoliberal and Anglo-Saxon countries only (Table 2.8).

Figure 2.4: Percentage of labour market job insecurity, age group 18–54

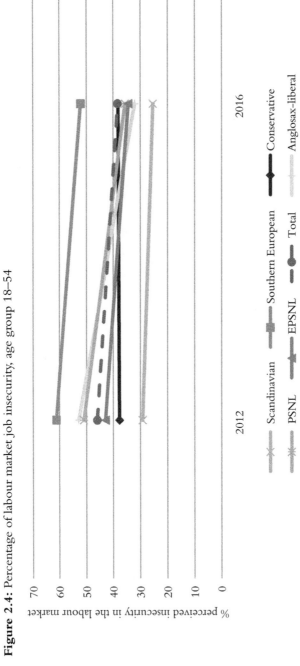

Note: % of employed individuals. Original question: If you were to lose or had to quit your job, how likely or unlikely is it that you will find a job of similar salary? Very +, Rather unlikely = 1.

Source: own elaboration on EQLS data.

Figure 2.5: Percentage of labour market job insecurity, young (aged 18–34) and adult (aged 35–54) workers

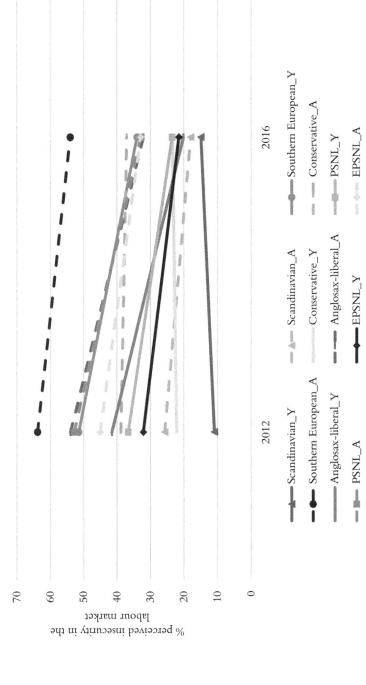

Note: the solid line is for young adults (18–34), the dotted line is for adult workers (35–54).

Source: own elaboration on EQLS data.

Table 2.7: Percentage of labour market job insecurity by age group

Country clusters		2012	2016
Scandinavian	young	10.9	14.91
	adult	25.72	17.98
	Δ (Y-A)	-14.82	-3.07
Southern European	young	51.47	33.98
	adult	63.82	54.0
	Δ (Y-A)	-12.35	-20.02
Conservative	young	22.16	23.42
	adult	38.82	37.1
	Δ (Y-A)	-16.66	-13.68
Anglosax-liberal	young	41.49	20.14
	adult	53.91	32.08
	Δ (Y-A)	-12.42	-11.94
PSNL	young	36.65	23.49
	adult	52.81	32.89
	Δ (Y-A)	-16.16	-9.4
EPSNL	young	32.11	21.49
	adult	45.03	32.91
	Δ (Y-A)	-12.92	-11.42

Source: own elaboration on EQLS data.

The interrelationship between subjective and objective job insecurity

The rich body of empirical research on job insecurity presented in Chapter 1 has highlighted the main factors both at the individual and macro levels that make people feel subjectively insecure. However, if empirical research has so far disentangled the macro and individual level factors that are associated with feelings of job insecurity, to our knowledge very little attention has been paid to the inconsistent profiles of individuals who do not fall into the consistent pattern, for example, feeling insecure in stable objective conditions or not feeling insecure in insecure objective conditions.

The focus on such inconsistent profiles is the value added of this study. Investigating the inconsistency between subjective and objective situations, how this varies across European countries and what factors may contribute to allocate individuals to one of the inconsistent profiles contributes to a better understanding of the mechanisms behind the perception of job insecurity and how policies can reach those most

Figure 2.6: Percentage of cognitive and labour market job insecurity, aged 18–54

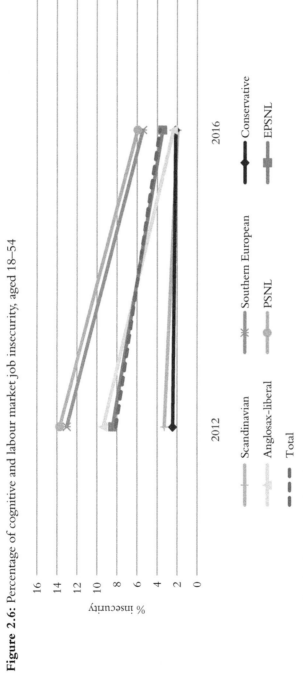

Note: % of employed individuals. Small absolute values for Scandinavian and Anglo-Saxon cluster.

Source: own elaboration on EQLS data.

57

Figure 2.7: Percentage of cognitive and labour market job insecurity, young (aged 18–34) and adult (aged 35–54) workers

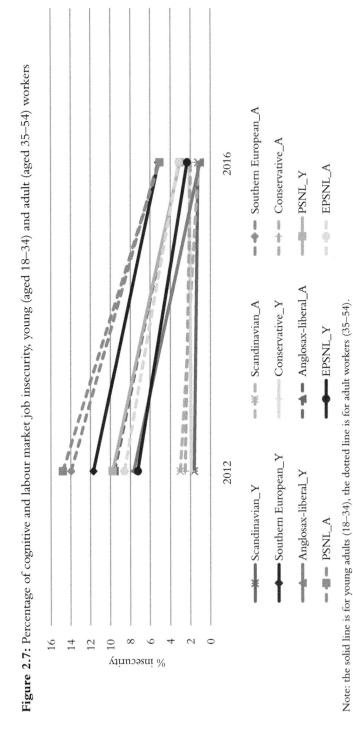

Note: the solid line is for young adults (18–34), the dotted line is for adult workers (35–54).

Source: own elaboration on EQLS data.

Table 2.8: Percentage of cognitive and labour market job insecurity by age group

Country clusters		2012	2016
Scandinavian	young	1.63	1.25
	adult	3.03	1.17
	Δ (Y-A)	–1.4	0.08
Southern European	young	13.97	5.2
	adult	11.69	5.16
	Δ (Y-A)	2.28	0.04
Conservative	young	1.92	2.13
	adult	2.54	2.0
	Δ (Y-A)	–0.62	0.13
Anglosax-liberal	young	7.65	1.05
	adult	9.6	3.1
	Δ (Y-A)	–1.95	–2.05
PSNL	young	9.78	3.07
	adult	14.81	5.06
	Δ (Y-A)	–5.03	–1.99
EPSNL	young	7.24	2.35
	adult	8.6	3.18
	Δ (Y-A)	–1.36	–0.83

Source: own elaboration on EQLS data.

in need. As highlighted in similar works in the field of objective and subjective poverty (Neumann et al, 2018), acknowledging and understanding the characteristics of the mismatch is important for policy implications. In fact, introducing policies aimed at reducing one dimension (for example, objective) may fail to obtain the desired outcome because of the other dimension (for example, subjective) which remains in place and is overlooked by the policy.

Therefore, the aim of this section is to investigate the interrelationship between the dimensions of objective and subjective job insecurity by focusing specifically on the inconsistent profiles of individuals who feel secure under one dimension but insecure under the other one. This section will first try to estimate the extent of such mismatch between the two dimensions of job insecurity in Europe. Second, the analysis will investigate what factors are more likely to be associated with inconsistent profiles of workers who, as an example, feel secure under one dimension (such as objective, having a permanent contract) but feel insecure under the other dimension (such as subjective, fearing to lose their job in the next six months) and vice versa. Building on the extensive literature on the role played by institutional filters posed by welfare state regimes (Esping-Andersen, 1990; Ferrera, 1996; Blossfeld et al, 2005, 2011; Burroni, 2016), and by the varieties of capitalism (Hall and Soskice, 2001), the analyses investigate whether and how the institutional setting and contextual factors, proxied by country clusters based on welfare models, may play a role in determining a mismatched profile. Moreover, the analysis will also take into consideration whether micro level characteristics like age may also play a role in determining the chances of falling within an inconsistent profile.

Inconsistent profiles

In order to reach the research aim of this study, a typology has been drawn that combines the dimension of objective and subjective job insecurity, defined as follows:

- 'Subjective insecurity' in this work is restricted solely to the aspect of cognitive job insecurity, defined as the perception of the possibility of losing one's current job. Due to its direct link with the contractual position, cognitive insecurity is more suitable than other aspects of job insecurity – such as labour market or income insecurity, related to the consequences of the event of job loss, or composite as affective insecurity – for empirically operationalizing the interrelationship with the objective dimension of job insecurity.
- 'Objective job insecurity' is defined on the basis of the contractual form with which the individual is employed.

The typology drawn in Table 2.9 identifies two coherent profiles (A and D) and two inconsistent profiles (B and C). The former refer to individuals who are consistently secure (profile A) or consistently insecure (profile D) in both the objective and subjective dimensions. The latter refer to individuals who are insecure in one dimension but secure in another one (profiles B and C). As an example, the people who fall into case B can be defined as 'negatively inconsistent' since they are objectively secure (namely are employed with a permanent contract) but feel subjectively insecure. The opposite case (C) can be defined as made up of 'positively inconsistent' individuals, who are objectively insecure (that is to say, employed with a non-permanent contract), but nonetheless feel subjectively secure.

The fact of belonging to one of the two mismatched profiles becomes the dependent variable explored in the logistic regression models presented in this section and, building on the literature presented in Chapter 1, the analysis is articulated in the following hypotheses.

Table 2.9: The interrelationship between objective and subjective job insecurity

		Subjective insecurity	
		Secure	Insecure
Objective insecurity	Secure	A Consistently secure	**B** **Negatively inconsistent:** **permanent but insecure**
	Insecure	**C** **Positively inconsistent:** **temporary but secure**	D Consistently insecure

Source: our elaboration based on Neumann et al (2018).

H1: negatively inconsistent

Hypothesis 1.a: we expect to observe that individuals working in contexts with relatively high labour market segmentation (for example, Southern European and conservative) are less likely to be negatively mismatched (since once becoming 'insiders', workers should feel protected). On the contrary, we expect to find a positive association of the chances of being negatively mismatched in post-socialist neoliberal and Anglo-Saxon clusters, where the dualism between insider and outsider is less pronounced.

Hypothesis 1.b: we expect to find that adult workers are positively associated with the risk of being negatively mismatched compared to their younger peers, due to the fast pace of innovation and their risk of obsolescence of skills.

H2: positively inconsistent

Hypothesis 2.a: we expect that protective and less segmented welfare state regimes, such as the Scandinavian one, are positively associated with the possibility of workers feeling positively inconsistent. Consistently, we expect to find that individuals have less chance of feeling positively inconsistent when living and working in Southern European and post-socialist neoliberal countries, characterized by low levels of job protection and a lower probability of transition toward protected jobs.

Hypothesis 2.b: overall, we expect to find that young people are more likely to be positively mismatched (compared to adult workers), in virtue of the optimism that may characterize the initial stages of career and fewer family responsibilities.

Findings

Descriptive statistics

A simple cross-tabulation of the distribution of subjectively and objectively insecure people helps identify the groups of interest and the extent of this phenomenon. Table 2.10 shows that, overall, the proportion of individuals falling into one of the two inconsistent profiles varies significantly. The number of individuals who are negatively inconsistent (corresponding to B in Table 2.9) – that is, are subjectively insecure despite being in a permanent position – is relatively small, around 10 per cent. On the contrary, the group of positively inconsistent individuals (corresponding to C in Table 2.9) is quite large, counting for about 70 per cent of workers employed with a fixed-term contract.

When considering separately the group of young adults from adult workers no substantial differences emerge, in particular for the case of negatively inconsistent individuals, which in both age groups involves about 9 per cent of the total population of workers employed with a permanent contract. While the case of positively inconsistent profiles seems to be slightly more common among young workers compared to their adult peers (+4 percentage points).

Regression models

Given this overview, it is now interesting to investigate how these inconsistent profiles are distributed across countries and across groups, to identify whether some institutional filters may play a role in shaping the chances of falling into one or the other inconsistent profile. In order to have a full and clearer picture of the associations exerted by predictors, and to compare estimates for young and adult workers, it is helpful to refer to the average marginal effects of the predictors of interest to grasp actual probabilities per each group (Leeper, 2018).

Average marginal effects plotted in Figures 2.8 and 2.9 indicate the difference in percentage points in the likelihood of experiencing the outcome

Table 2.10: Inconsistent profiles (age 18–54)

	Young and adult workers (18–54)		Young adults (18–34)		Adults (35–54)	
	Subjective insecurity (%)		Subjective insecurity (%)		Subjective insecurity (%)	
Objective insecurity (%)	Secure	Insecure	Secure	Insecure	Secure	Insecure
Permanent contract	90.3	**9.7**	90.4	**9.6**	90.2	**9.8**
Fixed-term contract	**71.4**	28.6	**73.5**	26.5	**69.2**	30.8
Total	87.8	12.2	86.8	13.2	88.1	11.9

Note: numbers in bold indicate inconsistent profiles

Source: own elaboration on EQLS data.

Figure 2.8: Average marginal effects of being negatively inconsistent by welfare regime

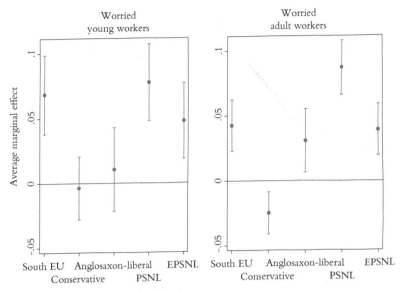

Note: reference category = Scandinavian cluster.

Source: own elaboration on EQLS data.

of interest (such as being negatively inconsistent in Table 2.8), given the fact of belonging to a certain country cluster (represented on the x axis). Values above the line (equal to 0) indicate a higher likelihood compared to the reference category (for example, the Scandinavian cluster), values below the line indicate a lower likelihood. As an example, the first dot in the left panel of Figure 2.8 indicates the difference (in percentage points) in the likelihood of having a permanent contract but being subjectively insecure for individuals living in the Southern European cluster versus the Scandinavian cluster (the reference category), given a 95 per cent confidence interval (the vertical bar).

Negatively inconsistent profiles

As far as the group of 'negatively inconsistent' individuals is concerned (employed with a permanent contract but feeling subjectively insecure, B in Table 2.9), the role of institutional filters seems confirmed (Figure 2.8): in countries with less labour market protection (like South-European countries) and a neoliberal approach (as post-socialist countries PSNL and EPSNL), individuals tend to 'worry' more than in Scandinavian countries. By contrast, young people in the conservative and in the Anglo-Saxon liberal cluster do not perceive different levels of concern compared to their peers in

Scandinavian countries. Things are a bit different when it comes to adult workers (right side panel of Figure 2.8). The pattern remains the same, with permanent workers in post- socialist countries and South-European countries showing higher levels of concern compared to Scandinavian peers. However, adult workers with permanent contracts living in the conservative cluster tend to 'worry' even less than Scandinavian peers (although to a limited extent of about -2 percentage points); while adult workers in the Anglo-Saxon cluster (unlike young workers in the same countries) feel subjectively insecure in their permanent position (although to a limited extent, of about +3 percentage points compared to adults in Scandinavian countries).

As far as individual-level factors are concerned, Table A2.1 (in the Methodological appendix) shows that for both young and adult workers being employed in the private sector increases the risk of feeling insecure despite having a permanent contract. For young workers, family responsibilities (proxied by household size or the presence of a partner) do not have a significant role in influencing (increasing or decreasing) their level of concern, possibly linked to a greater presence of dual-earner couples among young people or at least more equally distributed gender roles. On the contrary, the burden of family responsibilities does increase the extent of concern for adult employees, who have a permanent contract but see their sense of subjective insecurity increasing if they have a large family (4–5 or more people) or an unemployed partner.

Therefore Hypothesis 1.a is supported, although only partly. Contrary to what we hypothesized, both young and adult individuals working in the Southern European countries show higher chances of falling into the category of negatively mismatched. This seems to suggest that the segmented labour market characterizing these countries does not seem to provide protection as expected, neither for insiders nor outsiders. However, in line with the hypothesis, the segmented labour market that workers living in countries characterized by a conservative welfare model experience seems to protect both young and adult workers who indeed have the same or even lower (for adults) chances of being negatively mismatched than Scandinavian employees (the reference category). Moreover, again as expected by Hypothesis 1.a, in Eastern European countries (both Baltic and Central-Eastern European), both young and adult workers show a higher likelihood of being negatively mismatched, as well as adult workers in the liberal cluster, hence supporting the assumption that the neoliberal regulation of the labour market in these countries tends to increase the concern and feeling of insecurity of employees (widespread in post-socialist countries, limited to adult workers in UK and Ireland). The latter result is in line with Hypothesis 2.b, for which adult workers may be more positively associated with the category of 'negatively inconsistent' because of the fast pace of

Figure 2.9: Average marginal effects of being positively inconsistent by welfare regime (social-democratic cluster)

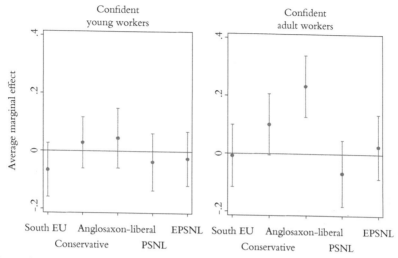

Note: reference category = social-democratic cluster (social-democratic is here used as a synonym of Scandinavian). Standard errors in parentheses, *** p<0.01, ** p<0.05, + p<0.1. Source: own elaboration on EQLS data.

innovation and their risk of obsolescence of skills, that seems to be evident especially in the liberal countries, but not in the others.

Positively inconsistent profiles

As far as the group of 'positively inconsistent' individuals are concerned (that is, employed with a temporary contract but not subjectively insecure), the differences among young and adult workers become quite visible (Figures 2.9 and 2.10). Indeed, for young workers the differences associated with the welfare state regime in regard to the chances of feeling insecure while employed with temporary contracts are visible but not as expected. Indeed, when considering Scandinavian countries as the reference category no significant differences emerge among young workers (left panel of Figure 2.9) while a relative advantage of Anglo-Saxon adult workers over Scandinavian peers is observable (right panel of Figure 2.9). However, when comparing the chances of being in a temporary position but feeling subjectively secure against the chances of those in Southern European countries (switching the reference category to Southern European countries, as in Figure 2.10), country differences emerge also for young workers. Indeed, young people living in the conservative cluster and in the Anglo-Saxon countries tend to have higher chances of falling into the category of positively inconsistent

Figure 2.10: Average marginal effects of being positively inconsistent by welfare regime (Southern-European cluster)

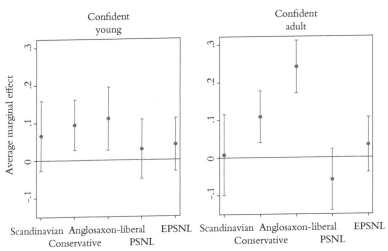

Note: reference category = Southern-European cluster. Standard errors in parentheses, ★★★ p<0.01, ★★ p<0.05, + p<0.1.

Source: own elaboration on EQLS data.

compared to their peers in Southern European countries, while young people in Scandinavian countries do not show a different attitude than their peers in Southern Europe. The same pattern is also observable among adult workers (right panel in Figure 2.10), where adult workers with a temporary contract have more chances of feeling subjectively secure in the Anglo-Saxon liberal cluster (+24 percentage points), and in conservative countries (+ 10 percentage points) compared to peers in Southern European countries. Moreover, Table A2.2 (positively inconsistent; in the Methodological appendix) shows that for positively inconsistent profiles most of the variation is captured by welfare state models, while micro level factors related to the sector of employment or family responsibilities do not show any significant association with the chances of being in this type of inconsistent profile.

Therefore, Hypothesis 2.a is only partly supported, insofar as the findings provide no support for a protective role of the Scandinavian model of labour regulation, where indeed employees do not feel more positively mismatched than in other low protective institutional contexts like the Southern European and post-socialist countries. Nonetheless, employees living in Southern European countries, characterized by lower probabilities of transition toward protected jobs, show a disadvantage in the likelihood of falling into the profile of positively inconsistent only compared to individuals living in the conservative and liberal cluster (both young and adult workers). These results suggest that Scandinavians with temporary contracts tend to worry a lot, or at least more than expected, and may call for a reflection on the issue of the quality of temporary contracts in the different institutional contexts. Therefore, it seems that – for different reasons – the segmented and highly regulated labour market of conservative countries as well as the low regulated liberal labour market of UK and Ireland provides more chances of feeling secure, despite being in a situation of objective insecurity, than the other welfare state systems, even the protective Scandinavian one (at least for adult workers). Moreover, results plotted in Figures 2.9 and 2.10 do not provide support for the hypothesis of greater likelihood of being positively mismatched for young adults compared to adults.

Conclusion

This chapter has a twofold aim: first, it described the extent of job insecurity in European countries, both considering the objective and the subjective dimensions. Second, it dedicated particular attention to the analysis of the interrelationship between these two dimensions and their non-automatic correspondence, focusing on some 'inconsistent' profiles where security in one dimension was flanked with insecurity in the other dimension.

The descriptive statistics showed that, for objective job insecurity in all countries considered, youth unemployment is higher than unemployment among other age groups. Youth unemployment (18–24) appears to follow a cyclical pattern, particularly regarding the financial crisis in 2008, after which youth unemployment rates rose in most countries. In most countries, they had declined after 2012, but once again increased from 2019 with the pandemic period.

The magnitude of youth unemployment shows clear variations across welfare regimes, particularly in Southern European countries with unemployment rates of 20 to 30 per cent before the crisis and a strong increase after it, with values in Greece and Spain even rising to above 50 per cent. In fact, in these countries the process of segmentation had been particularly strong in the phase of recession, since the fixed-term contracts of youth had not been renewed.

Lowest values of youth unemployment are observed in the employment-maintaining regimes of social-democratic and liberal countries.

Conservatives and social-democratic countries appear better able to protect their young workers from unemployment, even in the time of recession. In particular, in the German-speaking countries (Austria, Germany and Switzerland), even if regulation is very similar to the welfare regime in Southern European countries and flexibilization had been based on labour market segmentation, a combination of the 'dual training' system with active labour market policies has maintained comparatively low unemployment rates among its youth.

In the social-democratic countries, the generous welfare state and active reintegration policies reduce long-term labour market risks and appear to protect young people from unemployment even in periods of financial and economic crisis.

Eastern European countries initially suffered from youth unemployment, particularly after the system transformation following independence from the Russian Federation in the 1990s, reflected in high values in the early 2000s. After a second peak around the 2008 financial crisis, they have normalized.

With respect to subjective job insecurity, the figures elaborate on EQLS data from 2003 to 2016,[1] showing for cognitive job insecurity an increase of the share of employees who felt their job being at risk in the next six months (after the interview) in correspondence of the 2012 wave, probably a tail of the negative consequences of the economic crisis of 2008, but an overall decrease in the following wave of 2016. The decrease has been more robust for post-socialist countries, both those belonging to the Baltic area and the Central-Eastern European regions, as well as for Southern European countries, which settled on values slightly above 10 per cent in 2016, just a few percentage points higher than the other welfare state countries (8 per cent for Scandinavian and 6 per cent for conservative and Anglo-Saxon countries). Overall, both young and young adults tend to experience this type of job insecurity more frequently than adult workers in all country clusters – with the sole exception of post-socialist Baltic countries – confirming that early entrants and early career workers tend to perceive themselves at risk and their jobs not safe, at least compared to adult workers in their own countries.

A decrease has also been observed in the other type of job insecurity, that is, the share of employees who perceive themselves as insecure in terms of chances of finding a similar new job in case of loss of their current one. The main difference with respect to the previous type of job insecurity is the scale, much higher in the case of labour market job insecurity. Indeed, the idea of searching and not being able to find a similar job worries half of the employees working in Southern European countries, while it ranges from 40 per cent to 30 per cent in the other clusters, with the lower band represented by Scandinavian employees, where only one in four employees fears not being able of finding a similar job (25 per cent). Contrary to what was observed for cognitive job insecurity, in this case young and young adults are systematically less concerned with the chances of finding a new job in case of job loss, while adult workers in all country clusters show higher percentages of labour market job insecurity. This may be linked to the fact that older workers may find themselves less competitive and less employable on the labour market; it may also be due to the fast pace of technological change and a higher risk for them of obsolescence of skills. Yet, this result may also be associated with the position in the labour market hierarchy. Indeed, the question asks for the likelihood of finding a 'similar' job: since it is more likely that adult workers may be in a position that offered an internal career path, with responsibility and wage premia, such job characteristics may not be easily replicable in a new job. As a result, young workers may generally be more optimistic because they may associate low expectations to their entry jobs or attribute different values to their initial jobs, which likely do not include the same benefit and wage levels as those of mature workers.

Finally, employees who suffer both types of job insecurity, cognitive and labour market job insecurity (that is, who feel their job is at risk in the coming months and also are afraid of not being able to find a similar job in case of loss), are a minority in all countries considered. In this respect three main groups are identifiable, broadly corresponding to the different levels of regulation of the labour market. Employees in Southern European and post-socialist Baltic countries are those who worried the most in 2012 and experienced the largest decrease in 2016 from about 13 per cent to 6 per cent. Anglo-Saxon and post-socialist countries in the central European region also had values around 10 per cent in 2012; however, this lowered to an almost neglible share of 2–3 per cent, a level which remained stable in Scandinavian and conservative countries.

The second part of the chapter then focused on the interrelation between the objective and subjective dimension of job insecurity. For this exercise only cognitive job insecurity was considered, given that it is the most comparable type of subjective job insecurity with objective job insecurity.

By combining objective and subjective job insecurity, we drew up a typology, then narrowed the focus onto two inconsistent categories in which one type of security (for example, objective) does not automatically correspond to the other type of security (for example, subjective). These 'inconsistent' categories identify individuals who are secure in one dimension but insecure in the other one and thus are not perfectly matched in a consistent condition of completely secure or insecure worker. As an example, workers can be defined as positively inconsistent when they are insecure in objective terms (namely, employed with a temporary contract), but are subjectively secure (they do not consider their job at risk in the next six months). On the other hand, negatively inconsistent workers are those who are secure in objective terms (having a permanent contract) but nonetheless feel subjectively insecure (feeling likely to lose their job in the next six months).

Findings for the main dimension of interest, the welfare state model and labour market regulation, show a more complex picture than in previous research. The theory of welfare state regimes and variety of capitalism seems to explain only in part the subjective perception of job insecurity today. Probably the financial and economic crisis and the increase of insecurity due to several phenomena – such as unionization, financialization of the economy, globalization, and the digital revolution (Kalleberg and Vallas,

2017), together with recent welfare state reforms – may have changed the perception of insecurity for some (groups of) countries.

First, the model of Scandinavian countries, considered as one which reproduced a low level of job insecurity, does still protect from the probability of falling into an inconsistent category, but less than what was expected. As an example, the Scandinavian cluster is more protective than other welfare regime configurations toward permanent workers who feel insecure even if they have a secure job (negatively inconsistent group) but does not provide a greater relative advantage in terms of optimist mismatch.

In fact, the results show that in the Nordic system there is less probability of a worker being negatively inconsistent, compared to other welfare state models, but this advantage is no longer observable in the probability of being optimist inconsistent, namely insecure in objective terms but feeling subjectively secure. This could be linked to recent welfare state reforms in which conditionality for access to social protection and unemployment benefits has increased (Hussain et al, 2012; Burroni, 2016). If we add the fact that the rate of involuntary nonstandard work is very high in the Nordic countries, such as the segmentation between local and immigrant workers, we see a new tract of the Nordic model: the system does not protect (as it did before) temporary workers from a high level of social insecurity. According to the results, it seems that the new reforms put on the margins whoever is not inside the protected labour market or does not meet the requirements. As a consequence, the perception of insecurity has increased for these workers. For this reason, only people inside the system still perceived themselves as protected.

On the contrary, the other welfare state regime, the Anglo-Saxon one, seems to keep young and young adults in permanent positions, as well as adults in temporary roles, far from the perception of job insecurity, compared to other systems. It can be argued that good economic performances and a tradition of flexibility and high mobility in the labour market may contribute to protecting workers against subjective job insecurity, although through market mechanisms (Ebralidze, 2011).

Looking at two other welfare state models, the Southern European and conservative, indicated from previous studies as models in which the level of subjective job insecurity was expected to be very high due to the presence of a very segmented labour market, we find a process of diversification. Workers in the Southern European cluster have a higher probability of being negatively inconsistent, indicating that workers perceive greater job insecurity (compared to the Scandinavian one) even if working with permanent contracts. However, when it comes to observing how 'confident' workers of the Southern European cluster employed with temporary contracts (namely positively inconsistent) are, there is no observable difference with their Scandinavian peers, but a disadvantage compared to the liberal and conservative cluster. Indeed, the conservative model confirms its protective role: when it comes to the chances of falling into the negatively inconsistent profile (permanent workers feeling insecure) young and young adult workers in the conservative cluster have the same likelihood as their Scandinavian peers or, even slightly lower if adult workers. Similarly, adult employees with temporary contracts in conservative countries have similar chances of being 'confident' (that is, falling into the profile of positive mismatch) than their Scandinavian peers and, in general, employees of all ages have higher chances of being confident than their peers in the Southern European countries. Therefore, at least when it comes to subjective job insecurity and its non-automatic association with objective conditions employment, the two models of labour market regulation, the conservative and liberal cluster, seem to protect workers from subjective job insecurity through different mechanisms: the former with its segmentation and protection of insiders, the latter through the dynamism of its labour market.

Methodological appendix

Data

The analyses presented in Chapter 2 are based on cross-sectional data from the European Quality of Life Survey (EQLS). This database contains information on the current type of employment and specific questions on the perception of the risk of losing one's current job and on the possibilities of finding another suitable one. The unit of analysis is employed individuals, from 18 to 54 years of age, subsequently grouped into young people aged 18–34 and adults aged 35–54, residing in 28 member states of the European Union (including the UK). The total number is 10,615 young individuals and 19,957 adults.

Variables

Dependent variables

As far as the measurement of job insecurity is concerned, the literature has pointed to various indicators, methods and limitations as well (Kiersztyn, 2017). Building on the theoretical chapter (Chapter 1), the authors adopted the variables commonly used in literature:

• Objective job insecurity is operationalized as 1 if the individual has a permanent contract and equal to 0 if the individual works with various forms of fixed-term contracts (fixed-term, agency worker, apprenticeship), whereas no contracts or other residual forms are excluded.

- Subjective insecurity is operationalized as a dichotomous variable with a value equal to 1 for those who answer 'rather probable' or 'very probable' to the question 'How likely or unlikely do you think it is that you might lose your job in the next six months?'(value 0 for those who answer differently).

For the logistic regression models two dependent variables have been defined, following Table 2.9:

- Positively inconsistent: individuals who are objectively insecure but subjectively secure (temporary contract and no cognitive insecurity).
- Negatively inconsistent: individuals who are objectively secure but subjectively insecure (permanent contract and cognitive insecurity).

Independent variables

The main explanatory variable refers to the institutional context and it is proxied by the welfare regime and associated labour market regulation model. The grouping of 28 European countries included in EQLS into clusters follows the classic typology of welfare models outlined by Esping-Andersen (1990) and then updated by Ferrera (1996). For the post-socialist countries, we have followed the typology proposed by Bohle and Greskovits (2012), which divides these countries into a neoliberal model and an embedded neoliberal and neo-corporative model. The latter has been aggregated to the second model for reasons of parsimony. Therefore, the 28 EU member states included in EQLS have been grouped as follows:

- Scandinavian/social-democratic cluster: Denmark, Finland and Sweden;
- Southern European cluster: Greece, Spain, Italy, Portugal, Cyprus and Malta;
- Conservative cluster: Germany, Austria, France, the Netherlands and Luxembourg;
- Anglo-Saxon/liberal cluster: the United Kingdom and Ireland;
- Post-socialist neoliberal (PSNL) cluster (corresponding to Baltic countries): Estonia, Latvia, Lithuania, Bulgaria, Croatia and Romania;
- 'Embedded' post-socialist neoliberal (EPSNL) cluster (corresponding to Central-Eastern European countries): Slovak Republic, Czech Republic, Hungary, Poland and Slovenia.

Other independent variables are included as control variables and relate to: sector of employment (public versus private), family responsibilities, in particular household size, the presence of a partner and the individual labour market status of the partner. Finally, controls for gender, educational level and wave are included in the regression models.

Method

To investigate whether and to what extent the explanatory factors that have been identified for the institutional context and for individual characteristics are associated with the mismatched profiles, the analyses rely on a set of logistic regressions. The models estimate the likelihood of falling into one of the inconsistent profiles (for example, positively inconsistent), as opposed to the chances of being in the associated consistent group (for example, consistently secure). Models for young adults (18–34) and adult workers (35–54) are run separately.

Table A2.1: Estimates of logistic regression models for the probability of being negatively inconsistent (versus consistently secure) for young and adult people

Negatively inconsistent profile	Young (18–34)			Adult (35–54)		
Welfare state regime (ref. = Scandinavian)	(1)	(2)	(3)	(4)	(5)	(6)
Southern European	0.823***	.831***	0.812***	0.515***	0.514***	0.692***
	(0.214)	(0.215)	(0.274)	(0.130)	(0.130)	(0.159)
Conservative	−0.0683	−0.0678	−0.306	−0.444***	−0.445***	−0.416**
	(0.217)	(0.217)	(0.277)	(0.135)	(0.136)	(0.169)
Anglosax-liberal	0.161	0.167	−0.158	0.394**	0.392**	0.330+
	(0.266)	(0.267)	(0.366)	(0.156)	(0.156)	(0.198)
Post-socialist neoliberal (Baltic)	0.903***	0.909***	0.927***	0.904***	0.898***	1.016***
	(0.209)	(0.209)	(0.261)	(0.126)	(0.126)	(0.156)
Embedded post-socialist neoliberal (CEE)	0.625***	0.631***	0.620**	0.483***	0.479***	0.607***
	(0.217)	(0.217)	(0.273)	(0.132)	(0.132)	(0.161)
Sector of employment (private)	0.282**	0.283**	0.352**	0.384***	0.385***	0.370***
	(0.114)	(0.114)	(0.151)	(0.0689)	(0.0689)	(0.0826)
Household size (ref. = 1 person)						
Household size = 2 people	−0.144	−0.178		−0.125	−0.00988	
	(0.141)	(0.164)		(0.102)	(0.120)	
Household size = 3 to 4 people	−0.108	−0.139		−0.0643	0.0734	
	(0.132)	(0.151)		(0.0912)	(0.119)	
Household size = 5 or more people	−0.0355	−0.0660		0.149	0.298**	

Table A2.1: Estimates of logistic regression models for the probability of being negatively inconsistent (versus consistently secure) for young and adult people (continued)

Negatively inconsistent profile	Young (18–34)			Adult (35–54)		
Welfare state regime (ref. = Scandinavian)	(1)	(2)	(3)	(4)	(5)	(6)
	(0.193)	(0.206)		(0.120)	(0.146)	
Has a partner		0.0466			−0.159+	
		(0.110)			(0.0890)	
Partner's labour market status (ref. = employed)						
Partner's labour market status = unemployed			0.412			0.327**
			(0.265)			(0.154)
Partner's labour market status = inactive			−0.187			0.117
			(0.350)			(0.124)
Partner's labour market status = student			0.145			−0.211
			(0.417)			(0.736)
Controls:						
education	Y	Y	Y	Y	Y	Y
sex	Y	Y	Y	Y	Y	Y
wave	Y	Y	Y	Y	Y	Y
Constant	−2.362***	−2.362***	−2.600***	−2.426***	−2.423***	−2.588***
	(0.264)	(0.264)	(0.330)	(0.168)	(0.168)	(0.187)
Observations	5,612	5,612	3,255	12,691	12,691	9,107

Note: standard errors in parentheses, *** p<0.01, ** p<0.05, + p<0.1

Source: own elaboration on EQLS data.

75

Table A2.2: Estimates of logistic regression models for the probability of being positively inconsistent (versus consistently insecure) for young and adult people

Positively inconsistent profile	Young			Adult		
Welfare state regime (ref. = Scandinavian)	(1)	(2)	(3)	(4)	(5)	(6)
Southern European	−0.305	−0.326	−0.406	0.0319	−0.0345	−0.0643
	(0.244)	(0.245)	(0.381)	(0.249)	(0.249)	(0.316)
Conservative	0.163	0.159	0.157	0.504**	0.501+	0.528
	(0.246)	(0.246)	(0.377)	(0.257)	(0.257)	(0.333)
Anglosax–liberal	0.274	0.258	0.0327	1.440***	1.446***	1.660***
	(0.300)	(0.301)	(0.456)	(0.332)	(0.332)	(0.437)
Post-socialist neoliberal (Baltic)	−0.186	−0.188	−0.380	−0.289	−0.292	−0.399
	(0.262)	(0.262)	(0.383)	(0.260)	(0.260)	(0.327)
Embedded post-socialist neoliberal (CEE)	−0.113	−0.128	−0.0856	0.122	0.121	0.0380
	(0.250)	(0.251)	(0.383)	(0.259)	(0.259)	(0.327)
Sector of employment (private)	−0.0546	−0.0615	−0.159	−0.0150	−0.0186	−0.111
	(0.136)	(0.137)	(0.202)	(0.131)	(0.131)	(0.163)
Household size (ref. = 1 person)						
Household size = 2 people	0.191	0.272		0.0396	0.189	
	(0.181)	(0.206)		(0.182)	(0.219)	
Household size = 3 to 4 people	0.201	0.254		0.226	0.408+	
	(0.173)	(0.185)		(0.165)	(0.221)	
Household size = 5 or more people	0.103	0.161		0.247	0.446	
	(0.235)	(0.246)		(0.223)	(0.275)	

Table A2.2: Estimates of logistic regression models for the probability of being positively inconsistent (versus consistently insecure) for young and adult people (continued)

Positively inconsistent profile	Young			Adult		
Welfare state regime (ref. = Scandinavian)	(1)	(2)	(3)	(4)	(5)	(6)
Has a partner		-0.113			-0.214	
		(0.138)			(0.172)	
Partner's labour market status (ref. = employed)						
Partner's labour market status = unemployed			-0.0993			0.0418
			(0.346)			(0.305)
Partner's labour market status = inactive			-0.269			0.314
			(0.420)			(0.266)
Partner's labour market status = student			0.201			-0.240
			(0.602)			(1.268)
Controls:						
education	Y	Y	Y	Y	Y	Y
sex	Y	Y	Y	Y	Y	Y
wave	Y	Y	Y	Y	Y	Y
Constant	0.678**	0.688**	0.592	-0.133	-0.127	-0.117
	(0.299)	(0.300)	(0.439)	(0.303)	(0.303)	(0.361)
Observations	1,493	1,493	658	1,441	1,441	944

Note: standard errors in parentheses, *** p<0.01, ** p<0.05, + p<0.1.

Source: own elaboration on EQLS data.

3

Job Insecurity and Transition to Adulthood

This chapter will analyse the decision-making mechanisms and strategies of individuals who must act in conditions of objective and/or subjective job insecurity. It will focus on young people in Europe in conditions of low attachment to the labour market and their decision-making mechanisms with respect to the transition to autonomous living. The results will be contextualized at the macro level taking into consideration the role of the welfare state regimes offering a different set of constraints and opportunities in the various countries considered.

In particular, we will focus on the transition of 'leaving the parental home', because this is considered an important point in the process of becoming adult in the traditional theory of 'life courses'. Literature explains that there are different patterns of transition in different welfare state systems and that job insecurity is one of the determinants of postponement of this transition. Data show that the year of leaving the parental home is very different across Europe.

Then we will focus on how objective and subjective job insecurity affect housing autonomy of youth in different welfare state regimes. In particular, we will look at: Does their situation correlate to their decision about leaving home? How does this vary across welfare state system and countries? Is objective job insecurity relevant? Is subjective job insecurity relevant? And how are they linked to other factors (such as culture, housing affordability, access to credit and so on). How do young people make their decisions (what are their 'decision mechanisms')?

The rationale behind the choice of the countries is driven by the mixed-method design of the chapter. It integrates quantitative data aimed at illustrating statistical regularities around the phenomenon of leaving the parental home and qualitative data aimed at investigating the meaning and mechanisms behind such transition. Therefore, the first section provides an overview of the association between individuals' labour market situation and transition out of the parental home in seven European countries, as it emerges from quantitative data. The focus is on the condition of objective job insecurity in particular (that is, the lack of a permanent job as defined in Chapter 1). The following section addresses the same relationship for the same European countries with qualitative data, exploring both the objective and −especially − the subjective dimension of job insecurity, providing a more encompassing analysis of the decision process behind the decision to leave the parental home. Details about data and methods are provided in the Methodological appendix at the end of the chapter.

Leaving home and objective job insecurity: variations between and within welfare state regimes

This section explores the relationship between a condition of objective job insecurity, as proxied by the individual's labour market situation, and the transition out of the parental home for young people aged 16 to 40 years old (see the methodological appendix for more details on the sample). To do so, this section presents empirical analyses based on longitudinal data of the European Union Statistics on Income and Living Conditions database (EU-SILC) for seven countries, belonging to different welfare regimes.

The rationale for the choice of the countries to include in the analysis relies on the aim of comparing different welfare regimes and realizing a complementary mixed-method research design. To this end, the chapter takes into consideration a set of countries, each representative of different welfare state regimes, and for which we have access to both quantitative and qualitative empirical data about the chances of exiting the parental home. Therefore, the countries considered are: Greece and Italy as representative of the Southern European model (Ferrera, 1996); Bulgaria, Estonia and Poland as representative of Eastern European countries, the first two characterized by a post-socialist neoliberal (PSNL) welfare regime, the latter with a more 'embedded' post-socialist neoliberal (EPSBL) model (Bohle and Greskovits, 2012). Finally, Sweden is included as a representative country of the social-democratic welfare model and the United Kingdom as the reference for the liberal model in the European context.[1]

Starting from the countries belonging to the Southern European cluster (Figure 3.1), results of the quantitative analyses indicate that for young people in Greece having a job is relevant for making the transition out of the parental home, but whether the job is temporary or permanent does not seem to make a difference. Indeed, individuals who are employed with a temporary job do not show a different likelihood of exiting the parental home compared to their peers with a permanent job (the reference category), while a significant disadvantage (-1.5 percentage points) is observable for unemployed individuals who have lower chances of exiting the parental home, but not for those inactive or students. A significant disadvantage is observable for individuals

Figure 3.1: Average marginal effects of leaving parental home by labour market status (Greece and Italy)

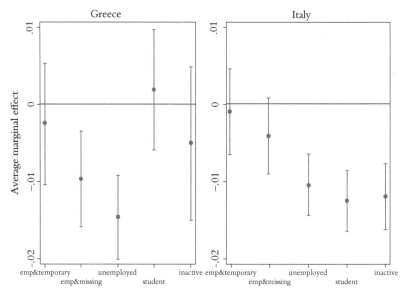

Note: reference = employed and permanent

Source: own elaboration based on EU-SILC longitudinal dataset (EU-SILC12–EU-SILC19).

who are employed but for whom information on the type of contract is not available (emp&missing). We are not able to identify whether lack of information on the type of contract may indicate a situation of unregulated job or is simply a result of lack of information in the survey due to multiple reasons, therefore any interpretation must be very cautious.

Similarly, for Italian young people (right panel in Figure 3.1) having a job seems to be the most important factor: whether it is temporary or not does not make any significant difference. Rather, not having a job (because unemployed or inactive, or student) decreases the chances of leaving the parental home (-1.5 percentage points compared to individuals who are employed and permanent).

The second group of countries belongs to the broad group of Eastern European countries. According to Bohle and Greskovits (2012) the welfare regimes of Bulgaria, Estonia and Poland can be grouped under the category of post-socialist welfare regimes, but with a distinction between a more neoliberal-oriented welfare regime in Estonia and Bulgaria, as opposed to a more 'embedded' neoliberal model for Poland.

The results of quantitative analyses for the three countries are shown in Figure 3.2. For all three countries, the lack of a stable job does not seem to be a critical factor influencing the chances of leaving parental home. As regards Bulgaria, no significant association between labour market status and chances

Figure 3.2: Average marginal effect of leaving parental home by labour market status (Bulgaria, Poland and Estonia)

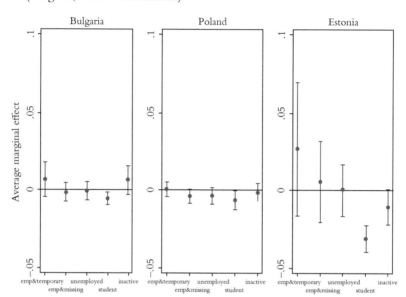

Note: reference = employed and permanent; due to collinearity, the variable about parental education has been dropped for Bulgaria.

Source: own elaboration based on EU-SILC longitudinal dataset (EU-SILC12–EU-SILC19).

of exiting the parental home emerges, with the only exception being for the status of student (which is negatively associated with housing autonomy). However, the characteristics of the sample may suggest that in this country the process of transition out of the parental home may take different patterns and as well as being influenced by other factors (such as cultural). Indeed, in the age period considered (10 years) only a very limited number of exits is observable (nr 70, 68 per cent of which happen with a partner) and about 14 per cent of individuals already lived together with their partner and their parents at the beginning of the observation period, an element which may explain the small number of exits to form an independent household.

As for Bulgaria, so also for Poland, where a significant association between individual labour market status and chances of exiting the parental home does not emerge, with the only exception being students. As for Bulgaria, Poland also shows a non-negligible share (10 per cent) of people who already live with partners and their parents at the beginning of the observation period. Moreover, for Poland, the relationship between lack of job and leaving the parental home seems to be mediated by the presence of a partner and by educational level: when adding the control for the presence of a partner, the negative association for unemployed (and student) individuals decreases, up to disappearing when also adding the educational level.

Finally, for Estonia a negative association between the individual labour market condition and the chance of leaving the parental home is only observable for students (-3 percentage points). Therefore, for Estonia too, objective job insecurity – at least as operationalized in these models – do not seem to be a key factor in influencing the chances of exiting the parental home. At the same time, as for the other countries, the lack of income from paid work that characterizes the condition of unemployed individuals does not seem to be associated with lower chances of exiting the parental home. It can be argued that other factors may play a significant role in the decision-making process associated with the transition out of the parental home. In this respect, the analysis of qualitative material can be of help in understanding the complex dynamics that lead to the decision of leaving parental household.

Finally, the last two countries taken into consideration are Sweden, belonging to the social-democratic welfare model and the UK, belonging to the liberal cluster.

In the case of Sweden (top panel of Figure 3.3), the association between individual labour market situation and the chance of exiting the parental home is significant and robust across several controls. Indeed, compared to employed individuals with a permanent contract, all labour market situations associated with labour market exclusion have a lower chance of exiting the parental home. With the exception of individuals in a situation of objective job insecurity (that is, employed people who hold a temporary contract), a negative association is observed for individuals who are involuntary excluded from the labour market (unemployed -13 percentage points) and voluntary excluded (students -10 percentage points and inactive -15 percentage points). This suggests that economic factors such as the availability of income from paid work may play a substantial role in the decision-making process about housing transition in Sweden.

On the contrary, in the case of the UK (bottom panel of Figure 3.3), the negative association between the stability of the employment contract and the transition out of the parental home is not observable, while a decrease of the chances of exiting the parental home emerges for unemployed (-2 percentage points) and students (-1.6 percentage points). On the contrary, the type of contract, temporary or permanent, does not seem to play any significant role in the decision to exit the parental home.

These preliminary analyses, narrowed down to the objective conditions of job insecurity, seem to suggest that the lack of a job may represent a significant factor in determining lesser chances of exiting the parental home, given the negative association with unemployed people observable in Greece, Italy, Sweden and the UK. However, a different picture emerges for Eastern European countries, where only students show a significant lower chance of exiting the parental home. With respect to this latter group of countries, characterized by a relatively high proportion of multi-family arrangements,

Figure 3.3: Average marginal effect of leaving parental home by labour market status (Sweden and United Kingdom)

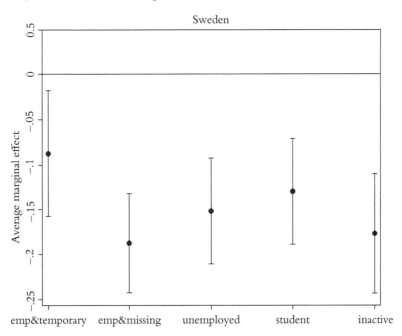

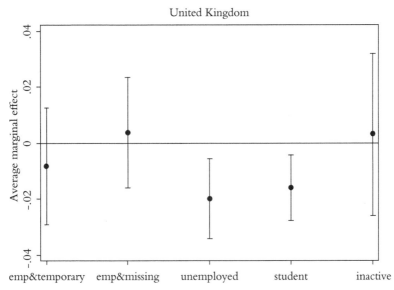

Note: reference = employed and permanent; due to collinearity, the variable about parental education has been dropped for Sweden.

Source: own elaboration based on EU-SILC longitudinal dataset (EU-SILC12–EU-SILC19).

it can be argued that other factors, not just those pertaining to the economic dimension, may also be at work. The following section will provide a more complex analysis of such transitions using qualitative empirical material and focusing on the subjective dimension of job insecurity.

Leaving home and subjective job insecurity across welfare state regimes: qualitative insights

In this part of the chapter, we are interested in looking at the relation between labour market attachment and housing autonomy, and at what are the conditions and the mechanisms that allow young people to leave the parental home or to make the decision to stay longer at home. As seen in Chapter 1, the objective condition of job insecurity matters, but the subjective perception of job insecurity can also affect these decisions.

As seen in the previous section, objective conditions of individuals do play a role in the chances of exiting the parental home, but the analyses leave some questions unanswered. Beyond the empirical regularities found in the models presented in the previous section, what are the mechanisms, the subjective conditions and expectations that drive the decision of young people to exit the parental home? This section aims to contribute to disentangling these aspects associated with one of the most important transitions to adult life.

Feeling insecure about their job, and having to suspend plans regarding their work because they don't know what will happen at the end of the contract, may lead to a similar attitude in the other spheres of family life and may lead youth to postpone their transition to adult life. We know that youth facing similar degrees of labour market flexibility can pursue different response strategies, depending on the nation-specific institutional setting created through the relevant welfare state system as well as labour and family policies. In fact, when we looked comparatively at our interviews in nine European countries, we found similarities and differences regarding the way in which young people perceived this relationship.

Overall, qualitative results[2] of the comparative analyses of interviews with youth 18–30 years old showed that, in a first group of countries, the self-perception of an individual's labour market position might affect decisions of leaving the parental home, even in different ways. In Italy, Poland and Greece, it was a matter of job insecurity; in Ukraine and Bulgaria, young people expressed more a feeling of insecurity due to low income attached to the contract and not the security of their jobs.

By contrast, in a second group of countries – the UK and Estonia – it was not only having a secure job but having enough money that affected decisions around leaving the parental home.

Finally, Germany, and partly Sweden, were single cases where there was a mediation of the institutional context in the perceived relationships between job insecurity and housing autonomy. In this case, job insecurity did not affect the decision to leave the parental home.

Let us look more deeply at the cases and the different mechanisms expressed by youth in the different country contexts.

A matter of job insecurity

In Italy, Poland and Greece, the decision about leaving the parental home was a matter of job insecurity. Italy was the country in which the link between job insecurity and housing autonomy seemed stronger. In fact, the reference to a permanent contract was often present in young people's accounts. This could be due to the kind of policies that only recently introduced some protection for fixed-term contracts and the general system of private and public insurance based on permanent contracts.

In this respect, we could generalize and say that young people still considered having a stable job and economic autonomy as a prerequisite for housing autonomy in Italy today:

'I really wanted to go and live alone in Turin. I've never taken this step, because first, I have a brother who is ill and so we try to help him, and secondly, because I'm often away, and it is useless to pay rent if I'm gone, because I have no fixed income.' (Anna, 27, female, higher education, temporary employment, Italy)

The attitude toward housing autonomy varied with age and area. It must be underlined that housing autonomy was not always considered as important in Italy as it was in other countries (Bertolini et al, 2021); the age when it did become important was later compared to other countries, both within our sample and in the official data.

Strong familiar links of mutual help were one of the motivations. Otherwise, informal social and financial support were also the main way young people could, in the end, actually leave the parental home.

Indeed, perhaps in connection with ever-decreasing job opportunities due to the economic crisis, it appeared that job insecurity in Italy prompted youth to consider either the most immediate present or the foreseeable future, which was dreamed about rather than planned. In this regard, not only did they postpone the transition from leaving home but they were also unable to plan the intermediary steps, how and where, for making this transition.

In Greece, most of the participants still lived with their parents, just like the majority of young people in Greece. 'This results mainly from the high rates of unemployment or precarious employment that render young people unable to cover the expenses of separate housing (Eurofound, 2014)' (Athanasiades et al, 2017).

In Poland, it seems that the more important element in making the decision is the level and the regularity of income. The sources of income, salary, financial support from parents, social transfers, scholarships and so on are not considered so important for leaving the parental home (Kubicki et al, 2017).

Ewa, for example, almost 30 years old, had a temporary job in public administration in a small town. She had a boyfriend, but still lived with her parents as she was not sure if she would keep her job position:

> 'To be sure that I can afford 100 per cent of my expenses and that I will have a stable job. And right, this is probably the thing about work, salary, flat etc. So as I'm saying, theoretically it doesn't bother me that I live with my parents, or let's say with my family, but on the other hand, if I had this security about the job and the salary, you know, I would prefer to stay by myself, for sure.' (Ewa, 30, female, higher education, temporary employment, Poland)

It was not only the type of contract, even if permanent contracts were preferred by Polish young people, but the financial situation and sufficient income that were important. However, the two aspects were strictly connected, as the lack of a job or an informal job often did not allow access to an adequate and regular income in order to leave the parental home. Informal jobs were often very low paid in Poland. It was possible to identify some common elements behind the decisions made: the balance between costs and resources is the stimulus that triggers the decision-making process.

In Poland, just as in Italy, the availability of family resources was very important in making this transition. In particular, regarding housing autonomy, one young person had access to a house belonging to the family, which helped this transition. Lech, for example, lived with his parents and younger brother in a small town surrounded by a rural area. He had no girlfriend and was registered as unemployed, although he worked informally from time to time on different commissions. He had plans of renting a flat together with his friend. However, his income was too low to move out of home:

> 'I've said, I will catch a job, hopefully ... I don't want to ... sometimes I want to get away from home, sometimes not. I know that if I move out, at least, they [his family] will not bother me anymore.' (Lech, 28, male, low education, no contract job, Poland)

Due to family conflicts, Daniel, after he came of age 18, moved in with his grandparents. He was still living with them at the time of the interview. He said their coexistence was smooth and peaceful, apart from the obvious conflicts caused by the generation gap. However, he would really like to move out and live with his girlfriend. The only obstacle was money:

> 'Now being independent has become my priority. Now I'm trying to do everything not to be dependent anymore. Cause I just feel, that in this age, you already have some experience, and living with your family, in quite a small flat, it's just tiring and irritating. It's been five years that I'm with my girlfriend, and after such a time it would be cool to live together, the only problem is just a lack of funds.' (Daniel, 23, male, medium education, unemployed, Poland)

In Ukraine and Bulgaria, we found another type of job insecurity preventing leaving home. In fact, the young people expressed more a feeling of insecurity due to low income attached to the contract rather than the security of their jobs. It seems to suggest that job security, as in the form of permanent contracts, is something no longer taken for granted for the young generation – and not even expected in some countries. Low income was the aspect that often prevented youth from leaving the parental home and also prevented them from making plans to leave, because they could not save money. This aspect was linked to all types of contracts and, sometimes, such as in the next section, pushed young people, especially in Ukraine, to plan to leave the country. In this case, leaving the parental home coincided with moving to a different country.

In Bulgaria, young people who experienced economic difficulties believed they would not be able to afford to live independently: 'the problem is not only the lack of jobs, but a lack of quality jobs providing proper remuneration' (Krasteva et al, 2018):

> 'A normal salary, which you can receive, is 600–700 leva. With a half of this, you can pay the rent. Apart from that, when the bills, water, electricity and anything else, the dwelling, are paid, at a given point of time, people cannot stand it.' (Milena, 21, female, medium education, unemployed, Bulgaria)

We must underline that Ukraine and Bulgaria, like Italy and Greece, were countries in which young people did not feel it was so urgent to leave the parental home. In Ukraine: 'Staying at the parents' home during studies, after graduation and even after entering the labour market was perceived normal among the majority of the interviewed respondents. However, normal does not necessarily mean desirable' (Sologub et al, 2018).

The same was true in Poland:

> 'We met and moved to his parents' place, and then we decided together with them to leave and rent something just for us. The period in

which we lived together [with his family] was quite difficult: always a few fights. Or some arguments or something.' (Marek, 25, male, low education, unemployed, Poland)

However, not all respondents articulated a strong desire to leave the parental home and, in any case, did not perceived lack of private accommodation as a significant shortcoming of their weak situation in the labour market or an obstacle for creating their own families.

Having enough money

In another group of countries, it was not having a secure job, but having enough money coming from the job or from the state, which affected the decisions of leaving the parental home. In the UK and Estonia, we found very similar feelings among young people.

In fact, in the UK living away from the parental home was linked more to having a good and reliable income; how this was obtained, whether through a fixed-term contract, permanent contract or social benefits from the government was not important. As we expected, in the UK, finances usually controlled a participant's ability to move out of the parental home. In fact, in the interviews it emerged that living away from home was attached to having sufficient income. Research confirms this: 'The lack of a permanent employment contract only became more of an issue if they wanted to secure a mortgage. Otherwise, having temporary contracts did not seem to affect their ability to rent (as long as they earned enough money to pay the landlord)' (Yoon, 2018). Here we saw how the institutional context affected decisions: in the UK, you did not need a permanent contract to rent a house. Also culturally, the tradition of buying a house and the transmission of economic resources through generations using housing equity were not usual. Then young people tended to move through renting houses:

> 'I mean probably I'd like to, well I wouldn't want to live on my own, I'd probably want to move in with my boyfriend, but I wouldn't want to do that on the wage I'm on at the moment, I just think I'd really struggle. I wouldn't be able to do anything! I'd have a house but I wouldn't be able to leave it!' (Sandy, 18, female, low education, temporary employment, UK)

In Estonia, the decision to move out or stay had more to do with having money and having any job, not necessarily the security of a permanent job. Andry, currently living with his own mother and girlfriend in his mother's apartment describes his plans as follows.

'Well in this sense I am satisfied [with current living conditions], but at the same time I would already want to find a job and then. When both me and my girlfriend would find a job and then finally we could move in together somewhere, to take a rented apartment.' (Andry, 21, male, low education, unemployed, Estonia)

Having institutional support

Sweden was another country in which subjective job insecurity did not stop young people from moving out of the parental home. Here, the interviews showed that there was no link between job insecurity and housing autonomy, but rather, a social norm in this country encouraged young people to leave the parental home early. In our sample, job instability or unemployment did not prevent young people from making this transition. For example, the lack of ability to afford a certain type of house did not hamper the respondents' housing autonomy in relation to their parents.

With regard to this, having a permanent job was not considered a condition for leaving the parental home. Here, it was not only a question of tradition but also the institutional contexts that offered protection for making this transition: 'This should partly be seen as a consequence of a housing policy that allowed students to rent a flat or a room in a shared flat at an affordable price, and there were benefits available to respondents who were unemployed, which covered their housing costs' (Strandh and Baranowska-Rataj, 2018).

In fact, the Swedish situation was similar to the German one. Interviews in Germany, and partly Sweden, were single case studies where we found the mediation of the institutional context in the perceived relationship between job insecurity and housing autonomy.

In Germany, 'It could not be generally shown that unemployment leads automatically to a delay in moving out of the parental home, but was definitely an important factor, which had to be taken into account' (Schlee, 2018). In fact, young people said they could count on income continuity, even if they became unemployed and had generous unemployment benefits or worked with a fixed-term contract. This was a big difference compared to other countries: generous unemployment benefits, extended also to young people looking for their first job, allowed precarious people to have income continuity, even in objective job insecurity. In this case, we could say that the regulation of the institutional context made it possible for young people to take decisions regarding their transition to adult life, such as leaving the parental home even in situations of objective job insecurity, because they felt they were able to save money even if their employment was precarious.

Some of these young people felt dependent because they officially received support:

'Well, as I am still dependent on the money from the employment agency [state support] that I somehow ... well at least as far as my rent is paid with that, because I then would have too much money ... From that point I am highly dependent, otherwise it wouldn't bother me that it is not going perfectly at the moment.' (Maja, 24, female, medium education, unemployed, Germany)

Finally, an important point to underline in the link between job insecurity and housing autonomy was accessibility to income, in order to earn enough to buy a house, and the tradition of leaving the parental home as an owner rather than a renter. This changed the perception of young people and their feelings about unstable job contracts and their effect on the decision of leaving the parental home.

In the UK, 'We found that housing autonomy in relation to owning one's own property was linked to the idea of a secure income. At the same time, the institutional dimension of job insecurity had a real impact on the accessibility of housing and financial services. Temporary contracts might be a real barrier to getting a mortgage' (Filandri and Bertolini, 2016; Yoon, 2018).

In Bulgaria, getting a mortgage remains more in the realm of wishful thinking than a real coping strategy. Young people tended to talk about this alternative but almost none of them did it:

'Now ... the question is ... I'm thinking about finding a possibility to get a credit [loan], but I want to complete my studies, in order to be able ... you know ... to be 100 per cent sure that I will be able ... to be able to repay it without problems.' (Poly, 25, female, medium education, permanent employment, Bulgaria)

The reason was that such a decision generated enormous economic risk, which young people were not ready to manage. This was well linked to young people's job situations:

Interviewer: Maybe it would be difficult to you to buy your own place now?

Ani: Absurd! In my current situation – there is no way! Without a proper job and taking into account the current level of salaries, and the prices ... You must be very bold and rather stupid to get a mortgage. (Ani, 24, female, higher education, unemployed, Bulgaria)

In Ukraine, taking credit from the state for accommodation was a very risky practice, due to financial instability and unreliability of financial institutions, the exchange rate falling, the country's negative experience with inflation after the collapse of the USSR and the weak rule of law in the country. In the opinions of the youth, rights for financial services were not protected in the country.

In Italy, both renting and obtaining a loan was strongly associated with having a permanent contract. This was one of the rational reasons why young people were looking for a permanent position in order to leave the parental home.

So it seems that, if there is a relationship between job insecurity and housing autonomy, it is different in different countries, as the literature underlines, as this relation is mediated by social cultural and institutional factors: first, the meaning of and pressure on leaving the parental home in different countries; second, the protection offered by the institutional context in the different countries; and third, the level of salaries associated with different types of contracts. Qualitative data also showed in-depth mechanisms that have to be taken into account in designing new policies for young people. The next section explores these mechanisms in more detail.

Beyond job insecurity: other factors influencing housing autonomy

So far we have been focusing on job insecurity and its consequences on the decision to leave the parental home. However, the literature has underlined how the choice of young people to leave the parental home is a complex one and that multiple factors (beyond the labour market situation) contribute to shape expectations, attitudes and behaviours of young people in different institutional and cultural contexts. This section will investigate some of the main trends emerging from qualitative empirical material.

Pressure by parents

The first element we found common in some countries was pressure by parents: although a specific question about this point was not present, it appeared to be an important element to consider during the interviews with young people. In fact, for young people leaving home was often a process of negotiation with parents, even if relationships were not good. In this case, leaving the parental home was an outcome of the bad relationship, a mechanism that pushed young people toward the exit strategy.

In Sweden and the UK, leaving the parental home was a strong social norm, also encouraged by the parents. Young people mentioned how their parents encouraged them to 'grow up'. An interviewee told us that:

'Dad had told [me] that … "It would be good for you to move out, go away and live by yourself and take responsibility for stuff" … [But he said that on the other hand] "there is no use you being in debt if

you can avoid it. If you don't need to be in debt, why would you be."
So, those are the two things I was weighing against each other. To me
it was quite clear that I wasn't ready to leave.' (Me, 24, male, medium
education, unemployment, Sweden)

By contrast, in the Southern European countries young people underlined
that their parents did not encourage them to leave the parental home. This
happened in Greece and Italy: 'It was important to note that living in the
parental home was not necessarily seen as a negative thing from the point of
view of the parents. In fact, some parents preferred their children to remain
in the parental home and were more than willing to cover their expenses
without urging them to get a job' (Athanasiades et al, 2017). One interview
illustrated this:

Interviewer: Do you feel pressure from your family in order to get a job?
Mirsini: No, not really. My parents don't won't me to leave home.
               My parents want to pay for my expenses.
Interviewer: Really? [laughter]
Mirsini: [laughter] Yes.
Interviewer: Are you an only child?
Mirisini: I have an older brother. But, this is their opinion. They
               want me to remain at home. And to pay for my expenses.
               Meaning that, they don't mind at all, even though things are
               hard, they want me to stay at home. I don't want to though.
               (Mirsini, 19, female, low education, unemployed, Greece)

However, living with parents after a certain age could sometimes be
problematic:

'Yes. I live with my parents ... and my sister in a house ... and it is really
hard for us to live all together there, not due to character differences
and it's not that ... we don't get along very well, it's just ... it's mostly
an issue of timing ... especially during rush-hours, meaning that,
when you want to get ready and leave for work and the bathroom is
occupied, meaning that there are difficulties in our daily routine ...
which sometimes can be unbearable.' (Victoria, 27, female, higher
education, unemployed, Greece)

The same results were found in a very different context in some cases
in Germany:

'I have everything I need here.' (Daniel, 21, male, medium education,
unemployed, Germany)

'Yes, we live in a rented flat ... And we are five people at home, all in all. My parents, mum, dad, myself and two younger sisters ... And yes ... everything is working out well at home.' (Finn, 18, male, low education, unemployed, Germany)

In other cases, parents in Germany encouraged children to move out, to take care of their own responsibilities: in the case of Tom, he perceived pressure to move out because his parents said if he remained 'lazy', did not care about his education or employment situation, or trying to improve it, as well as not helping with housework, he had to move out:

'They want me to start a new apprenticeship and for me to get a real life, a "normal" life. They don't want that I laze around the whole day. They think it's important for me to assume responsibility, now. That's the reason I have to move out.' (Tom, 20, male, medium education, unemployed, Germany)

In Germany, some interviewees mentioned having a more public spirit because they take care of their parents and support them in their daily life, for example, in the case of parents with disabilities.

In Poland, young people told us about a process of negotiation between a child leaving the parental house and their parents. Although we might perceive the final decision as individual, rather the process of decision-making was collective: other members of the family were also involved.

Another reason was having bad relationships with their parents. This pushed young people toward an exit strategy. In Estonia, part of a sample of young people were early leavers who had left the parental home because of bad relationships with parents. In this case, they did not care about their job situation. They often moved from one rental apartment to another. They got caught up in a vicious circle that could lead to a vulnerable situation as, even though they had left home early, they could not count on familiar support: 'This group seemed to be the most vulnerable as there were several young people who had prison episodes or experienced domestic violence. The lack of parental support was visible in their biographies and affected other areas of their life as the coping strategies often used by their peers who had supportive parents (for example returning home or getting financial support in case of job loss or other financial difficulties) were not available to them' (Reiska et al, 2018).

In the German national report (Schlee, 2018), sometimes growing up in a household with less individual freedom was underlined, perhaps because the parents were very traditional; this could lead youth to move out of the parental home in order to realize their own aspirations.

In Poland, we found Marcin (19) who had been put in an orphanage at the age of 15 due to bad family conditions:

'Well, earlier it sucked, at home it wasn't too good, and this is how I got to the orphanage.' (Marcin, 19, male, low education, unemployed, Poland)

Starting a family

Another reason to leave the parental home was starting a new family. In some countries, the transition of leaving the parental home and the transition of starting a new family were strongly connected.

In Poland, the general social norm regarding housing autonomy was that getting married and starting one's own family was the last moment when parental ties should be cut. Most of our interviewees perceived marriage as an important steppingstone to 'real' adulthood. Zbigniew said:

'I would like to move out, but now I've got time. When there will be a girl, a wedding, then I will think about moving out. When I'll have some money, then of course, I can move out. But now I can't. I live with my family. I've got time.' (Zbigniew, 25, male, low education, unemployed, Poland)

In Bulgaria marriage or living as a couple was also as reason for leaving the parental home, both for women and men. Viktor told us:

Viktor: I'm about to get married.
Interviewer: To your girlfriend?
Viktor: Yes. We, with my girlfriend, decided to start live separately
                [from our parents] and moved to a rented flat. (Viktor, 28,
                male, medium education, permanent employment, Bulgaria)

In Ukraine, marriage was another opportunity to move out of the parents' home. It increased the income of the couple and their chances of affording to rent their own apartment. Here, we could see that leaving home in a couple could also be considered as a strategy against job insecurity.

In comparison to other western countries, young people in Greece continued to live in the parental home until they decided to start their own family, with the sole exception of students who moved out in order to go to university in another town or abroad (Petrogiannis, 2011). This situation worsened during the 2008 financial crisis.

In Italy, we needed to take regional differences into account. It was interesting to note that, in Catania (in the south of Italy), young people living with their families until a concrete plan was made to create a new family of their own was considered as normal and taken for granted. They linked exiting the parental home with the creation of a stable partner relationship and the decision to marry and have children. In short, the importance of family obligations (Finch, 1989, 2007) and the persistence of a traditional view of what leaving the parental home meant was more evident in the Catania sample than in the Turin sample (in the north of Italy).

'The fact that I still live with my [parents] I do not know, maybe in Sicily is a normal thing, because only when I get married I can go out from my parental home. This is something normal in Sicilian [tradition]. [laughing] For us it is normal ... For now, I consider a normal thing living with my parents because all of my friends are living with their parents but also when someone is employed, he/she cannot go away from home because we are in Sicily and /one cannot escape from parental home [laughing]. Only for that. So I live in a very normal way, this thing to live with my family.' (Concita, 23, female, medium education, unemployed, Italy)

By contrast, among the Swedish respondents, housing autonomy was in general closely linked to independence and not to forming a family:

'I don't live by myself right now because, as I've said, I don't have an income, I don't get any support at the moment, but I'm looking for my own place ... it's, as I've said, a bit depressing.' (Eugen, male, medium education, unemployed, Sweden)

Similar, in the UK moving out of the family home was not linked to starting a family, instead it was more about young people having their 'own space' and independence.

'[If] I had a job, I'd have my own space, you know, mix with other people.' (Donna, 21, female, unemployed, UK)

Leaving for studying

Leaving for studying is an aspect mostly mentioned by the tertiary educated who started their studies at a university in another town; this tended to be the case in Germany, Sweden, Estonia and the UK, for example.

In Estonia, 'there was quite a large group of interviewees who had followed this traditional trajectory: they stayed in the parental home until taking their diploma from upper secondary education and becoming legally adult, and then moved to university or, in a fewer cases, to start a family' (Reiska et al, 2018). This was also linked to the fact that, in Estonia, young people could use formal support for accommodation in a students' residence when starting university, as in Germany, Sweden and the UK.

In Italy, it happened especially to young people from the south of Italy, moving to a university in the north. It must be underlined that in Italy moving out of home for studying was mainly (financially) supported by parents. But the traditional path was to leave home late, after finishing studies and finding a job.

The Polish situation was similar in some respects to Italy. The right moment to leave the parental house was when one could afford it. This was an opinion that was expressed about people who had already finished their education. The rule for youth who were still in education was different. As education was generally valued among all generations of Poles, there was a common belief that, if parents had sufficient financial resources, they should provide for their children until they finish their education.

> 'I think, that everyone should, if a person is in her twenties, and if you study, after the studies you just should move out, and then if he or she has a job, they should move out. It's just how I think.' (Pawel, 19, male, medium education, unemployed, Poland)

In Poland, a strong belief that the right time to leave the parental home was just after finishing school and university was observed. When Anna was 17, she was thrown out of her home by her mother:

> 'I was 17 when I was expelled from school, cause I was … One year earlier, I mean I jumped over one year, cause they said I'm talented enough to start the school earlier and so on. And three, three and a half weeks before the finals they've just expelled me – for my absences, and I just had them mainly because of my mum who kicked me out of home a half year earlier.' (Anna, 23, female, medium education, no contract job, Poland)

To realize aspirations

In Bulgaria, leaving for university and then maybe later returning to the parental home, was part of the process to become an adult. Other reasons expressed by young people were linked more to their freedom and their will to realize their aspirations. These reasons were much stronger in Sweden and Germany, where 'respondents showed instead great awareness in the choices they made, what they aimed for and what possible outcomes could be' (Strandh and Baranowska-Rataj, 2018). The argument of choosing to move from the parental home in order "to be independent and to get on by [themselves]" was expressed several times. Independence, including residentially independent, seemed to be central in the process of becoming an adult in these countries. They also expressed awareness of what it meant for their independence to choose to live on their own:

'And that it is not all the time like: "Go and tidy your room" or something like that. That you have your own apartment, that you can do whatever you want to do, hmm, and nobody keeps telling you things like "do this or do that" ... Standing on my own two feet, hmm. Not being dependent on my parents. Not living at home anymore. Do what I want to do, hmm. Yes ... Enjoy the freedom I have at home.' (Ben, 21, male, low education, unemployed, Germany)

Institutional support can make the difference in the choices and opportunities offered. In particular, the subjective perception of job insecurity seems to play a role in decision-mechanisms around choices in which the imaginary of the future plays a fundamental role. It is very evident if we compare these two interviews – one from Italy, the other from Germany:

'If there is no work, there is no autonomy in my opinion; it is the most important thing there is ... when there is work there is hope ... Since there is no work, how do you do it? It cannot be done. That is the problem ... Unfortunately, I repeat, society today does not give us young people much hope.' (Erika, 29, medium education, unemployed, lives with family of origin, Italy)

'Concerns about the effect of insecurity, not really. They [the supervisors] said we shouldn't worry, because after two years of training, we can do advanced training and therefore we can continue to work for the company, in all likelihood. In this case, I feel safe about the job situation after my apprenticeship.' (Tina, 18, medium education, unemployed, lives with parents, Germany)

Reasons to stay

Our sample included young people still living at home, especially in Bulgaria, Greece and Italy. What were the reasons expressed?

The first motivation in all the countries was economic, as already explored in the first section. Usually young people who expressed this motivation were not satisfied. Often they wanted to leave due to their poor financial situation. Sometimes they used a strategy to accumulate money for leaving. This happened in nearly all the countries.

Another interesting reason was expressed, especially by young people who were satisfied about their residential situation. In Bulgaria, a group of factors could be best described as a reluctance of the respondents to leave their parents' house because they felt comfortable and did not see a reason to change anything:

> 'Well, they are not bothered. There is enough space for everybody.' (Anton, 25, male, higher education, temporary employment, Bulgaria)

> 'I like that I'm adult ... that I live with my mother and father.' (Eva, 22, female, low education, unemployed, Bulgaria).

> Interviewer: You said that at the moment you live with your parents? Have you ever thought about your own place or moving from your parents' place?
>
> Katya: Well, honestly speaking ... I don't see a point to rent something, because this will put me to expense. And, after all, I have my own place, my own room, my own space [laughing]. (Katya, 30, female, higher education, temporary employment, Bulgaria)

This situation was very similar to what was expressed by the majority of Italian people staying at their parents' home. With regard to interviewees belonging to the younger age group in this country, it seemed that leaving the parental home was not perceived as an urgent need, but was rather an idea which they translated into a more practical plan when engaged in stable relationships. Considering those aged 25 or over who still lived in the parental home, the desire to move out was usually expressed as being more urgent, while living in the parental home seemed something that needed an explanation:

> I have also thought about going to live alone, but then I also thought that, for now, anyway, since my parents are also at a certain age, then, perhaps, seeing as one of my siblings comes and goes and the other one has now moved away, so, maybe ... I'm in no rush for now, I also like staying there. They have given me so much, so I think it is right to give them something too. Then when I need to leave, because I'll have a partner, then, of course I will. That's all.' (Franco, 29, male, low education, no contract job, Italy)

> 'If I think about how I would live, of course, undoubtedly I'd like to be able to live more independently, precisely to be autonomous with regard to housing. It's something that excites me, that I'd like to be able to do even now. In fact, as I said, if I'm not doing it right now it is only because I'm waiting for something bigger.' (Dario, 29, male, higher education, permanent employment, Italy)

In Estonia, staying longer at home was not so common but, looking at the reasons expressed by young people still living at the parental home, the main reason was similar to that expressed by Bulgarian youth – the comfort. 'Two girls living with parents did not want to move out because of the mutual help provided by their parents and to their parents. One of them lived on the second floor of their grandparents' house with her own family and felt this would be her own one day in the future. The other felt insecure because of a disability and feared she might not cope on her own' (Reiska et al, 2018).

An interesting point: a group of young men, most of whom were unemployed or working unofficially and living outside two of the biggest towns of Estonia, tended to justify their motivation not in terms of economic reasons but in terms of what was normal in Estonia, "staying with parents longer [was] a normal and sensible thing to do".

> 'It's just different nowadays. Before, you left home, left school, got married ... Yeah ... and a job, got an apartment, stuff. Well, um ... Yeah ... things are different now. People just continue living at their parents' home, their parents work and they then live off their parents' income. And they also continue sneaking around.' (Erki, 24, male, low education, unemployed, Estonia)

Finally, in the majority of countries, but especially in Bulgaria, Italy and Germany, we found cases in which young people had to provide care for elderly relatives and leaving was not an easy decision:

> 'I live with my grandmother and I take care for her. She is not young. You know that an elder person requires care, elderly are like the children.' (Ana, 20, female, medium education, unemployed, Bulgaria)

Ukraine was a particular case in which the way of leaving the parental home derived from tradition, helping to resolve the problem of the lack of accommodation in villages or towns. Young people knew they could stay with their parents because: 'Traditionally, newly married couples were expected to live with parents of one of the partners. Later, they started to build a new house next to the parents' house. This tradition was internalized by many citizens of small towns and villages in Ukraine nowadays as well' (Sologub et al, 2018). This was socially acceptable and sometimes even expected behaviour.

> 'Of course they would like to have me living with them, to be close to their child ... Well, no, I wouldn't live separately from parents. It's not because I am a mommy's son, no, I just love my house. I have my own yard ... and it cannot be compared with a life in a flat. To live

in apartment is awful! It sucks ... these elevators! ... But, you know, sometimes you need to change atmosphere. Yes, you need to miss home, to arrive sometimes, be there a bit and then again to go to another city.' (Taras, 23, male, higher education, unemployed, Ukraine)

Finally, as our sample was constructed to include vulnerable people in terms of labour market situation, we also found problematic cases in terms of socialization in all the countries. In some cases, there were respondents who did not want to leave the parental home because they had socialization problems and also a very limited social network, reasons why they were afraid to live alone:

> 'I would move [out] from time to time from my grandfather to teach him. But I would always return to him ... Sometimes I think with fear of what will happen with me without him, but I try not to think about this ... It would be nice to take a child from the orphanage to have someone to take care of me when I get old. Frankly, I need a person-insurance ... I'm pretty happy. I wish I have a solid guarantee that the situation will be stable. Then, I would 100 per cent be happy.' (Diana, 26, female, higher education, permanent employment, Ukraine)

> 'What do you mean, separately? To live alone? It is easier to hang [myself] from boredom than to live alone. Whom will I talk to? No way, it is really boring to live alone.' (Oleksandr, 26, male, medium education, unemployed, Ukraine)

Conclusion

In this chapter, we have investigated the relationship between job insecurity and one of the most important transitions to adult life in the perspective of life-course studies, namely the decision to leave the parental home and live autonomously from the family of origin. Building on the different theoretical approaches that explain the mechanisms behind such relationships, seen in Chapter 1, this chapter approached the issue by taking into consideration both the objective and the subjective dimensions of job insecurity and combined different types of data to better grasp the unfolding of the different dimensions of job insecurity on young people's strategies of autonomy.

A preliminary overview of the association between objective job insecurity (proxied by having a temporary job) and autonomous living in different European countries was carried out using the longitudinal panel of EU-SILC dataset. As underlined by the literature, the expectations were of finding a heterogeneity in the behaviour of young people in different institutional contexts due to the different welfare policies and the varying degrees of economic and social support to young people in different welfare regimes. In addition to labour market and welfare state conditions, cultural factors were also expected to play a role in influencing the choice of autonomous living. However, for the seven countries considered, the results of discrete time longitudinal models do not support the hypothesis of a negative association of job insecurity with autonomous living. This means that, at least based on the models specified, it is not possible to observe a significant lower probability of exiting the parental home for young people in temporary positions (compared to their peers in permanent positions). Similarly, no variability seems to emerge across young people in the different countries. Rather, the results suggest that what matters is having a job: with the only exception of the Eastern European countries, in all other countries unemployed individuals have significantly lower chances of exiting from the home of the family of origin.

However, the analyses focus on the actual behaviour of young people, and the transition to autonomous living is a complex decision. Various factors may be at work underneath, influencing these results; several of these may be hard to measure and operationalize in a quantitative research design. Therefore, this preliminary investigation has been complemented and integrated with qualitative research investigating the perception of job insecurity and its link with the decision of leaving parental home.

The qualitative analysis, based on a sample of 386 young people in nine European countries, highlighted that there is a relationship between job insecurity and housing autonomy, but this relation is mediated by social, cultural and institutional factors: first, the meaning of and the pressure on leaving the parental home in different countries; second, the protection offered by the institutional context in the different countries; third, the level of salaries associated with the different types of contracts.

Overall, qualitative results show that, in a first group of countries, the self-perception of an individual's labour market position might affect decisions of leaving the parental home, even in different ways. In Italy, Poland and Greece, it was a matter of job insecurity; in Ukraine and Bulgaria, the young people expressed more a feeling of insecurity due to the low income attached to their contracts and not the security or otherwise of their jobs.

By contrast, in a second group of countries, the UK and Estonia, it was not only having a secure job but having enough money that affected decisions to leave the parental home. Finally, Germany, and in part Sweden, were single cases where there was a mediation of institutional context in perceived relationships between job insecurity and housing autonomy. In this case, job insecurity did not affect the decision.

To explain this transition, we need also to take into consideration other factors, such as the pressure of parents toward autonomy that are very strong in some countries (such as Sweden or Germany), and the countries in which strong familiar links prevent leaving home (such as Italy, Greece, Poland or Bulgaria), and also the association of leaving the parental home with a starting a new family or leaving early for motivation as studying (Germany, Sweden, Estonia, UK).

Qualitative data also show that, even if the actual timing differs, the aspiration to autonomy becomes important at some point for young people in all the countries considered. As sociological and psychological studies prove, it is important to gain autonomy from parents in the process of identity formation. At that point, both objective and subjective job insecurity become important in offering opportunities or constraints to leaving the parental home. Qualitative results also show different paths to autonomy in different welfare state systems. In Eastern European countries, often young people form a new family within the parents' home. In fact, due to high job insecurity and low wages, several generations often live together in the same house.

We also observe a similarity of welfare policies for the youth of Eastern European countries, such as Bulgaria and Poland, with those of Southern European countries, such as Italy and Greece, while the Estonian situation seems more similar to that in the UK.

In this respect, the combination of the findings of quantitative and qualitative analysis exhibit a certain degree of variation and may at first sight seem inconsistent. Nonetheless, these results provide a different standpoint on the issue of job insecurity and can rather be considered as complementary, as they illustrate different parts of the broader picture.

Indeed, with quantitative data we observed actual behaviours, while the qualitative analysis mainly focuses on attitudes and perceptions. As an example, the latter can indeed provide a greater understanding of the meaning of a permanent or temporary job in a certain institutional and cultural context, as well as on the framing of one's own working career in an individual's life course, as opposed to the dichotomous value attributed to such variables in the quantitative analyses.

Moreover, the samples observed in the quantitative and in the qualitative analyses differ in their composition, with mainly young people at risk of social exclusion and generally younger (up to maximum 29 years old) included in the qualitative sample.

In conclusion, the combined investigation of overall trends and mechanisms of decisions and perceptions behind the decision to leave the parental home highlights the key role played, first, by having or not having a job and, second, by the perception of job insecurity (that is, the subjective dimension) in attributing meaning and in shaping the life course of young people within different institutional contexts. Indeed, assuming that public policies may actively improve individuals' objective labour market situation, they must also be effective in shaping the perceptions and attitudes of young people.

In fact, as labour markets become ever more flexible, as we have seen in Europe after the reforms of the last 20 years, it requires people to become very autonomous, able to build a career characterized by frequent changing of job and/or periods of unemployment. Very low levels of autonomy, as in the welfare states system in the countries of Southern and Eastern Europe, can push young people to become 'discouraged' and then inactive or not in education, employment or training (so-called NEETs).

Institutional support can make the difference in the choices and opportunities offered. In particular, the subjective perception of job insecurity seems to play a role in the decision-mechanisms surrounding choices in which the imaginary of the future plays a fundamental role.

Methodological appendix

Quantitative data and method

The empirical analyses were performed using the longitudinal data from the European Union Statistics on Income and Living Conditions database (EU-SILC). In order to increase the chances of observing the desired outcome, several waves of EU-SILC longitudinal data were pooled together, from EU-SILC 2012 (with observations starting in 2009 and ending in 2012) to EU-SILC 2019 (observations starting in 2016 and ending in 2019). The longitudinal database follows individuals for a maximum of four years, per each wave. In order to avoid the risk of duplicating households when pooling together different waves, only individuals followed for four years were included, dropping cases of individuals followed for a shorter period, which might have appeared in several waves.

The sample is composed of individuals residing in the seven countries of interest, in the age range of 16–40, who lived with their parents at the beginning of the period of observation. The age bracket is extended to increase the chances of observing exits from the parental home, which happen at various ages in different countries (generally later in Southern European countries and earlier in Nordic and Eastern European countries).

The dependent variable is the event of exiting the parental household, which is operationalized as a dummy variable (equal to 1 if the individual does not live with parents, equal to 0 if parents are household members). The information about living with parents (or not) is recorded in EU-SILC on a yearly basis, together with other time-varying covariates. This organization of the dependent variable requires adopting a person-period scheme with a number of rows per each individual equal to the number of years in which he/she is followed (for example, if the subject was censored, the panel expired and the subject did not make the transition, the subject had four rows; if the subject made the transition in the second year, he/she would have two rows in the dataset. Once the event occurred, the subject exited from the risk set and was no longer observable).

The major explicative variable included in the models is the individual's labour market situation, operationalized as a categorical variable, combining information about occupational status and type of contract in six modes:

- employed with permanent contract (the reference category)
- employed with temporary contract
- employed with missing information on contract (due to a high number of missing values in the variable PL140)
- unemployed
- students
- purely inactive individuals (retired, disabled, homemakers).

Other independent variables included as controls are:

- the presence of a partner: the literature highlighted a strong role played by marriage and consensual unions in determining the pattern of exit from the parental home, therefore whether the partner is present in the new household or not is included in the regression model;
- level of education: a categorical variable with 3 modes indicating the highest level of education attained;
- parental education: a categorical variable as a proxy for the social status of the family of origin. This to test whether a higher social status (or at least higher cultural resources) may help (or restrain) youth in making the transition to autonomous living. A higher social status may indeed support youth leaving home with economical resources;
- age: a categorical variable grouping into three modes the age range of the sample: young (16–24), young adults (25–34), adults (35–40).

The method used for the empirical analyses is event history analysis, with models for discrete-time data (Bernardi, 2006; Box-Steffensmeier and Jones, 2004; Mills, 2011). Event history discrete-time models estimated the hazard rate, which is defined as the probability that an event occurs at a particular time t, conditional on the fact that the event did not occur before t. The survival function expressed the probability that an event did not occur before time t (Mills, 2011: 181).

When the dependent variable is binary and the time intervals are discrete (for example, a one-year interval), the recommended model is logit regression. Observations in a dataset organized according to a person–period scheme cannot be considered independent among them, therefore the models include robust standard error clustered on individuals (Bernardi, 2006).

Separate models are run for each country and for each model estimates of the average marginal effects (AMEs) are computed and plotted, in order to make the results comparable across different countries.

Qualitative data and method

The qualitative interviews with youth had been collected in the nine countries involved in the EXCEPT project (Bulgaria, Estonia, Germany, Greece, Italy, Poland, United Kingdom, Sweden, Ukraine). The 386 qualitative interviews were conducted according to common criteria. Common criteria were defined and followed in constructing the sample in each country, in order to include: temporary workers, unemployed people, NEET and non-contractual workers (including some successful stories); young people aged 18–30, all education levels, but oversampling 'low educated'; at least 20 young people involved in policies for each country; an equal number of male and female. The comparative qualitative research approach was based on the same agreed and shared, but at the same time flexible, tools in the nine countries: interview outline; sampling plan; codebook; synopsis; tools for implementation and monitoring of the entire process.

This methodology is quite innovative (Bertolini et al, 2018; Unt et al, 2021; Bertolini and Hofäcker, 2023) with respect to other research projects based on cross-national comparative analysis of qualitative interviews carried out by different research teams. The comparative qualitative analysis was developed by using directly the empirical material collected in each country and organized in synopses, along with country reports. This was made possible by writing the synopses, that comprise a thematic summary of the interview plus selected quotation in a common language (English), therefore granting to each researcher the access to the whole empirical body of interviews. Indeed, synopses were not only a way to organize the large empirical material collected, but also a strategy to overcome the language barrier that always emerges when designing cross-national research that adopts the qualitative interview tool. In literature and in previous cross-national comparative researches (see, for example, Bertolini et al, 2014; Hantrais, 2009; Quilgars et al, 2009; Livingston and Hasebrink, 2010; Bird et al, 2013;), the most common strategy adopted in cross-national analysis is to build the comparative analysis grounding it on the analysis already performed on the empirical material of each country. In other words, a common path is to elaborate cross-national comparative report by using country-specific reports as a source.

4

Objective and Subjective Employment Insecurity and Mid-career Workers

Introduction

In this chapter, we will look at the relationship between objective and subjective insecurity in mid-career, often referred to as an age range spanning from the late twenties until the early fifties. In previous research, this phase has often been portrayed as a phase of relative stability in employment lives. Following a phase of (difficult) establishment within the labour market during early career (see, for example, Chapter 2), individuals are more often found in more stable forms of employment. Notably, however, this pattern has been shown to apply particularly for men, who are more often found in permanent, stable full-time employment than in flexible employment forms, although the risk of ending up in the latter varies with educational attainment and welfare state background (Blossfeld, Mills and Bernardi, 2006). In contrast, women's employment has often been more discontinuous due to childcare phases (Blossfeld and Hofmeister, 2006). The still disproportional engagement of women in childcare and household activities (Eurostat, 2019c) not only leads to employment interruptions, but often also implies reduced working hours when returning to work up until children reach school age (Eurostat, 2020). Looking at the development in employment insecurities in mid-career thus requires a gender-specific perspective, differentiating between the labour market experiences and perceptions of men and women.

In this chapter, we will apply such a perspective, looking at the gender-specific experience of objective employment insecurity and the subjectively perceived insecurity of men and women. We will start by providing an overview about the overall labour force attachment of the two genders over time by contrasting their overall employment rates. Particular attention in this respect will be given to women's employment during motherhood and early childhood years. We will then turn to different types of objective insecurity, first considering atypical employment. Here we will look at major trends in part-time employment, which is known to play a particular role for women in reconciling work and family during early childhood years. We shall also investigate in how far fixed-term-employment, whose importance loomed large for early career employees, is also found among mid-career employees of both sexes. A final focus on unemployment concludes the part on objective employment insecurity. Following an interim summary, we shift our focus to the perception of employment insecurity by mid-career employees, again differentiating results by gender: How is subjective insecurity perceived by men and by women? And how far does this perception vary with the type of job mid-career employees hold? Finally, we will investigate how job insecurity impacts on key indicators in the quality of life for men and women: Are mid-career employees in atypical employment forms deprived in terms of their quality of life? And how far is this effect mediated by both macro level and micro level factors? A final summary concludes the chapter.

Overall employment rates

We begin our empirical overview of mid-career workers' objective employment conditions with a consideration of the long-term development in the labour force attachment of men and women in Europe. Figure 4.1 provides an aggregate overview of trends in EU countries since the early 1980s. To delineate mid-career workers, the standard OECD age range of 25–54 years is used. Figure 4.1 shows the well-known gradual, yet not complete, convergence of male and female employment rates known from earlier publications (for example OECD, 2012; Eurofound, 2016; Eurostat 2020). Since the early 1980s, men's employment in EU countries has remained persistently high, meandering between 80 and 90 per cent of the respective age group. Women's employment rates have gradually risen throughout the same period from around half of women in 1980 to around 75 per cent in 2020. Yet, there remains a gender cleavage in employment rates of around 10 percentage points.

Even though this overall trend of gender convergence could generally be observed in virtually all European countries, its magnitude and development over time has varied considerably between (groups of) countries.

To capture these cross-national differences, Figure 4.2 breaks down employment rates in mid-career to the country-level. Given the persistently high engagement of men in employment in most countries, the figure displays women's employment trends only. Countries are sorted by welfare regimes in order to better capture context-specific patterns. In order to outline most recent trends – to which the following sections on objective and subjective employment insecurity will also refer – figures focus on trends in the last two decades (covering the time-period from 2000–20).

Figure 4.1: Employment rate of men and women, aged 25–54, EU-27, 1983–2020

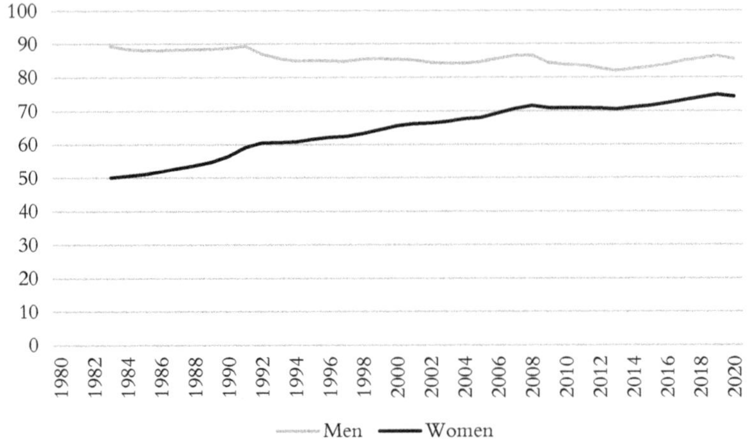

Source: OECD, 2021a.

Results from Figure 4.2 point to marked cross-national differences in the development of female employment rates. Particularly in Scandinavian countries, female employment has been traditionally high, reflected in continuously high employment rates throughout the last two decades. In most other countries, a more recent increase in women's employment can be observed.

This is particularly visible in conservative Central European countries, as well as in Ireland, where female employment rates have persistently risen to values around 70–80 per cent since the turn of the millennium. Southern European countries have long appeared to be on a similar path; yet, setbacks after the financial crisis in 2008 have at least temporarily slowed down the increase. Eastern European countries, where female employment rates have been traditionally high during socialism, have experienced massive setbacks in female employment after the system change in the 1990s. More recent trends displayed in Figure 4.2 point to a modest recovery since the 2000s, though with considerable cross-national variation in terms of starting points.

The observable cross-national variation of the generally increasing trend in women's employment points to contextual factors at the national level that mediate the overall trend. Previous literature has referred to various factors, including labour market and family policies (for example, Ostner and Lewis, 1995; Hofäcker, 2006; Cippolone et al, 2014; Ferragina, 2019), as well as cultural norms (Pfau-Effinger and Smidt, 2011; Pfau-Effinger, 2012) and gender-based expectations (Lück, 2006). High employment of women in social-democratic countries, for example, was frequently explained by a strong dual-earner orientation in public policies, reflected in

Figure 4.2: Employment rate of women, aged 25–54, 2000–20, by welfare regime

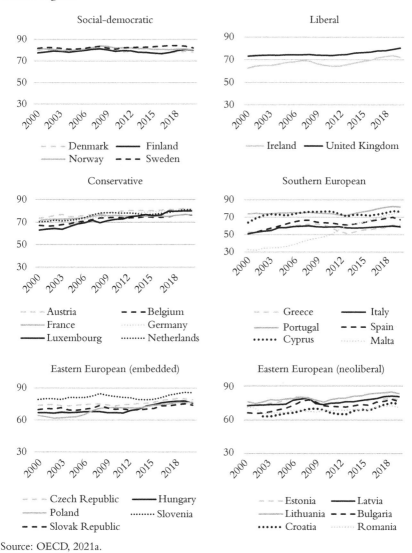

Source: OECD, 2021a.

extensive policy support for work-family reconciliation as well as sufficient supply of jobs through the large public employment sector. In contrast, both conservative as well as Southern European countries long followed a strong male breadwinner orientation, reflected in insufficient reconciliation support and a welfare system that penalized the dual employment of both spouses. Only more recent reforms to this system have improved employment opportunities for women.

Notably, contextual factors do not only impact on the incidence of women's employment, but also on its continuity throughout the life course. Particularly when support for work-family reconciliation is scarce, women often tend to interrupt employment around childbirth and return only when children have reached kindergarten or even school age. Such employment interruptions often make up one of the major reasons for the yet incomplete convergence of gender-specific employment rates. It is also one major factor in the explanation of still persistent gendered labour market inequalities in terms of labour market outcomes, for example, with regard to wages earned or the level of job security. In order to empirically capture such interruptions with a simple stylized measure, Table 4.1 presents evidence on maternal employment rates in various European countries. On the one hand, figures are reported separately by the age of the youngest child (differentiation between 0–2, 3–5 and 6–14 years), assuming that mothers will interrupt employment particularly during early childhood years. On the other hand, figures are also subdivided by the number of children, assuming that employment interruptions will more likely occur in families with larger numbers of children. Figures are reported for the most recent year available (2019), and are clustered again by welfare regimes to reflect contextual differences.

All in all, findings from Table 4.1 confirm the expected pattern that maternal employment increases with the age of the youngest child and declines with the number of children. At the same time, cross-national comparison reveals some striking parallels to overall employment patters reported earlier: Scandinavian countries not only have the highest female employment rates but also exhibit the highest degree of employment continuity around childbirth. In both Denmark and Sweden, employment rates of women with pre-school children are only marginally lower than that of mothers with school children; likewise, employment rates hardly differ according to the number of children. This is likely an effect of the high coverage rates of public early childhood education and care institutions in the two countries (56.0 per cent in Denmark and 46.3 per cent in Sweden for children aged 0–2 years in 2019; see OECD, 2021b). The only notable exception is Finland where employment rates of mothers with children aged 0–2 years respectively with three children or more are significantly lower. This may be particularly due to less developed childcare options in Finland (coverage rate of 33.4 per cent in 2019; OECD, 2021b) and less flexible labour market options (see Grönlund et al, 2017). In liberal and conservative countries, the generally modest level of maternal employment appears to be more sensitive to age and number of children as, particularly for young mothers with small children, maternal employment rates are clearly lower, particularly in Germany. Only in the Netherlands, where widespread part-time options allow for a better reconciliation of work

Table 4.1: Maternal employment rates by number/age of children, 2019

	Age of youngest child			Number of children		
	0–2	**3–5**	**6–14**	**1 child**	**2 children**	**3 children+**
Denmark	73.8	84.3	85.9	80.3	83.6	80.7
Finland	52.9	81.6	88.8	78.2	79.8	65.1
Sweden	82.0	86.1	88.7	86.1	86.9	82.9
United Kingdom	66.1	71.5	80.6	79.0	75.6	55.4
Ireland	65.5	66.6	70.7	72.3	69.1	59.2
Austria	68.7	78.2	83.1	81.8	78.4	58.0
Belgium	65.4	72.4	78.0	76.3	76.5	58.6
France	60.0	73.8	80.1	76.8	76.1	53.0
Germany	56.4	75.5	82.5	78.0	73.5	48.1
Luxembourg	75.8	75.2	77.4	78.1	77.1	64.6
Netherlands	77.9	77.4	82.4	79.6	82.7	73.4
Cyprus	67.0	72.2	76.1	72.9	75.1	61.5
Greece	54.7	58.8	62.1	60.5	59.9	55.2
Italy	52.1	56.8	60.3	60.3	55.8	41.4
Malta	62.3	68.7	69.4	72.9	64.5	50.2
Portugal	79.6	87.0	84.3	84.4	84.1	73.1
Spain	61.3	68.1	69.9	69.7	67.8	49.1
Czech Republic	21.7	78.9	92.3	68.6	67.7	53.9
Hungary	16.2	73.5	86.5	69.2	62.3	37.2
Poland	58.1	68.2	78.7	75.4	68.5	50.9
Slovakia	19.2	70.9	86.0	67.2	60.2	38.5
Slovenia	80.4	86.4	90.2	88.2	86.9	76.3
Bulgaria	44.3	68.0	80.4	77.9	62.3	40.7
Croatia	74.1	72.2	79.6	79.7	77.9	62.1
Estonia	30.4	82.5	88.4	75.0	70.4	51.7
Latvia	71.9	73.3	86.1	80.3	76.4	72.4
Lithuania	74.3	80.6	84.8	82.4	82.8	59.2
Romania	59.1	63.4	72.5	73.1	65.9	44.2

Source: OECD, 2021b.

and care (see the next section on part-time employment), such patterns are less pronounced.

Maternal employment rates in Southern European countries appear to be generally lower with values around 50–60 per cent.

Mothers of three or more children, in particular, appear to reduce their labour market activity. This pattern is indicative for the still largely 'familialist' Southern European model (Esping-Andersen, 1999) in which public childcare is generally underdeveloped, normative expectations are traditional (for example, Naldini et al, 2016) and labour force participation is rather dependent on available family support. Only Portugal, where support for a dual-earner model has expanded (Tavora, 2012), deviates from this traditional pattern of employment during early childhood years. Finally, Eastern European countries exhibit no unique picture, but with a few exceptions: maternal employment appears to be strongly sensitive to age of children (when in some countries, employment drops to less than 30 per cent for women with toddlers) and partly also to number of children. Previous research has explained this pronounced differential in employment participation with the interplay of different factors, including the lack of sufficient early childcare options (Hofäcker et al, 2013; Bicakova and Kaliskova, 2021), lesser previous labour market experience (Gauthier, 2016), traditional gender role expectations and the return to more traditional family values (Lobodzinska, 1996; Ma, 2010).

Contextual factors – reflected in labour market, social and family policies – thus impact on both the overall incidence as well as the continuity of male and female employment. It stands to reason that the level of security associated with a certain type of job may also be dependent on such characteristics. We investigate this in more detail in the following sections. In doing so, we discuss two types of uncertain employment that are relevant to mid-career employees: part-time employment and fixed-term employment.

Part-time employment

Part-time employment represents a flexibilization of employment contracts with regard to working times. According to standard international classifications such as that of the OECD (1997), part-time work has been defined as employment of 30 weekly working hours or less. Particularly for mid-career employees in their family phase, reduced working hours may provide a welcome means to better reconcile work and family life. Comparative evidence even shows that some women over 40 continue to work in part-time positions out of their own preference (OECD, 2010: 238). At the same time, remaining in part-time work for longer may hamper further career development and may be detrimental in terms of earnings potential, union membership and overall job security (OECD, 2010: 220ff.). A consideration of part-time employment thus requires a more detailed consideration of its motives. For this reason, the following two tables provide evidence on both the overall incidence of part-time work for the age group 25–54 years (Table 4.2) as well as the question of whether part-time employment was chosen voluntarily or was involuntary, that is, respondents preferred to work more hours but were not able to do so (Table 4.3). Given that part-time employment only plays a marginal role for men – in the EU only 8 per cent of men work part-time as compared to 30 per cent of women (Eurostat, 2020) – we focus on figures for women only. In order to capture the importance of part-time work particularly around motherhood, Table 4.2 presents figures on part-time and full-time employment for women with a child aged 0–12 years.

Figures from Table 4.2 show that the recent increases in female employment among mothers (see previous section) have predominantly been due to increases in full-time employment, whereas in many countries, full-time employment has remained largely stagnant or has even declined. At the same time, there exists considerable cross-national variation both in the relative importance of part-time employment as well as its degree of voluntariness. In Scandinavian countries, female employment is predominantly full-time, with part-time employment making up for less than 10 per cent of employment. Furthermore, the majority of part-time work in these countries is voluntary, with only a temporary surge in involuntary part-time employment after the financial crisis in 2008, which restricted the number of available jobs. All in all, figures reflect the employment-promoting labour market policies in Scandinavian countries which keep employment high among women and provide sufficient options for full-time work if requested.

In both conservative and liberal countries, part-time work is of considerable importance for women, with part-time employment rates between around 10 and 30 per cent. In Germany, the UK and (particularly) the Netherlands, part-time work is still the dominant work form among mothers with young children. The extraordinarily high part-time rates among Dutch women is the outcome of the explicit promotion of part-time employment for women throughout the 1980s and 1990s (Visser, 2002). Even though this model has been criticized for its detrimental effects on gender equality in the labour market (OECD, 2019a), figures for the voluntariness of part-time employment (see Table 4.3) suggest that part-time employment indeed is 'what most Dutchwomen want' (Booth and van Ours, 2013: 264). Similar conclusions can be drawn for most other conservative and liberal countries, where most recent figures for involuntary part-time work are low. The only exceptions are France and Luxembourg, where full-time employment is more dominant.

In both Southern and Eastern European countries, women's employment predominantly takes place in full-time work, with only Spain and Italy continuously exhibiting two-digit figures for female part-time employment. If it occurs, however, part-time employment is predominantly regarded as being involuntary in Southern European countries, where more than half of female part-timers would prefer a full-time job. Unlike in most other

Table 4.2: Shares of full- and part-time employment for women with a child aged 0–12 years, 2000–19

Country	Working hours	2000	2005	2010	2015	2019
Denmark	Full-time	na	na	73.5★	72.0	72.5
	Part-time	na	na	9.4★	8.7	9.1
Finland	Full-time	na	na	63.8	61.6	65.7
	Part-time	na	na	7.0	7.4	7.9
Sweden	Full-time	na	na	68.6	74.6	76.7
	Part-time	na	na	10.7	8.5	8.5
United Kingdom	Full-time	27.0	29.0	29.9	34.5	39.7
	Part-time	35.7	35.0	34.1	32.6	33.7
Ireland	Full-time	na	29.7★	29.4	36.9	42.7
	Part-time	na	28.0★	26.4	25.1	24.9
Austria	Full-time	na	36.7	35.9	34.6	36.1
	Part-time	na	33.3	38.4	41.5	42.4
Belgium	Full-time	36.8	42.2	46.5	49.0	51.6
	Part-time	25.9	24.9	23.9	22.1	21.6
France	Full-time	na	50.3	53.9	53.8	57.2
	Part-time	na	17.7	17.7	15.6	14.7
Germany	Full-time	na	22.7★	26.7	31.8	35.7
	Part-time	na	38.6★	39.1	38.6	37.5
Luxembourg	Full-time	34.0	35.3	39.9	46.7	51.4
	Part-time	22.0	28.1	27.8	19.1	16.7
Netherlands	Full-time	13.6	16.2	20.5	24.6	30.1
	Part-time	51.3	55.4	57.2	51.7	50.0
Cyprus	Full-time	53.1	58.5	64.8	60.5	62.9
	Part-time	8.3	8.9	8.8	8.2	10.5
Greece	Full-time	45.2	48.5	57.9	54.0	59.9
	Part-time	5.6	7.6	9.5	8.6	9.3
Italy	Full-time	na	33.1	34.5	34.9	36.7
	Part-time	na	19.7	20.1	20.5	20.6
Malta	Full-time	na	na	na	42.5	53.0
	Part-time	na	na	na	16.8	14.9
Portugal	Full-time	67.8	68.1	67.6	70.5	75.7
	Part-time	7.7	6.7	4.9	6.0	5.7

Table 4.2: Shares of full- and part-time employment for women with a child aged 0–12 years, 2000–19 (continued)

Country	Working hours	2000	2005	2010	2015	2019
Spain	Full-time	37.2	40.2	43.1	45.1	50.1
	Part-time	8.2	14.5	15.3	15.2	15.4
Czech Republic	Full-time	na	55.2	52.9	56.7	60.8
	Part-time	na	4.1	3.9	4.9	6.1
Hungary	Full-time	51.4	48.5	48.5	53.6	58.0
	Part-time	3.2	3.9	3.7	3.9	3.4
Poland	Full-time	na	51.8★	57.9★	62.8	64.3
	Part-time	na	9.7★	7.6★	6.3	6.0
Slovakia	Full-time	na	54.2	51.7	49.8	54.7
	Part-time	na	1.7	2.5	4.9	5.0
Slovenia	Full-time	na	80.6	83.8	80.6	79.7
	Part-time	na	3.6	6.5	7.0	6.9
Bulgaria	Full-time	na	57.3	60.3	61.3	66.4
	Part-time	na	1.2	0.9	1.6	1.0
Croatia	Full-time	na	na	na	66.3	72.7
	Part-time	na	na	na	3.4	4.0
Estonia	Full-time	58.8	58.5	56.2	59.6	60.3
	Part-time	4.6	4.7	5.6	9.1	10.1
Latvia	Full-time	na	58.6	59.3	66.2	71.9
	Part-time	na	6.9	7.7	6.7	5.8
Lithuania	Full-time	na	63.8	64.7	68.8	74.0
	Part-time	na	11.1	6.1	7.6	4.8
Romania	Full-time	na	58.3	60.2	59.7	63.9
	Part-time	na	5.6	6.0	5.5	4.5

Note: ★ = next available year.
Source: OECD, 2021b.

European countries, part-time employment is not being regarded as a means of work-family reconciliation but rather as a precarious and insecure work form. This impression is corroborated by further literature that highlights that in Southern European countries, part-time employment is rather perceived as primarily meeting 'employers' demand for greater external flexibility at the contract level' (Mastrierei and Leon, 2019: 72). Notably, this perception appears to have increased throughout the economic crisis in the early 2000s.

Table 4.3: Relative shares of involuntary part-time employment among all female part-timers aged 25–54 years, 2000–20

	2000	2010	2020
Denmark	16.6	19.6	14.0
Finland	na	na	na
Norway	12.8	18.8	7.1
Sweden	na	31.2	8.4
United Kingdom	6.9	10.4	8.1
Ireland	12.4	25.1	11.4
Austria	16.4	9.7	8.3
Belgium	18.6	9.9	4.1
France	24.0	29.3	35.3
Germany	11.5	17.8	7.6
Luxembourg	5.7	8.0	11.6
Netherlands	2.8	4.6	4.6
Cyprus	na	32.8	58.3
Greece	64.8	71.4	70.8
Italy	35.0	46.6	61.8
Malta	na	8.4	4.8
Portugal	56.5	65.7	55.8
Spain	24.6	52.9	52.7
Czech Republic	na	na	na
Hungary	30.4	41.6	19.0
Poland	47.4★	26.3	18.7
Slovakia	na	na	na
Slovenia	na	14.1	9.2
Bulgaria	na	61.3	52.3
Croatia	na	26.2	43.9
Estonia	na	26.9	6.9
Latvia	na	45.0	19.3
Lithuania	51.6	48.9	33.9
Romania	na	46.7	32.9

Note: ★ = next available year.

Source: OECD, 2021a.

Figures for Eastern European countries suggest that, particularly in the years after the system change, part-time employment was perceived similarly, reflected in high shares of involuntary part-time work. However, in all countries except Croatia, involuntary part-time employment has declined more recently.

Fixed-term employment

Fixed-term employment flexibilizes the 'normal employment relationship' by restricting the duration of a contract to a predefined period. In the previous Chapters 2 and 3, we have seen that this work form has been extensively used to flexibilize the employment relationships of young labour entrants. Table 4.4, which displays the share of fixed-term employment for men and women aged 25–54 years, shows that this has been much less the case for mid-career workers where it is not a widespread work form, making up for around or below 10 per cent of employment overall. The only exceptions are a few countries, particularly in Southern Europe, where it has been more frequently used in general (Spain, Portugal, Finland). Figures are particularly low in the other Eastern European countries, with the sole exception of Croatia.

In most countries, women display a higher likelihood of being in temporary employment, thus confirming findings from earlier analyses (OECD, 2014, 2002; Eurostat, 2008). Previous literature has explained the somewhat higher incidence of fixed-term employment among women by their specific preference for more flexible types of work, respectively their higher share in sectors where temporary contracts are overrepresented (Salladarré et al, 2007). Nonetheless, differences are modest and decrease over time.

Unemployment

In the previous sections, we had looked at different ways in which employment can be flexibilized. We conclude our elaboration of objective insecurity with a consideration of unemployment patterns among mid-career men and women, before subsequently turning to the analysis of subjectively perceived insecurity.

To that end, Table 4.5 presents figures on the development in unemployment rates within the age group 25–54 years throughout the last two decades, divided by gender. Unemployment rates in mid-career generally appear to be modest. Particularly in Southern European countries, unemployment surpasses a two-digit margin, especially around the financial crisis of 2008, mounting to values as high as 20–30 per cent in some countries. Unemployment rates decline again in the following decades

Table 4.4: Share of fixed-term employment (as % of dependent employment), aged 25–54, by gender, 2000–20

Country	Gender	2000	2005	2010	2015	2020
Denmark	Men	4.6	5.3	5.5	5.1	6.0
	Women	8.7	9.6	7.8	8.3	9.7
Finland	Men	9.5	9.8	9.2	10.0	9.9
	Women	16.6	18.6	16.9	15.7	15.8
Norway	Men	4.7	5.5	4.3	4.5	4.7
	Women	9.2	10.3	8.1	8.4	7.3
Sweden	Men	9.9	10.7	10.0	10.9	9.8
	Women	14.0	13.9	13.4	13.8	13.3
United Kingdom	Men	4.3	3.6	4.0	4.1	3.5
	Women	6.5	5.0	5.2	5.1	4.4
Ireland	Men	2.2	1.4	6.2	6.5	4.8
	Women	4.0	2.1	7.5	6.5	6.0
Austria	Men	3.0	4.1	4.6	4.9	4.5
	Women	4.7	5.1	5.2	5.5	5.7
Belgium	Men	4.5	4.6	5.2	6.7	7.7
	Women	10.0	9.0	7.8	8.0	8.4
France	Men	10.3	9.0	9.7	12.1	10.7
	Women	13.1	11.8	12.6	14.5	13.3
Germany	Men	7.1	8.4	9.1	9.1	8.6★
	Women	8.1	8.7	10.3	10.1	8.9★
Luxembourg	Men	1.5	3.1	4.8	7.7	5.8
	Women	3.5	4.3	6.6	7.7	6.5
Netherlands	Men	6.7	9.5	12.0	14.0	12.1
	Women	12.3	11.8	14.5	15.8	13.8
Cyprus	Men	6.6	8.9	6.6	13.2	9.0
	Women	13.2	19.4	22.1	24.2	17.8
Greece	Men	10.2	8.9	10.4	10.6	8.6
	Women	13.8	13.1	13.5	11.6	11.6
Malta	Men	1.5	2.1	2.7	4.9	5.6
	Women	4.8	4.2	4.9	6.9	8.4
Italy	Men	7.1	8.3	9.2	12.4	13.6
	Women	10.5	13.1	13.2	14.2	15.5
Portugal	Men	14.8	15.7	20.6	20.2	16.1
	Women	18.2	17.8	21.7	20.0	17.6

Table 4.4: Share of fixed-term employment (as % of dependent employment), aged 25–54, by gender, 2000–20 (continued)

Country	Gender	2000	2005	2010	2015	2020
Spain	Men	26.7	29.0	22.6	24.8	16.1
	Women	29.4	32.8	24.8	24.9	25.8
Czech Republic	Men	4.8	5.3	5.1	7.0	5.1
	Women	5.5	6.8	7.5	10.7	7.6
Hungary	Men	6.5	6.7	9.4	10.4	4.8
	Women	5.3	5.9	8.5	10.1	6.0
Poland	Men	9.8★	23.4	23.9	25.3	15.4
	Women	8.0★	20.8	23.0	26.0	17.6
Slovakia	Men	3.9	3.7	4.5	8.7	5.1
	Women	2.9	3.2	4.7	10.3	6.6
Slovenia	Men	8.7	11.0	10.6	13.9	7.4
	Women	10.1	13.8	14.4	14.8	10.1
Bulgaria	Men	na	5.7	4.4	4.4	3.6
	Women	na	5.2	3.5	3.8	3.0
Croatia	Men	na	9.9	10.0	19.2	12.6
	Women	na	10.3	12.4	18.6	15.3
Estonia	Men	4.0	2.8	4.3	3.4	2.1
	Women	1.3	1.4	2.0	2.4	2.2
Latvia	Men	8.4	10.2	8.5	3.6	2.7
	Women	3.9	5.4	4.4	2.1	2.5
Lithuania	Men	5.9	7.2	2.7	1.9	1.0
	Women	2.6	3.1	1.5	1.4	0.7
Romania	Men	1.9	2.3	1.0	1.5	1.5
	Women	2.0	1.6	0.8	0.9	0.7

Note: ★ = last available year.

Source: OECD, 2021a.

in Southern European countries, even though in Greece and Spain, they remain comparatively high. Eastern European countries show a pattern with a 'double peak' of employment: one in the early 2000s, likely due to the repercussions of the system change in the 1990s, and a second one around the financial crisis. Since then, unemployment rises have declined substantially so that, by 2020, unemployment rates in Eastern Europe are at a rather modest level.

Table 4.5: Unemployment rate, aged 25–54, 2000–20

Country	Gender	2000	2005	2010	2015	2020
Denmark	Men	3.4	3.5	7.3	5.4	4.4
	Women	4.9	4.4	6.6	6.0	5.5
Finland	Men	7.2	6.5	7.4	7.9	5.9
	Women	8.8	7.3	6.3	7.5	5.8
Norway	Men	2.5	3.8	3.4	4.2	4.1
	Women	2.2	3.6	2.5	3.8	3.6
Sweden	Men	5.3	6.2	6.3	5.8	6.5
	Women	4.5	6.3	6.6	5.8	7.1
United Kingdom	Men	4.7	3.8	6.6	3.8	3.5
	Women	3.8	3.3	5.3	4.2	3.1
Ireland	Men	4.2	4.0	15.4	9.5	4.7
	Women	2.9	2.8	10.2	8.2	4.1
Austria	Men	2.8	4.5	4.6	5.5	5.0
	Women	3.5	5.3	4.2	4.9	5.0
Belgium	Men	4.9	6.6	7.2	8.2	5.1
	Women	7.6	8.4	7.5	7.1	4.9
France	Men	6.6	7.0	7.6	9.5	7.0
	Women	9.2	8.8	8.3	9.0	7.1
Germany	Men	6.6	10.6	7.1	4.7	4.1
	Women	7.5	10.2	6.2	4.0	3.1
Luxembourg	Men	1.4	2.9	3.0	5.0	5.2
	Women	2.9	5.3	5.0	6.9	6.2
Netherlands	Men	1.9	3.6	3.1	5.0	2.8
	Women-	3.3	6.1	4.6	6.3	3.0
Cyprus	Men	2.9	3.6	5.5	12.9	6.6
	Women	6.7	5.6	5.3	13.2	7.6
Greece	Men	6.2	5.4	9.5	20.9	13.1
	Women	15.1	14.3	15.5	28.7	20.0
Italy	Men	6.3	5.1	6.5	10.4	8.0
	Women	12.1	8.9	8.9	12.2	10.4
Malta	Men	5.1	4.6	5.3	4.1	3.4
	Women	4.5	5.8	5.8	4.7	3.9
Portugal	Men	2.7	6.1	9.3	10.8	5.6
	Women	4.4	8.4	12.1	11.6	6.4

Table 4.5: Unemployment rate, aged 25–54, 2000–20 (continued)

Country	Gender	2000	2005	2010	2015	2020
Spain	Men	8.0	6.0	17.9	18.9	12.6
	Women	18.9	10.7	18.9	22.4	16.6
Czech Republic	Men	6.0	5.3	5.2	3.7	2.1
	Women	9.9	9.3	8.0	5.8	2.8
Hungary	Men	6.2	6.0	10.7	5.6	3.6
	Women	5.0	6.9	10.1	6.6	4.1
Poland	Men	12.1	14.5	7.9	6.2	2.6
	Women	16.0	17.7	8.7	7.1	3.0
Slovakia	Men	15.2	13.2	12.4	9.1	5.8
	Women	15.8	15.7	13.3	12.2	6.7
Slovenia	Men	5.4	5.2	7.1	7.3	4.0
	Women	5.8	6.2	6.8	10.2	5.3
Bulgaria	Men	14.9	9.1	9.8	9.1	5.3
	Women	15.1	9.0	8.8	7.8	4.6
Croatia	Men	na	9.3	9.2	13.3	6.9
	Women	na	12.7	11.2	15.6	6.6
Estonia	Men	15.0	8.6	17.4	5.3	5.8
	Women	12.9	6.8	12.7	5.8	6.0
Latvia	Men	15.2	9.6	21.2	10.4	8.9
	Women	12.8	9.5	14.9	8.6	6.9
Lithuania	Men	17.7	7.4	20.0	9.5	8.1
	Women	13.5	8.4	13.5	7.8	6.7
Romania	Men	6.9	6.7	6.7	6.9	4.6
	Women	6.3	6.0	5.7	5.2	4.2

Source: OECD, 2021a.

Gender-specific developments do not seem to follow a clear-cut pattern. In a number of countries, women's unemployment is somewhat higher than that of men in the early 2000s. The financial crisis in 2008 has shifted this gender balance somewhat, as male unemployment figures often rose by a larger margin than that of women, sometimes even overtaking them. By 2019, unemployment rates of men and women seem to have normalized again and show generally fewer differences than before the crisis, though it is often still rather women who exhibit slightly higher unemployment figures (see also Eurostat, 2020).

Reasons for this gender difference identified in previous literature have included difficulties for women to successfully re-enter employment after 'family breaks' (Bicakova 2016) as well as with continued care responsibilities (Eurofound, 2016). So it is not surprising that – particularly in Southern European countries, which combine the strongest exposure to the financial crisis with only a weak support for work-family reconciliation – not only is unemployment highest but also the gender gap is most pronounced to the disadvantage of women. In contrast, in countries with employment-sustaining policies, such as particularly the Scandinavian ones, overall unemployment as well as related gender differences have remained rather modest.

Objective employment insecurity: interim summary

Taking together the results from the previous sections, a few general conclusions can be drawn with regard to objective employment insecurity.

In line with findings from previous research (for example, Blossfeld and Hofmeister, 2006; Blossfeld, Mills and Bernardi, 2006), mid-career still appears to be a rather stable phase in employment life, particularly when being compared with the preceding results on youth and early-career (see Chapters 2 and 3). Employment rates are comparatively high and have gradually converged between men and women, while unemployment rates are rather modest. Fixed-term employment forms are also of a lesser significance than for younger employees, suggesting a generally safer anchorage of mid-career employees in the labour market. Only part-time work appears to be of higher importance, particularly for women aiming to combine work and family tasks during early parenthood years.

Notwithstanding the general finding of higher employment stability in mid-career, there appear to be pronounced gender differences in the degree of establishment within the labour market. Despite recent increases, women's employment rates still lack behind that of men. Women more often interrupt their employment careers due to childbirth and apparently face higher difficulties re-entering employment. They are also more often found in atypical work forms, particularly part-time work. Even though our results suggest that these work forms meet an existing demand for work-family reconciliation and thus are chosen voluntarily, women's employment stability appears to be lower than that of men.

Our results also point to notable and largely systematic differences in the spread of flexible work forms as well as in gender differences across European welfare regimes:

- Smallest differences appear to surface in Scandinavian countries, where employment rates for both sexes are high, unemployment rates are low and women tend to work mostly full-time. Deviations from the standard work model are rare and – if they occur – are largely of a voluntary nature.

- The opposite picture can be found in Southern European countries, whose economies have been hit particularly hard by the economic recession in 2008, reflected in persistently high unemployment rates. Against this background, fixed-term employment – which was a dominant work form for young people in the South – stretches well into mid-career, with up to one third of the population still being affected by it. Further to this picture of higher employment insecurity in general, women's employment appears to be most insecure in these countries. Employment rates of women in Southern Europe are among the lowest while at the same time, female unemployment is high and significantly above that of men. Part-time employment among women is rather rare, and if it occurs it is often involuntary.

- Eastern European countries initially have displayed a similar picture, reflected in high overall unemployment rates, particularly in the time-period from the 2000s to the early 2010s. Flexible work such as part-time or fixed-term employment were hardly available for Eastern European men or women, and if it occurred it was frequently involuntary. However, our results suggest that the situation in these countries changed for the better in the late 2010s so that employment insecurity by 2019/20 was well below that of Southern European countries.

- Conservative and liberal countries take an intermediate position within these polar opposites. While being only modestly affected by the financial crisis, women's employment still lags behind that of men in these countries. This is reflected in still clearly lower employment rates, but also in lower working hours of women which are predominantly found in part-time work. Yet, the fact that in the majority, reduced working hours are accepted voluntarily suggests that overall, women do not perceive their unemployment as being particularly uncertain.

Subjective employment insecurity

In the following, we will systematically contrast these patterns of objective insecurity with the subjective perception of labour market insecurity in order to investigate the relationship between the two dimensions for employees in mid-career. To what degree do employees in this relatively stable phase of employment life perceive their labour market position as being uncertain? And how far does this perception vary between welfare regimes and according to gender?

To begin with, we first focus on cognitive job insecurity (see Chapter 2), that is, the perceived likelihood of the risk of losing one's job in the following six months. Table 4.6 reports the percentage of employees aged 25–50 years[1]

Table 4.6: Subjective perception of job loss worry, employees aged 25–50, by gender, 2003–16

Country	Gender	2003	2007	2011	2016
Denmark	Men	9.4	6.3	8.0	6.8
	Women	7.1	7.4	14.0	6.3
Finland	Men	6.4	13.1	14.4	5.7
	Women	7.3	15.6	9.4	9.1
Norway	Men	na	2.8	na	na
	Women	na	2.3	na	na
Sweden	Men	8.6	4.8	5.5	10.8
	Women	7.4	2.1	2.4	10.4
United Kingdom	Men	8.0	6.1	12.4	8.1
	Women	6.8	7.9	15.4	6.2
Ireland	Men	7.5	5.7	15.1	12.1
	Women	6.5	2.1	20.9	1.9
Austria	Men	3.9	2.2	2.5	5.4
	Women	7.1	6.7	4.0	5.0
Belgium	Men	9.0	4.4	5.7	10.9
	Women	6.7	9.3	5.9	9.4
France	Men	7.8	10.8	10.9	8.8
	Women	7.8	7.6	15.2	9.0
Germany	Men	5.9	6.1	3.8	4.9
	Women	4.1	3.9	3.9	5.2
Luxembourg	Men	7.8	4.0	4.7	8.4
	Women	6.9	8.2	7.0	4.5
Netherlands	Men	2.7	3.6	3.5	5.3
	Women	2.5	1.5	5.0	7.3
Cyprus	Men	11.5	6.9	28.1	14.0
	Women	9.9	7.9	37.5	20.1
Greece	Men	11.0	6.8	34.2	12.3
	Women	12.9	10.1	32.9	15.3
Italy	Men	4.2	8.0	13.8	8.2
	Women	10.7	10.5	17.9	11.5
Malta	Men	10.7	2.3	11.7	7.5
	Women	5.6	4.3	7.3	4.3
Portugal	Men	9.5	13.6	21.6	7.2
	Women	9.6	15.0	24.8	8.6

Table 4.6: Subjective perception of job loss worry, employees aged 25–50, by gender, 2003–16 (continued)

Country	Gender	2003	2007	2011	2016
Spain	Men	6.5	7.6	19.6	12.1
	Women	13.4	9.9	20.7	11.7
Czech Republic	Men	16.1	7.0	18.2	10.7
	Women	18.6	12.9	22.6	14.2
Hungary	Men	7.8	7.8	10.3	10.1
	Women	9.3	9.6	14.4	8.4
Poland	Men	15.6	9.4	14.6	5.5
	Women	16.8	10.2	16.7	12.8
Slovakia	Men	19.4	11.7	19.9	8.7
	Women	14.7	15.5	21.5	10.6
Slovenia	Men	12.4	9.6	9.8	10.7
	Women	6.8	12.6	10.1	12.5
Bulgaria	Men	44.7	17.6	23.5	4.9
	Women	57.6	25.3	19.7	6.3
Croatia	Men	na	13.4	29.0	10.1
	Women	na	10.9	31.4	18.2
Estonia	Men	17.6	12.0	13.3	10.2
	Women	18.9	9.2	15.0	15.3
Latvia	Men	39.0	9.3	21.1	12.4
	Women	21.9	14.1	30.6	9.7
Lithuania	Men	32.5	15.8	19.3	7.0
	Women	33.5	18.2	21.5	14.6
Romania	Men	14.8	10.2	22.6	10.8
	Women	18.8	17.8	17.9	7.2

Source: own elaboration on EQLS data.

who either perceived this risk as being 'very likely' or 'rather likely' on a 5-point-scale, using data from the European Quality of Life Survey, covering the period from 2003–16.

Table 4.6 shows that, generally, the perceived insecurity of job loss is rather low, particularly in Scandinavian, liberal and conservative countries where the relative share of those fearing job loss remains mostly below 10 per cent. Only around the economic crisis in 2008 did the share of those fearing job loss rise, but it drops again in the fourth EQLS wave in 2016. These patterns appear to be in line with the picture of mid-career being characterized by relative career stability in the afore-mentioned countries. Southern European countries deviate from this pattern in as far as perceived job insecurity increases in the third EQLS wave, signifying the post-crisis period, where up to a third of Greek and Cypriot employees and around a fifth in Portugal and Spain are apparently afraid of losing their jobs. This pattern is much in line with the increase in unemployment and atypical work reported in the previous sections. In the following years, this perceived insecurity declines to around pre-crisis level, but remains above that of the afore-mentioned countries. Patterns of job loss worry in Eastern European countries display two peaks, as also observed for objective insecurity (see the earlier section on this). The first is in the first wave, that is in a time-period when these countries still suffered from the repercussions of the system transformation. In this period, some countries display extraordinarily high levels of job loss worries among almost half (Bulgaria) or around a third of employees (Latvia, Lithuania) while a number of other countries clearly remain below that level. A second peak in job loss worries is reached after the financial crisis, when in virtually all Eastern European countries, more than 10 per cent of Eastern European employees report job loss worries, with highest values reached in the same countries as before, as well as in the Czech Republic, Croatia and Slovakia. In most countries, however, these worries decline again in the subsequent years. In Southern European countries, perceived risks of job loss thus follow a largely cyclical pattern with rapid increases in job loss worries after the financial crisis.

There appears to be no clear-cut pattern with regards to gender differences across countries, not even in those countries which were identified as exhibiting clear gender differences in objective employment insecurity. The only pattern that seems apparent is that the economic crisis has harmed somewhat more the perceived job security of women, even though in most countries gender differences are also not particularly pronounced throughout this period.

The perceived job security of those having a job – the so-called 'labour market insiders' – thus appears to be rather high in mid-career. In Table 4.7, we contrast this perception with the perceived likelihood of re-entering employment when becoming unemployed, that is, the re-employment opportunities when becoming a 'labour market outsider'. In Table 4.7, we report the cumulated percentage of those who report considering it 'very likely' or 'rather likely' they would 'find a job of similar salary?' on a 5-point-scale. As the question was only asked in the last two waves, we can report figures for 2011 and 2016 only. As before, findings refer to employees aged 25–50 years, with results reported separately for men and women.

Table 4.7: Likelihood of re-employment after job loss, employees aged 25–50 years, by gender, 2011 and 2016

Country	Gender	2011	2016
Denmark	Men	57.4	72.6
	Women	61.4	74.8
Finland	Men	57.5	61.8
	Women	73.3	79.5
Norway	Men	na	na
	Women	na	na
Sweden	Men	75.5	78.5
	Women	82.5	81.3
United Kingdom	Men	44.6	55.3
	Women	44.9	56.0
Ireland	Men	29.6	52.6
	Women	24.8	57.8
Austria	Men	60.5	52.5
	Women	53.5	53.3
Belgium	Men	46.2	43.0
	Women	50.0	49.6
France	Men	59.4	42.9
	Women	55.8	44.6
Germany	Men	37.5	48.8
	Women	44.6	54.5
Luxembourg	Men	46.6	45.9
	Women	53.1	49.6
Netherlands	Men	52.3	55.2
	Women	52.9	59.2
Cyprus	Men	27.0	31.5
	Women	16.8	29.6
Greece	Men	7.3	13.4
	Women	10.7	9.4
Italy	Men	24.0	22.3
	Women	21.6	21.2
Malta	Men	17.6	51.7
	Women	24.1	54.7
Portugal	Men	27.7	36.1

(continued)

Table 4.7: Likelihood of re-employment after job loss, employees aged 25–50 years, by gender, 2011 and 2016 (continued)

Country	Gender	2011	2016
	Women	20.9	36.4
Spain	Men	25.4	28.5
	Women	17.3	36.8
Czech Republic	Men	33.7	51.5
	Women	30.0	46.7
Hungary	Men	34.6	45.4
	Women	30.3	45.0
Poland	Men	43.0	47.6
	Women	34.0	49.4
Slovakia	Men	37.8	42.0
	Women	34.6	41.5
Slovenia	Men	38.2	49.3
	Women	33.5	38.0
Bulgaria	Men	34.1	56.6
	Women	28.8	45.7
Croatia	Men	36.4	33.3
	Women	26.3	27.1
Estonia	Men	54.8	61.0
	Women	46.7	63.5
Latvia	Men	50.0	64.4
	Women	30.4	58.2
Lithuania	Men	48.1	56.9
	Women	23.3	50.6
Romania	Men	44.6	50.0
	Women	37.6	48.9

Source: own elaboration on EQLS data.

In the majority of cases (though not in all), the perceived likelihood of re-employment after job loss is higher for 2016 than it is for 2011. Considering previous results on objective and perceived job insecurity, this finding may suggest that, while closely after the financial crisis of 2008, the strained labour market situation enforced individual worries of difficulties about re-entering employment, the gradual economic improvement in the following years promoted a greater optimism regarding labour market opportunities after a job loss. However, there remain marked variations in this assessment across countries. The highest level of optimism concerning re-entry prospects in case of job loss is found in Scandinavian countries where by the year 2016, between around 60 and 80 per cent of respondents expect to find a new job in case of job loss. This result seems plausible given the strong focus on fostering employment and the modest to low level of unemployment and employment flexibilization observed in these countries. Notably, even though figures in 2011 are lower, still more than half of the population in all Scandinavian countries displayed this relative optimism even shortly after the financial crisis. Another notable finding is that for all countries and both points in time, women's perception of re-employment chances is more positive than that of men, reconfirming the strong support for women's employment provided in these countries. A completely reverse situation prevails in Southern European countries: Particularly in the years after the financial crisis, less than 30 per cent of Southern European respondents – and even less than 10 per cent of men in Greece – expected a successful employment re-entry once becoming unemployed. These findings correspond with the higher levels of objective employment insecurity, and particularly the sharp rise in unemployment throughout this period. Even though perceived re-employment chances have improved in the following years, Southern European figures remain the lowest in the sample. Eastern European figures initially (2011) exhibited a similar pessimism as, particularly in post-socialist neoliberal economy countries, only around a third of respondents expected successful employment re-entry. Yet, in most countries, notable increases until 2016 suggest that in the perception of mid-career workers in Eastern Europe, not only the job security of the 'insiders' has improved throughout economic recovery, but also the re-employment chances of (temporary) employment 'outsiders' are viewed more positively.

Conservative and liberal countries take an intermediate position between the two poles when mostly around half of mid-career employees in these countries perceive their re-employment prospects positively; a picture somewhat more pronounced in the fourth (2016) than in the third (2011) EQLS wave, though the margin remains modest. The only notable exception is Ireland, where by 2011, only around a quarter of respondents perceived re-employment chances favourably, in line with the pronounced increase in unemployment throughout this period. Yet, with the subsequent economic recovery, figures almost doubled, thus again converging with the other countries of the afore mentioned group.

Determinants of subjective job insecurity and re-employment chances in mid-career

In the previous section, we investigated the cross-national differences in subjective employment insecurity, pointing to notable cross-national differences between welfare regimes. In this section, we will complement this perspective with a more detailed investigation of individual factors that impact on subjectively perceived employment security. Which individuals fear most that they will lose their job? How far do perceived probabilities of employment re-entry after unemployment differ between socio-economic groups? And how far is perceived employment insecurity driven by the actual experience of insecure work forms?

To this end, we estimate logistic regression models using dichotomous measures of job loss worry and perceived employment re-entry as dependent variables.[2] We use information from wave 3 and 4 of EQLS, in which both indicators were included and control for cross-wave differences by using a wave dummy for 2011 (where objective and subjective employment insecurity was higher). Informed by our previous finding that objective employment insecurity may differ between genders, we estimate separate models for men and women. Following the regime classification of Bohle and Greskovits (2012) applied earlier (Chapter 3), we differentiate six welfare regimes: social-democratic, liberal, conservative, Southern European, embedded post-socialist and liberal post-socialist countries. As independent individual-level variables, we include dummy variables for low (ISCED 1/2), medium (ISCED 3/4) and higher education (ISCED 5 and higher) to reflect differences in human capital, assuming that higher human capital will shield from uncertain employment (see Chapter 1). To consider effects for the family situation – which was shown to be particularly influential for women's employment – we include a dummy for the presence of minor children in the household. The influence of insecure work forms is approximated by respective dummies for part-time and non-permanent employment. Table 4.8 reports β-coefficients and significance levels. Considering the nested nature of our data, we estimate robust standard errors, clustered by country.[3]

The results from Table 4.8 first of all confirm the differences between regimes already outlined in the previous sections. For both sexes, social-democratic and liberal countries display the lowest levels of job loss worries and high expected re-employment probabilities. While there is no observable difference between the two groups with regard to job loss worries, Scandinavian countries particularly stand out with the highest likelihood of re-employment; likely due to their system of active employment support. Conservative countries make up a peculiar case. With regard to job loss worries, men in these countries perceive their situation as even more safe than do respondents in Scandinavian or Anglo-Saxon countries. However, with regard to re-employment probabilities after unemployment, they significantly fall behind Scandinavian countries. These findings reconfirm the characterization of conservative countries as reflecting 'insider-outsider-regimes', not only with regard to their structural characteristics, but also for their subjective perceptions of employment security: while men as sheltered

Table 4.8: Logistic regression to explain job loss worries and re-employment probabilities among mid-career workers, aged 25–54, 2011 (that is, post financial crisis)

		Men		Women	
		Worry of job loss	Likelihood of re-employment	Worry of job loss	Likelihood of re-employment
Regime (ref.: social-democratic)					
	Liberal	−0.001	−0.161★★	0.010	−0.221★★
		(0.014)	(0.054)	(0.026)	(0.041)
	Conservative	−0.057★★	−0.148★★	−0.043	−0.193★★
		(0.011)	(0.045)	(0.028)	(0.039)
	Southern	0.039	−0.336★★	0.611	−0.393★★
		(0.025)	(0.045)	(0.038)	(0.034)
	Eastern (embedded)	0.034★	−0.196★★	0.049+	−0.294★★
		(0.016)	(0.044)	(0.029)	(0.033)
	Eastern (liberal)	0.077★★	−0.143★	0.109★★	−0.286★★
		(0.018)	(0.057)	(0.036)	(0.039)
Survey wave					
	2011 (ref.: 2016)	0.040★★	−0.064★★	0.069★★	−0.101★★
		(0.012)	(0.020)	(0.011)	(0.020)
Socio-demographic controls					
	Education: medium (ref.: low)	−0.036★	0.046+	−0.012	0.022
		(0.015)	(0.027)	(0.016)	(0.022)
	Education: high (ref.: low)	−0.067★★	0.169★★	−0.048★★	0.111★★
		(0.013)	(0.028)	(0.016)	(0.022)
	Children in household (ref.: no children)	−0.003	−0.024	0.013	−0.010
		(0.008)	(0.016)	(0.010)	(0.013)
Type of employment					
	Non-permanent (ref.: permanent)	0.109★★	0.021	0.133★★	0.00
		(0.018)	(0.018)	(0.021)	(0.015)
	Part-time (ref.: full-time)	0.047★	0.007	−0.003	−0.001
		(0.020)	(0.029)	(0.011)	(0.17)
Nagelkerke R^2		0.098	0.099	0.105	0.118
N		5173	5173	6428	6428

Note: significance levels: ★★<=0.01, ★ <=0.05, + <=0.10.

Source: Eurofound, 2018 (own calculations; unweighted). Average marginal effects. Robust standard errors, clustered by country.

employed 'insiders' perceive their labour market situation as highly stable, both genders are more worried about their employment prospects once becoming an 'outsider'. For Southern European countries, this picture is even more pronounced. Re-employment chances after unemployment are perceived most negatively in these countries, likely due to the widespread unemployment after the 2008 crisis. These bad economic conditions also may be the reason why – compared to conservative counties – Southern European men and women also perceive their current job to be less stable. Eastern European countries fall in between these country groupings. While their subjective labour market perceptions are not as favourable as in Central Europe, they exhibit more critical perceptions of their job stability, but better re-employment prospects than in Southern Europe. Over and above, this applies to both sub-groupings, even though the more liberally oriented countries perceive a higher level of job loss worries than the 'embedded' systems in Central and Eastern Europe. In line with the descriptive overview in the previous sections, both measures of employment insecurity appear to be more critical in 2011, that is in the time-period closer to the economic crisis.

Results also point to considerable variations at the individual level. In line with our expectations, educational attainment shelters against negative perceptions of employment security, as higher educated individuals generally exhibit lower job loss worries and higher perceived re-employment chances. Notably, this effect follows a gradual step-wise pattern for men, while for women, only those with highest educational levels appear to be shielded from subjective employment insecurity. No strong effect is observed with regard to the presence of children in the household. Only with regard to re-employment chances do women tend to be more pessimistic, a finding in line with the previously described difficulties of mothers to re-enter employment once becoming unemployed or inactive.

Turning to employment characteristics, atypical work forms apparently promote employment insecurity for mid-career employees, though with variations between the two genders and the dimension investigated. For men, both temporary employment as well as part-time employment have detrimental effects on the perceived likelihood of a job loss. This is in line with the still strong orientation of men as male breadwinners in predominantly safe and 'normal' employment. Men in work forms which deviate from this pattern thus regard their labour market position as being less stable. For women, only non-permanent employment is associated with higher job loss worries, while this is not the case for part-time employment. Given the more widespread use of part-time work among women and the often voluntary decision for this work form as a means to reconcile work and family, this finding seems plausible. For both women and men, no effects are found for atypical employment with regard to re-employment probabilities. Transitions back into employment apparently are perceived as being more related to individual human capital and contextual conditions at the national level, rather than being dependent on the type of job previously held.

Consequences of objective and subjective employment insecurity in mid-career

So far, we have investigated the spread of objective and subjective employment insecurity and its various determinants. In this final section, we now turn to the 'outcomes' of employment insecurity, that is, the question of how far objective and subjective employment insecurity impact on key dimensions in the overall quality of life, more specifically satisfaction with one's own job, satisfaction with one's current overall living standard and satisfaction with family life. These three dimensions serve as proxies for key spheres in the life of mid-career men and women. We investigate in how far EQLS respondents that experience objective or subjective employment insecurity are disadvantaged with regard to any of the three dimensions. To this end, we draw back to three indicators[4] from the EQLS waves 3 and 4, that were measured on a 10-point scale (with 1 meaning 'very dissatisfied' and 10 meaning 'very satisfied').

Given that answers to satisfaction items often suffer from an upward basis (with respondents tending towards more positive answers), we dichotomized the respective variables differentiating between values 1–7 and 8–10 which resulted in almost a median split of answers for all three variables. We used the respective dichotomized variables as dependent variables in logistic regression, including dummies for welfare regime, survey wave and socio-demographic controls as in the previous section. In addition, we included measures of objective (fixed-term employment, part-time employment) as well as subjective employment insecurity (dichotomized measures for job loss worry and perceived re-entry chances) as further determinants in separate model. To investigate gender differences, we again calculated spate models for men and women (see Tables 4.9 and 4.10), again with robust standard errors clustered by country.

For both genders, results for the logistic regression models point to pronounced regime differences in satisfaction. Male and female respondents in Scandinavian countries enjoy highest satisfaction with their living standard and their family life, while the opposite is the case for Southern and Eastern European countries. Respondents from liberal and conservative countries mostly take an intermediate position in between these poles. Similar rankings are observed for job satisfaction, though the pattern of Scandinavian exceptionalism is somewhat less pronounced. Levels of job satisfaction in conservative countries are comparatively positive among both genders in

Table 4.9: Logistic regression to explain outcomes of employment insecurity among mid-career workers, aged 25–54, 2011 (that is, post financial crisis); men

| | Satisfaction with ... | | | | | |
| | Job | | Living standard | | Family life | |
	M1	M2	M3	M4	M5	M6
Regime (ref.: social-democratic)						
Liberal	-0.093★	-0.089★	-0.105★★	-0.102★★	-0.120★	-0.115★
	(0.042)	(0.044)	(0.024)	(0.022)	(0.047)	(0.049)
Conservative	-0,065	-0,063	-0.093★	-0.088★	-0.137★★	-0.134★★
	(0.044)	(0.045)	(0.041)	(0.039)	(0.048)	(0.050)
Southern	-0.165★★	-0.142★★	-0.246★★	-0.227★★	-0.151★★	-0.134★
	(0.049)	(0.050)	(0.029)	(0.026)	(0.055)	(0.056)
Eastern (embedded)	-0.157★★	-0.139★★	-0.263★★	-0.248★★	-0.200★★	-0.187★★
	(0.042)	(0.044)	(0.022)	(0.021)	(0.047)	(0.049)
Eastern (liberal)	-0.164★★	-0.141★★	-0.332★★	-0.317★★	-0.195★★	-0.180★★
	(0.041)	(0.042)	(0.020)	(0.019)	(0.051)	(0.053)
Survey wave						
2011 (ref.: 2016)	0.024	0.032★	-0.018	-0.012	-0.011	-0.006
	(0.016)	(0.016)	(0.020)	(0.019)	(0.014)	(0.015)
Socio-demographic controls						
Education: medium	0.030	0.022	0.071★★	0.065★★	-0.005	-0.010
(ref.: low)	(0.021)	(0.021)	(0.018)	(0.018)	(0.015)	(0.015)
Education: high	0.158★★	0.137★★	0.215★	0.196★★	0.055★★	0.044★★
(ref.: low)	(0.024)	(0.024)	(0.021)	(0.022)	(0.013)	(0.014)

Table 4.9: Logistic regression to explain outcomes of employment insecurity among mid-career workers, aged 25–54, 2011 (that is, post financial crisis); men (continued)

	Satisfaction with …					
	Job		Living standard		Family life	
Children in household	0.048**	0.051**	0.007	0.011	0.088**	0.090**
(ref.: no children)	(0.013)	(0.013)	(0.014)	(0.014)	(0.016)	(0.017)
Type of employment (objective)						
Non-permanent	-0.059**		-0.074**		-0.033+	
(ref.: permanent)	(0.021)		(0.021)		(0.017)	
Part-time	-0.070+		-0.083*		-0.020	
(ref.: full-time)	(0.036)		(0.034)		(0.024)	
Subjective employment insecurity						
Job loss worry		-0.188**		-0.160**		-0.080**
		(0.014)		(0.021)		(0.017)
Re-employment chances		0.053**		0.063**		0.039**
		(0.018)		(0.018)		(0.015)
Nagelkerke R^2	0.056	0.075	0.133	0.144	0.046	0.054
N	5159	5159	5171	5171	5153	5153

Note: significance levels: **<=0.01, * <=0.05, + <=0.10.

Source: Eurofound, 2018 (own calculations; unweighted). Average marginal effects. Robust standard errors, clustered by country in paratheses).

Table 4.10: Logistic regression to explain outcomes of employment insecurity among mid-career workers, aged 25–54, 2011 (that is, post financial crisis); women

| | Satisfaction with ... | | | | | |
| | Job | | Living standard | | Family life | |
	M1	M2	M3	M4	M5	M6
Regime (ref.: social-democratic)						
Liberal	-0.014	-0.018	-0.147**	-0.131**	-0.029	-0.020
	(0.037)	(0.044)	(0.015)	(0.015)	(0.059)	(0.059)
Conservative	-0.044	-0.047	-0.116**	-0.103**	-0.096	-0.086
	(0.043)	(0.046)	(0.038)	(0.038)	(0.058)	(0.060)
Southern	-0.134**	-0.126*	-0.248**	-0.221**	-0.148*	-0.125+
	(0.050)	(0.052)	(0.0299)	(0.028)	80.065)	(0.066)
Eastern (embedded)	-0.132**	-0.122**	-0.284**	-0.267**	-0.175**	-0.155*
	(0.039)	(0.042)	(0.016)	(0.018)	(0.66)	(0.067)
Eastern (liberal)	-0.098*	-0.073	-0.329**	-0.306**	-0.220**	-0.192**
	(0.040)	(0.044)	(0.021)	(0.023)	(0.059)	(0.062)
Survey wave						
2011 (ref.: 2016)	0.007	0.022	-0.048*	-0.032+	-0.039+	-0.029**
	(0.20)	(0.020)	(0.019)	(0.017)	(0.020)	(0.020)
Socio-demographic controls						
Education: medium (ref.: low)	0.051**	0.051**	0.061**	0.059**	0.013	0.014
	(0.018)	(0.017)	(0.018)	(0.017)	(0.016)	(0.015)
Education: high (ref.: low)	0.159**	0.150**	0.213**	0.199*	0.077**	0.070**
	(0.025)	(0.024)	(0.023)	(0.022)*	(0.016)	(0.015)

Table 4.10: Logistic regression to explain outcomes of employment insecurity among mid-career workers, aged 25–54, 2011 (that is, post financial crisis); women (continued)

	Satisfaction with ...					
	Job		**Living standard**		**Family life**	
Children in household	0.003	0.008	-0.008	-0,002	0.035★★	0.038★★
(ref.: no children)	(0.015)	(0.015)	(0.016)	(0.016)	(0.011)	(0.012)
Type of employment (objective)						
Non-permanent	-0.083★★		-0.056★★		-0.048★★	
(ref.: permanent)	(0.018)		(0.015)		(0.015)	
Part-time	0.004		0.019		0.006	
(ref.: full-time)	(0.018)		(0.022)		(0.016)	
Subjective employment insecurity						
Job loss worry		-0.226★★		-0.159★★		-0.081★★
		(0.017)		(0.022)		(0.018)
Re-employment chances		0.007		0.062★★		0.043★★
		(0.012)		(0.015)		(0.012)
Constant	0.213	0.205	0.599★★	0.431★★	1.616★★	1.440
Nagelkerke R²	0.044	0.070	0.121	0.138	0.045	0.052
N	6402	6402	6421	6421	6418	6418

Note: significance levels: ★★<=0.01, ★ <=0.05, + <=0.10.

Source: Eurofound, 2018 (own calculations; unweighted). Average marginal effects. Robust standard errors, clustered by country in paratheses).

conservative countries, likely reflecting the more pronounced levels of job protection in these countries. While women appear to be similarly satisfied with their job in the less regulated and flexible market system of liberal countries, male job satisfaction ranks somewhat lower. Job satisfaction is lowest in Southern and Eastern European countries, that is in contexts where a critical labour market situation was accompanied by weak welfare state protection against labour market and income risks. Men's satisfaction with family life is highest in Scandinavian countries, where policies supporting reconciliation between work and family are most pronounced. For women in the flexible labour market system of liberal countries as well as in conservative countries, similar satisfaction levels with family life are observed. In the other countries – that is, in Southern Europe and both groups of Eastern Europe, characterized by more strained labour markets and less generous reconciliation policies – we observe clearly more negative satisfaction levels. Satisfaction levels thus strongly correlate with institutional patterns in labour market, social and family policies.

On the individual level, education has a positive effect on all three dimensions of satisfaction, which is particularly pronounced for respondents with higher education (ISCED 5 or more.) Results thus reaffirm the shielding effect of human capital for avoiding negative life-course and labour-market outcomes (see Chapter 1).

Particularly interesting are the effects for indicators of objective and subjective employment insecurity. Atypical work forms impact negatively on satisfaction in all three dimensions discussed, even though the effect apparently varies by gender (see models M1, M3 and M5 in Tables 4.9 and 4.10). Non-permanent employment affects all three dimensions negatively: having a limited contract reduces not only the satisfaction with the job itself, but is also associated with lower satisfaction with one's own living standard, likely due to the lower pay and social security levels associated with it. Negative effects for the satisfaction with family life seem to suggest that there are also 'spill-over' effects into the private sphere of life, even when controlling for other relevant socio-economic characteristics.

While the effect for non-permanent employment appears to be similar across genders, there are gender-specific variations in the consequences of part-time work. For women, working part-time is not associated with significant reductions in job satisfaction, satisfaction with one's living standard or satisfaction with family life. This finding appears to be consistent with earlier considerations about the frequent use of part-time employment as a largely voluntary reduction of working hours to better balance family and work duties. This is not the case for men, where part-time work reduces job satisfaction (even though the effect is only marginally significant) and has strong negative effect for the satisfaction with their own living standard. For men, part-time work represents a deviation from stable full-time employment that is still being regarded as a certain norm. For those (few) men who are working part-time, it not only reduces their material revenues (reflected in the negative effect on living standards) but also seems to negatively affect their subjective satisfaction with their job.

Notably, however, it is not only the objective insecurity associated with atypical jobs that reduces individual satisfaction. In addition, subjectively perceived insecurity also appears to have a similar impact (see models M2, M4 and M6 in Tables 4.9 and 4.10). This particularly applies to job loss worries that strongly reduce all three types of satisfaction for both men and women. Individuals fearing to lose their job are not only less satisfied with the job they currently hold, but are also more likely to perceive their living standard as being endangered. Such perceived insecurities apparently also reduce satisfaction with family life. The picture appears to be reversed for the perceived likelihood of finding re-employment after a possible job loss. Individuals who perceive their chances of re-employment positively are more likely to also be satisfied with their current employment and the respective living standard. Only for women, the perception of one's own re-employment chances is non-significant. For both sexes, perceived re-employment chances impact positively on the satisfaction with family life, suggesting that reduced stress through higher labour market security also benefits family life. Taken together, results demonstrate that it is not only contextual conditions or the objective characteristics of a job, but also the perceived labour market (in)security that has repercussions for men's and women's well-being in mid-career.

Conclusion

The analyses in this chapter have shown that, in general, mid-career employment resembles a phase of relative stability in employment. Employment rates of both genders are high, after a marked increase of female labour market participation throughout recent decades. At the same time, atypical work forms are of relatively modest importance in mid-career. Fixed-term employment is clearly less widespread than in early career and mostly only occurs to a notable degree when the overall economic situation is strained (for example, throughout economic crises). Part-time employment is particularly observed for women around childbirth; yet the previous discussions show that it is largely perceived as a voluntary solution and does not impact negatively on women's satisfaction levels.

The picture for objective employment security is largely mirrored by our analyses of subjective perceived insecurities which are also lower than for the previous life phase (see Chapters 2 and 3). Job loss worries are generally less pronounced among mid-career employees, who also evaluate their re-employment probabilities better than, for example, older workers (see

Chapter 5). Yet, for those who are in insecure employment, job loss worries are significantly higher. Particularly men, for whom every atypical form of employment represents a deviation from the dominant mid-career norm of continuous employment, tend to perceive their labour market situation more critically once being caught in such work forms.

Further analysis show that perceived and objective insecurities are not only critical on their own behalf, but are also consequential for various other dimensions of life: they reduce job satisfaction, satisfaction with one's own living standard and also impact negatively on family life. Labour market disadvantages thus translate into disadvantages in the quality of life.

Nation-specific contextual conditions apparently can mediate the afore-mentioned negative influences. The Scandinavian model of active labour market policies and a generous welfare state support is most effective in this respect, reducing both the extent of objective labour market risks to a minimum, but also promoting lower levels of perceived job insecurity. In contrast, the situation seems most critical in Southern European countries which were hit particularly hard by the crisis, reflected in rising objective insecurities and higher job loss and re-employment worries. In Eastern European countries, the situation was largely similar after the system change and partly also throughout the Euro crisis. More recent figures show clear signs of recovery on both the objective and subjective level. Conservative and liberal countries fall in between these opposite poles, with modest levels of both objective and subjective insecurities. Conservative countries in particular reveal signs of an insider-outsider labour market in which job loss worries are modest, yet, there is concern about re-entry chances once losing employment in mid-career.

In addition to these macro level influences, individual attributes are significant in mediating objective and subjective insecurities. Results underline the high significance of human capital in avoiding labour market risks. In particular, those with higher education are best able to avoid labour market insecurities and their negative spill-over effects on their quality of life.

Finally, our results also show that it is important to focus on both objective and subjective dimensions of employment (in)security. Not only does their simultaneous consideration provide a more complete picture of remaining instabilities in a generally stable phase of the life course, both are also consequential for individual quality of life in this life phase and related social inequalities.

5

Job Insecurity and Its
Consequences for Older Workers

Introduction

With regard to their employment and concepts of employment insecurity, older workers make up a particular group on the labour market. According to established concepts in life-course theory (for example, Kohli, 1985; Mayer and Schoepflin, 1989), these workers are in the final phase of their employment career and will, after completing this phase, enter into a terminal state (in work terms) of retirement. Unlike younger workers, older employees thus have an alternative and socially accepted state as pensioners to which they can transit. This potential 'alternative role' as pensioners receiving public and/or private retirement benefits may reduce their readiness to accept insecure forms of employment as temporary solutions and instead opt for transiting into the 'safe harbour' of retirement. This may be even the more the case, given that today's older workers often can draw back to high levels of employment protection and legally established seniority rights which cannot be easily dismantled (Blossfeld, Buchholz and Hofäcker, 2006). At the same time, in many European welfare states, pension benefits received during retirement are often substantially based on previous earnings from income. Metaphorically speaking, pension benefits thus can be regarded as the 'balance sheet' of the previous career, implying that those with higher pension contributions will also receive higher pension pay-outs. Vice versa, those with lower contributions – originating for example from lower earnings and interrupted or fragmented careers – will receive lower benefits. Particularly if these benefits are not sufficient to guarantee a decent standard of living in old age, these employees are thus dependent on additional earnings; they thus (need to) remain longer on the labour market, even if this implies accepting unfavourable and insecure types of jobs.

Throughout recent decades, older workers' employment has undergone major transformations. From the oil crises in the 1970s up to the mid-1990s, many European countries actually followed a strategy of promoting 'early exit' of older workers to buffer the negative implications of globalization and the persistent labour market effects of the oil crises (Blossfeld, Buchholz and Hofäcker, 2006; Ebbinghaus, 2006; Hofäcker, 2010). However, faced with the projected effects of demographic ageing on the financial sustainability of national pension systems, many countries revised their labour market and pension policies. This included the closing of financially generous early retirement options and increasing investments into so-called 'active ageing policies' (for example, Hofäcker, Hess and König, 2016). In reaction to this, employment rates among older workers started to rise again (Ebbinghaus and Hofäcker, 2013). These overall employment trends represent the relevant contextual background for developments in the objective and subjective employment characteristics of older employees. The next section will thus first provide a stylized overview of key developments in older workers' employment trends since the 1980s. Following this quantitative overview of the extent of older workers' employment, the following sections will take a look at the qualitative aspects of their employment. The third section will first take a look at selected characteristics of objective employment (in) security, distinguishing different types of employment with particular focus on the atypical work forms outlined in Chapter 1 and their development over time. The fourth section will subsequently investigate how far older workers perceive their employment as being (in)secure and how this perception has changed over time. As indicated, earlier insecure employment (in the previous career but also in old age) may not only be immediately detrimental but may also negatively affect pensions savings and future old age income. A potential effect of the spread of insecure employment forms discussed in the previous chapters of this book may be that old age income becomes insecure as well. In the fifth section, we will thus discuss the future insecurity of old age income prospects, considering the pension-related perceptions of today's older employees and pensioners, but also considering the long-term pension effects of the spread of atypical employment among younger labour market generations.

Employment trends among older workers

To begin with, Figure 5.1 presents a stylized overview of the development in older workers' employment rates since the 1980s, averaged for the current EU-27 countries. To better assess age-specific patterns, figures are given for age groups, ranging from the early fifties to the late sixties and beyond. For illustrative reasons, figures are presented here for men only.[1]

Ideal-typically, the development of employment rates among older people can be subdivided into two successive phases. From the 1980s until the late 1990s, employment rates of older men, particularly in the years immediately

Figure 5.1: Age-specific employment rate for men aged 50–69, 1983–2020

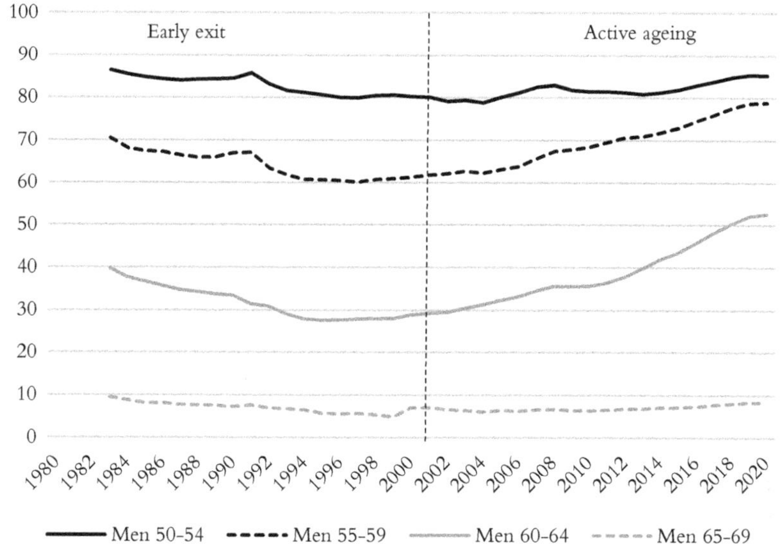

Source: OECD, 2021a.

preceding retirement (that is, the late fifties and early sixties) have been almost constantly declining so that by the millennium turn, less than one third of those aged 60–64 years and less than two thirds of those aged 55–59 years were still actively participating in the labour market. This downward trend reflects a policy of early retirement many European welfare states pursued throughout this time-period (see, for example, Kohli et al, 1991; Ebbinghaus, 2006). Faced with the negative labour market effects of the oil crises in the 1970s, many national governments allowed older employees to leave the labour market before the legal retirement age, financially supported through generous pension and early retirement benefits (Gruber and Wise, 1999, 2004) or additional welfare state programmes, such as unemployment or disability insurance (Guillemard, 1991). In particular, lower-skilled workers who were at high risk of losing their job in increasingly strained labour markets accepted these financially generous 'early exit' offers. Tendencies of flexibilization within employment were marginal among this group of workers. During the 'early exit' period, older employees were either in the labour market (employed) or outside it (retired or in transitionary welfare state systems). Job mobility among older workers was low (Blossfeld, Buchholz and Hofäcker, 2006) and, even among atypical work forms, only part-time work was used on a larger scale – yet, less as a measure of employment flexibilization per se, but rather as a means to gradually exit from employment by reducing working hours in the final years (Delsen, 1990).

This strategy, however, changed as European countries increasingly became aware of the future challenges of demographic ageing for national pension systems, generated by a rising number of (retired) pension recipients and a declining number of (employed) contributors. In response to this shift, many countries implemented policies of 'active ageing' (Hofäcker, Hess and König, 2016), promoting longer working lives and later retirement transitions. Such policies particularly included the closing of the previously generous early retirement options and pension-based incentives for later retirement. In some countries, these were complemented by measures promoting the employability of older workers, such as active labour market training and measures of lifelong learning. In consequence, employment rates among older workers started to rise again, reflected in a steep increase across virtually all age groups in Figure 5.1. More detailed analyses of retirement transitions additionally revealed, that in the course of this policy shift, labour market pressures on older workers, particularly those with lower skills, have increased: given the closure of early retirement pathways, they increasingly need to work longer for financial reasons (Hofäcker, Hess and König, 2019), even if this contradicts their actual retirement preferences (Hess, 2018; Stiemke and Hess, 2020). Given the absence of early exit options, it seems reasonable to assume that these workers in particular will increasingly tend to remain in employment, even if this implies accepting more flexible and insecure work or potentially risking unemployment. In the next section, we look at the development of such insecure work forms over time.

The average rates for the EU-27, however, obscure relevant variations between the countries in the course and magnitude of the early retirement and active ageing trend. Figure 5.2 thus gives a differentiated profile of country-specific employment trends, ordered by welfare regime.
As in the former figure, results are being displayed for men only. Since early exit trends have been most pronounced for employees immediately approaching retirement age (that is, 60–64 years), Figure 5.2 focuses on this age group only.

Figure 5.2 points to notable differences in the employment trends of older workers over time, that can roughly be clustered across welfare regimes (Blossfeld, Buchholz and Hofäcker, 2006; Blossfeld, Buchholz and Kurz, 2011; Hofäcker and Ebbinghaus, 2013), Particularly in liberal (represented here by the UK, Switzerland and Ireland) and social-democratic countries (Finland, Norway, Sweden, Denmark), male employment rates in their early sixties have fallen only modestly and are nowadays around 60 to 70 per cent. Different explanations are being put forward for these seemingly similar results. With the exception of Finland, social-democratic countries only marginally developed early exit pathways for older workers. Instead, active labour market policies actively promoted the continuation of older workers' employment while continued education and training oriented at

Figure 5.2: Country-specific employment rate for men aged 60–64, 1983–2020

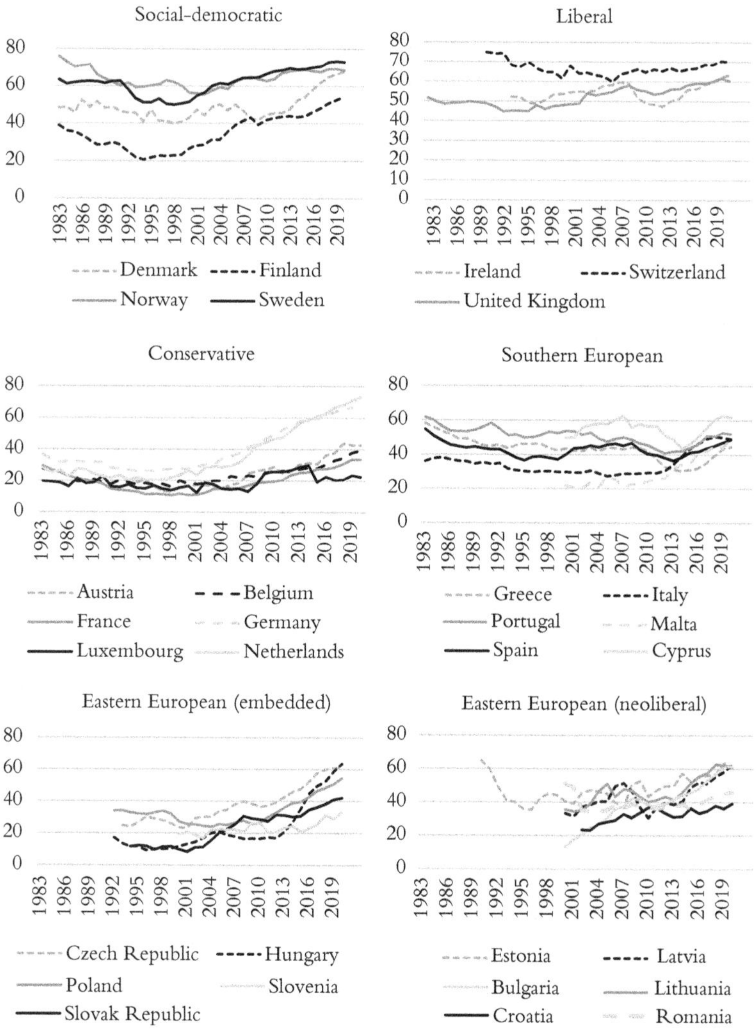

Source: OECD, 2021a.

the principle of 'lifelong learning' across the life course ensured that skills and qualifications of older workers did not become obsolete (Hofäcker, Hess and König, 2016). Under these conditions, employment of older workers remained rather stable. In contrast to this state-based support for labour market maintenance, older workers in the residual welfare states of liberal countries often remained in employment longer for financial reasons, given that public pension systems only weakly replace previous salaries and need to be backed up by additional private or occupational savings. Particularly for workers with lower human capital, this has frequently meant that they need to remain employed for financial reasons (for example, Flynn and Li, 2016). This financial need is reflected in still substantial labour market mobility in late career.

In contrast to these, conservative Central European countries particularly (Austria, Belgium, France, Germany, Luxembourg and the Netherlands) actively promoted an early exit from employment throughout the 1990s, leading to male employment rates in their early sixties dropping to as low as 30 per cent. Both public pension systems as well other welfare state systems (such as unemployment and disability insurance) were used to promote early retirement. This intensive use of early exit schemes has often been explained by the interplay of multiple institutional factors (Blossfeld, Buchholz and Hofäcker, 2006): standardized educational systems with little focus on retraining throughout the life course promoted the obsolescence of older workers' qualifications, while at the same time, rigid labour markets with high levels of employment protection and seniority wage systems increased the cost of older workers' employment. Against this background, early exit options were used as a strategy to dissolve this labour market unbalance by offering older workers attractive retirement pathways well before mandatory retirement ages. In turn, labour market mobility before retirement was low; if becoming unemployed, older workers often remained in this state or used it as pathway into (early) retirement (Buchholz, 2008). While the drop in employment rates among older workers in conservative countries was among the highest in Europe, their recovery during the 'active ageing' era was equally remarkable. Particularly in Germany and the Netherlands, employment rates among older workers skyrocketed after the millennium turn, reaching almost Scandinavian levels in 2020, while they rose only modestly in France and Belgium (see Figure 5.2). More detailed analyses suggest that this increase in employment was more due to the closing of retirement pathways rather than the investment into active ageing, and that continued employment is often involuntary (Hess, 2018) and due to financial reasons (Hofäcker, Hess and König, 2019). Herein lies a potential for possibly accepting more flexible forms of employment in order to continue drawing wages.

Southern European countries share a number of institutional similarities, particularly with regard to overall labour market rigidity and early retirement options throughout the 1990s. Throughout the last decades, employment rates declined similarly, but remained somewhat higher (partly due to the higher share of self-employment). At the same time, both the extent of policy reforms as well as the reversal throughout the last decades was comparatively modest so that employment rates remained around 50–60 per cent.

No unique picture can be observed for Eastern European countries. Central European countries, like Poland, Hungary or the Czech Republic, have followed a development similar to that of conservative countries, further fuelled through the economic crisis of the 1990s. It featured a decline to modest or low employment in the 1990s, and a subsequent recovery, even though the magnitude varied substantially between countries (around 60 per cent in Hungary and the Czech Republic, 30 to 40 per cent in Slovenia and Slovakia). Institutionally, labour markets in these 'embedded' countries have also been described as being rigid, leaving little opportunities for redundant workers in the formal labour market. Baltic countries, in particular, followed a somewhat more liberal approach, adopting the recommendations of supranational organizations such as the World Bank. They thus more resemble a liberal pathway, reflected also in higher levels of employment among older workers. Both groups of Eastern European counties furthermore share low generosity in national pension systems, promoting old age poverty. Occasional evidence suggests that given these risks and the limitations of the 'official' job market, older workers often resort to informal work to ensure a basic minimum income in old age.

The patterns described may be long-term historical developments in the labour market for older workers. Yet, at the same time they reflect general institutional foundations that create the background for older workers' employment and their objective/subjective security for in the present, but also their earnings and retirement prospects in the future. We thus will come back to these differential contextual backgrounds in the discussion of trends in the afore mentioned dimensions.

Objective employment insecurity

How uncertain are the employment trajectories of older workers? In order to answer this question, we will first explore the objective dimension of employment insecurity. We will begin by looking at insecurity of employment as such, that is, the risk of becoming unemployed and remaining in this state. We will then turn to different ways in which employment can be flexibilized, looking at the permanency of employment (fixed-term employment), the number of working hours (part-time employment) and self-employment.

(Long-term) unemployment

To what extent are older workers affected by unemployment, and how far does their risk of being unemployed differ from that of other age groups? In order to investigate this question, Table 5.1 presents the unemployment rates of older workers (aged 55–64) in European countries for the time-period 2010–20 and compares it to that of mid-career workers (aged 25–54). Figures are given for the total population (that is, both sexes) and are presented for selected countries, reflecting different welfare regimes.

Table 5.1: Unemployment rate of older (55–64 years) and mid-career workers (25–54 years; in brackets) in European countries, 2010–20

Regime	Country	2010	2015	2020
Social-democratic	Denmark	4.8 (6.7)	3.2 (5.7)	4.1 (4.8)
	Finland	6.5 (6.9)	8.0 (7.7)	7.5 (5.8)
	Norway	1.4 (3.0)	1.6 (3.4)	2.0 (3.9)
	Sweden	5.8 (6.4)	5.3 (5.8)	5.8 (6.8)
Liberal	UK	4.5 (6.0)	3.6 (4.0)	3.7 (3.3)
	Ireland	7.9 (13.0)	5.8 (8.9)	3.0 (4.0)
Conservative	Austria	2.5 (4.0)	4.7 (4.9)	4.0 (5.2)
	Belgium	4.6 (7.3)	5.6 (7.7)	4.2 (5.0)
	France	5.9 (8.0)	7.4 (9.3)	5.8 (7.1)
	Germany	7.7 (6.6)	4.7 (4.4)	na
	Luxembourg	2.3 (3.9)	4.7 (5.8)	4.1 (5.7)
	Netherlands	4.4 (3.8)	8.1 (5.6)	2.7 (2.9)
Southern Europe	Cyprus	5.1 (5.5)	17.4 (12.9)	5.0 (6.6)
	Greece	14.2 (12.1)	18.6 (24.4)	12.5 (16.2)
	Italy	3.6 (7.5)	5.5 (11.2)	5.0 (9.0)
	Malta	4.5 (5.8)	6.0 (4.1)	3.1 (3.4)
	Portugal	8.9 (10.7)	12.5 (11.2)	5.9 (6.0)
	Spain	14.2 (18.4)	18.6 (20.6)	12.5 (14.5)
Eastern (Central and Eastern European)	Czech Republic	4.0 (6.4)	7.8 (4.6)	3.7 (2.4)
	Hungary	7.9 (10.4)	5.8 (6.0)	3.0 (3.8)
	Poland	7.1 (8.3)	5.4 (6.6)	2.1 (2.8)
	Slovenia	4.0 (7.0)	7.8 (8.7)	3.7 (4.6)
	Slovakia	7.1 (12.8)	5.4 (10.5)	2.1 (6.2)
Eastern (neoliberal)	Bulgaria	9.3 (9.8)	9.4 (9.1)	4.4 (5.3)
	Croatia	7.2 (9.2)	12.2 (13.3)	4.1 (6.7)
	Estonia	16.3 (15.1)	6.0 (5.5)	6.5 (5.9)
	Latvia	16.0 (18.0)	9.3 (9.5)	8.1 (7.9)
	Lithuania	14.4 (16.7)	8.7 (8.6)	9.9 (7.4)
	Romania	4.5 (6.7)	4.8 (6.9)	3.4 (5.0)

Source: OECD, 2021a.

Table 5.1 clearly points to notable differences in unemployment rates across countries, with highest values in Southern European and Baltic countries, reaching double-digit figures in 2010. In contrast, overall unemployment was lower in most other countries, particularly in the employment-oriented Scandinavian ones. In most countries, overall unemployment rates declined over time, sometimes after a temporary increase in the mid-2010s.

Table 5.1 also shows, that older workers' employment rates seem to follow that of the 'core' working population, in that they are high in countries where overall unemployment is high and vice versa. Notably, older workers are clearly not at a higher risk of becoming unemployed than their younger counterparts. In the majority of countries, older unemployment rates are below that of mid-career workers. At first sight, this result may be surprising, given the occasional labour market disadvantages of older workers in terms of education and training, employment protection and wage levels. Yet, this pattern may reflect the previously described 'alternative exit option' available to older workers: older workers in difficult labour market situations may make use of the opportunity to permanently leave the labour market and enter into (early) retirement.

In order to investigate unemployment and its impact on employment insecurity, it is important to look at its incidence, but also its potential duration. Is unemployment just a temporary state from which employees may return after a certain amount of time, or do they become trapped permanently in this state? To investigate this question, Table 5.2 presents the relative share of long-term unemployment among those unemployed, with long-term unemployment reflecting unemployment of more than 12 months.

With regard to age-specific patterns, the picture appears to be the reverse for long-term unemployment. While older workers are at a lower risk of becoming unemployed, their risk of remaining long-term unemployed is often higher than among mid-career workers. In the majority of countries, long-term unemployment makes up for more than half of older workers' unemployment, with particularly high figures in Southern, Eastern European and conservative countries, that is, countries with the most rigid labour markets that have most seriously been affected by unemployment, as discussed. Figures are clearly lower in the 'active ageing' regimes of Scandinavia, likely reflecting their high investment into retraining and active labour market policies. As for overall unemployment, patterns of long-term unemployment among the older workforce seem to closely follow that of the entire population. In countries in which long-term unemployment is generally high, it is also high among the older workforce; this points to the influence of general labour market characteristics rather than age-specific regulations.

Taken together, the risk of becoming unemployed is modest among older workers in intergenerational comparisons. Yet, when becoming unemployed,

Table 5.2: Long-term unemployment rate of older (55–64 years) and mid-career workers (25–54 years; in brackets) in European countries, 2010–20

Regime	Country	2000	2005	2010	2015	2020
Social-democratic	Denmark	41.0 (24.7)	48.5 (24.5)	36.8 (23.9)	41.5 (32.4)	na
	Finland	56.5 (34.0)	49.8 (28.9)	42.8 (27.4)	47.2 (27.8)	32.4 (17.6)
	Norway	32.7 (14.7)	37.5 (24.5)	42.4 (24.5)	46.8 (28.3)	38.4 (24.7)
	Sweden	49.3 (26.6)	na	31.5 (21.8)	36.2 (21.8)	24.1 (14.5)
Liberal	UK	43.4 (32.9)	38.8 (25.0)	42.7 (36.9)	40.9 (35.0)	29.0 (22.1)
	Ireland	48.6 (44.9)	46.4 (38.2)	56.0 (50.9)	75.3 (60.0)	na
Conservative	Austria	50.6 (25.5)	56.0 (28.1)	56.3 (26.6)	52.5 (30.5)	48.8 (25.4)
	Belgium	79.4 (61.9)	74.8 (58.6)	80.0 (52.4)	76.3 (53.4)	66.6 (42.9)
	France	69.6 (45.3)	64.0 (45.0)	56.7 (41.9)	63.1 (44.6)	59.7 (37.7)
	Germany	69.1 (51.0)	69.8 (54.4)	62.2 (48.3)	60.5 (44.3)	na
	Luxembourg	26.4 (24.9)	54.0 (28.9)	41.5 (29.5)	42.7 (33.1)	45.1 (28.3)
	Netherlands	na	62.5 (46.5)	52.1 (30.5)	68.1 (45.5)	48.7 (27.5)
Southern Europe	Cyprus	39.2 (27.6)	47.0 (25.7)	24.3 (21.1)	68.4 (47.1)	49.0 (28.1)
	Greece	57.1 (56.9)	52.8 (54.0)	52.0 (46.2)	84.8 (74.3)	75.8 (66.4)
	Italy	64.2 (63.8)	56.4 (51.0)	58.9 (49.0)	65.2 (59.2)	59.6 (53.3)
	Malta	56.5 (66.6)	75.6 (56.0)	49.6 (52.6)	69.6 (45.6)	31.0 (25.0)
	Portugal	69.4 (47.9)	67.6 (50.8)	72.7 (54.1)	76.4 (60.2)	na
	Spain	58.4 (45.0)	49.9 (25.9)	54.7 (36.6)	70.9 (51.9)	52.8 (31.1)
Eastern (embedded)	Czech Republic	45.6 (53.3)	58.8 (57.7)	41.9 (46.4)	57.4 (50.8)	31.0 (21.8)

Table 5.2: Long-term unemployment rate of older (55–64 years) and mid-career workers (25–54 years; in brackets) in European countries, 2010–20 (continued)

Regime	Country	2000	2005	2010	2015	2020
	Hungary	61.7	57.4	55.1	64.0	35.9
		(52.6)	(48.4)	(52.0)	(48.8)	(27.1)
	Poland	42.9	61.6	36.2	50.7	29.7
		(41.5)	(56.0)	(28.0)	(40.8)	(20.3)
	Slovenia	86.8	65.3	60.7	63.0	59.7
		(67.9)	(50.1)	(44.5)	(53.7)	(38.7)
	Slovakia	59.9	76.3	65.9	66.8	57.5
		(59.9)	(71.1)	(61.3)	(64.3)	(44.7)
Eastern (neoliberal)	Bulgaria	64.1	67.2	53.1	68.9	49.4
		(58.9)	(61.8)	(46.1)	(61.2)	(46.0)
	Croatia	na	79.4	71.2	83.2	47.5
			(63.6)	(57.5)	(65.3)	(26.6)
	Estonia	48.3	58.7	41.4	44.0	24.0
		(49.4)	(59.3)	(48.4)	(43.9)	(18.0)
	Latvia	65.0	50.9	50.9	51.1	37.5
		(61.3)	(49.4)	(47.9)	(47.8)	(26.8)
	Lithuania	51.5	69.4	46.7	55.1	42.3
		(51.4)	(57.0)	(43.7)	(45.7)	(28.7)
	Romania	61.7	61.9	44.1	41.6	31.8
		(56.4)	(59.0)	(34.5)	(46.4)	(29.0)

Source: OECD, 2021a.

it is often of longer duration for older than for younger workers. The risk of (long-term) unemployment – in general as well as among the younger population – appears to be highest in strongly regulated labour markets, and lowest in countries with an active employment policy orientation.

Fixed-term employment

In the opening chapters of this book, it has been shown that temporary employment in particular represents a significant employment risk for younger employees. Fixed-term employment rates among young labour market entrants are disproportionately high, and the insecurity arising from this type of employment adversely affects home-leaving transitions.

For older employees, fixed-term employment plays a clearly less prominent role. Figure 5.3 displays the relative incidence of fixed-term employment (as a percentage of overall dependent employment), differentiating between younger (aged 15–24), mid-career (aged 25–54) and older workers

Figure 5.3: Fixed-term employment by age group in EU-27, 2000–20

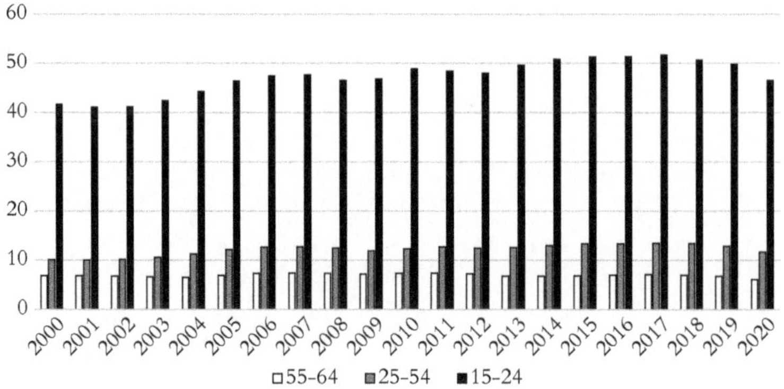

Source: OECD, 2021a.

(55–64 years) for EU-27 countries. It becomes evident that fixed-term employment clearly plays the largest role among younger employees, where it accounts for 40–50 per cent of employment. For mid-career and older workers, rates are lower, and among the older workforce, it makes up for constantly less than 10 per cent of employment. Furthermore, while for the younger generation fixed-term employment appears to follow cyclical variations, its share among older workers is constantly low, suggesting that, for them, it does not systematically act as a 'buffer' in periods of economic downturns. These results suggest that, as shown in earlier research, fixed-term jobs rather 'serve as entry ports into the world of work' (OECD, 2002: 137) for the young. For older workers, the widespread use of such work forms is, on the one hand, inhibited by their high levels of employment protection and seniority rules. On the other hand, the negotiation of fixed-term employment also does not seem rational from an employer perspective, given that older employees only have a limited time of further employment before retirement.

These averaged results are reflected also in country-specific patterns of fixed-term employment which remain below 10 per cent among older employees for the majority of countries displayed in Figure 5.4. The only notable exceptions with values continuously above 10 per cent are Poland, Spain and Portugal, likely reflecting the generally higher use of such contracts in these countries or their increasing usage to avoid unemployment among older workers (Lewandowski, 2017).

Part-time employment

Another form of flexibilization of work in later life may be that in terms of working time (see Chapter 1). Figures 5.5a and b thus display the incidence

Figure 5.4: Country-specific fixed-term employment rate, all persons, aged 55–64, 2000–20

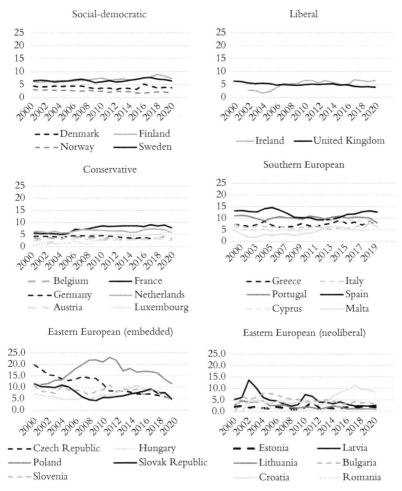

Source: OECD, 2021a.

of part-time employment – defined as working 30 hours or less – across age groups in EU-27 countries. As part-time work is known to vary by gender, we report patterns for men (Figure 5.5a) and women (Figure 5.5b) separately. With regard to age groups, we again differentiate between young (15–24), mid-career (25–54) and older workers 55–64.

Figures 5.5a and b confirm the well-known gender bias in part-time employment with figures being clearly higher among women (between 20 and 40 per cent) than among men (between 5 and 20 per cent). In contrast to fixed-term employment, part-time work plays a more prominent role in late-career employment, particularly among older women. Around the

Figure 5.5a: Incidence of part-time employment by age groups, men

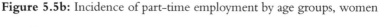

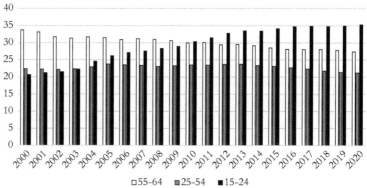

Source: OECD, 2021.

Figure 5.5b: Incidence of part-time employment by age groups, women

Source: OECD, 2021a.

millennium turn, more than a third of older women were in-part-time employment, more than in other age groups. This picture changed in the following two decades, with part-time rates declining to around a quarter of employment, while respective rates have risen among younger women. Recent declines may be attributed to generational changes in women's employment, as women approaching older age in more recent years likely had higher levels of labour market integration than previous cohorts. For older men, part-time employment has been of lesser importance, constantly making up for less than 10 per cent of dependent employment.

Yet again, the average values or the EU-27 hide considerable cross-national variations in the use of part-time work among older workers. Figure 5.6 thus breaks down part-time rates among older workers by country. Given that, as discussed, part time work is only of considerable importance among women,

Figure 5.6: Country-specific part-time employment rate for women, aged 60–64, 2000–20

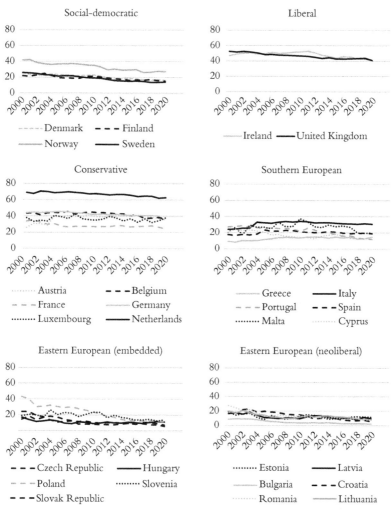

Source: OECD, 2021a.

we restrict our analyses to female part-time rates. Figure 5.6 shows that older women's part-time rates are rather low in most Southern European (with the partial exception of Italy and Malta) and Eastern European countries (with the exception of Poland where rates have fallen from initially higher levels). As shown earlier (see Chapter 4), these are countries where in general, the standard full-time employment rates prevail among both sexes and reductions in working time are rather rare. At the opposite end, female part-time rates are rather high in both liberal countries, UK and Ireland, and among most of the conservative countries. It is these countries that had long promoted a more traditional division of labour among the sexes, with women often taking the role of secondary earners. Even though, in general, women's part-time rates have declined over time in favour of higher labour market integration, part-time employment is still largely prevalent among the older generations. Scandinavian countries take an intermediate position between the two poles with part-time making up around a third of older women's employment.

It needs to be noted, however, that particularly for older employees, reduced working hours may not necessarily imply flexibilization and increased insecurity. On the one hand, older women particularly may actively choose part-time employment, given the established traditional division of labour. On the other hand, part-time employment may also act as 'bridge' into retirement when employees reduce their working hours in order to 'phase out' their employment lives (Delsen, 1990). Only when older employees are forced into part-time employment against their will (for example, when they would prefer to work full-time, but do not succeed in finding a job), part-time employment may have precarious implications. In addition to looking at the incidence of part-time employment, it is thus important to also look at the degree of choice associated with it.

Figure 5.7 presents additional evidence on the voluntariness of part-time employment among older employees. Involuntary part-timers are considered as those working part-time who would prefer to work full-time. Again, analyses focus on women only, given their overrepresentation in part-time employment.

Results from Figure 5.7 show that part-time employment in older age is predominantly voluntary, with involuntary rates of part-time employment

Figure 5.7: Incidence of involuntary part-time employment in EU-27 countries, women aged 55–64, 2000–20

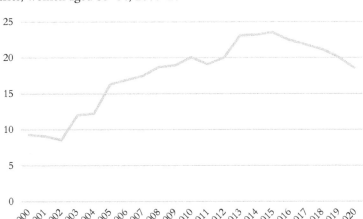

Source: OECD, 2021a.

among women aged 55–64 within the EU-27 hardly exceeding a quarter of part-time employment as a whole. This observation seems in line with earlier evidence from the OECD suggesting that 'personal constraints are not the main reason for voluntary part-time work among older workers' and that rather 'personal preferences drive the choice for part-time work, which can be used as an alternative to retirement – and thus, inactivity – for older workers with eroded labour market attachment' (OECD, 2010: 238). Notably, the percentage share of involuntary part-time work has increased over time, from around 10 per cent in the early 2000s to almost a quarter in the late 2010s. As further analyses show, this increase is mainly due to trends in Southern European countries (Figure 5.8).

Here, involuntary part-time rates have climbed steeply from 10–20 per cent to 40–60 per cent in the time span.[2] As further analyses of involuntary part-time rates in EU countries show, this increase in involuntary part-time employment has not been an exclusive trend among older workers, but has taken place similarly across other age groups as well. Horemans et al, (2016) relate this trend to the repercussions of the economic crisis of the late 2000s that particularly affected Southern European labour markets. Under these conditions, women had to draw back to part-time jobs given the lacking availability of full-time employment. Even though the share of part-time employed women in Southern Europe has been rather modest, the involuntary 'push' into part-time employment may have been detrimental for the long-term security of women affected by it, as it often increased poverty risks (Horemans et al, 2016). Notably, these trends largely continued after the immediate labour market crisis, pointing to the emergence of a potentially precarious work form (Denia and Guilló, 2019). Similar patterns are observed for some Eastern European countries, particularly Bulgaria and Romania, where figures were similarly high, though with strong cyclical variations. Yet, these figures need to be seen against the background of very low overall rates of part-time employment in these countries (see Table 5.6). Thus, part-time employment is rarely chosen among older women; if taken up, it is largely due to the absence of a full-time job.

Self-employment

In the previous sections, we have focused exclusively on flexibilization within dependent employment. However, flexibilization of employment relationships may also mean that a rising number of workers are no longer in a contractual relationship with an employer but may become self-employed. Figure 5.9, which compares the incidence of self-employment across age groups, shows that the incidence of self-employment is indeed higher among older workers than among mid-career workers, for both men and women. Furthermore, men are clearly more likely to be self-employed than women.

Figure 5.8: Country-specific incidence of involuntary part-time employment for women, aged 55–64, 2000–20

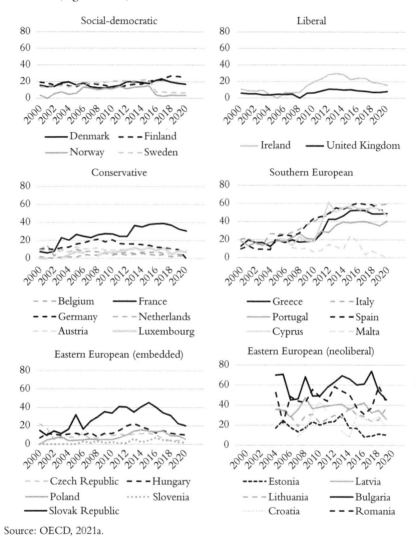

Source: OECD, 2021a.

For both older men and women, self-employment rates have declined over time, suggesting that especially among the older population, many self-employed were (or still are) employed in the primary sector whose relative importance has decreased. These patterns corroborate earlier findings on age and gender differences as well as over-time trends, such as from the OECD (2019).

Again, the incidence of self-employment varies considerably between countries. As Figure 5.10 – which presents the self-employment rate for

Figure 5.9: Incidence of self-employment by age group, 2000–20

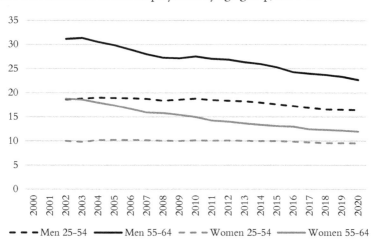

Source: Eurostat, 2021a.

men only – shows highest levels of self-employment among older workers are found in Southern European countries, some Eastern European countries and Ireland, that is in countries which exhibit generally higher self-employment rates in general due to a still substantial (though declining) agricultural sector (Eurostat, 2019a: 82).

There are various reasons given for the overrepresentation of self-employed among the older workforce: on the one hand, older workers may exhibit better preconditions for being self-employed, for example, through longer work experience and better access to capital and credit (Hatfield, 2015: 13). In addition to this positive rationale, self-employment may equally arise from labour market obstacles that hinder older workers from finding a 'regular job'. Against this background, self-employment may provide an alternative opportunity for older workers to remain in employment (Eurostat, 2019a: 81). Self-employment rates per se do not differentiate these types. One available proxy to further investigate whether self-employment reflects active entrepreneurship or is rather a precarious form of work is the differentiation of own-account self-employment and self-employment with employees. It can be assumed that due to the small size of own-account 'solo self-employed' businesses, their income is more volatile and they 'probably accumulated less wealth over their life course' (Horemans and Marx, 2017: 35). Figure 5.11 thus differentiates between self-employed as own account workers and those with employees.

Results show that both forms of self-employment are prevalent among the older workforce in Europe, yet, the relative share of own account workers is somewhat higher. This average picture is also reflected in

Figure 5.10: Country-specific incidence of self-employment for men, aged 55–64, 2000–20

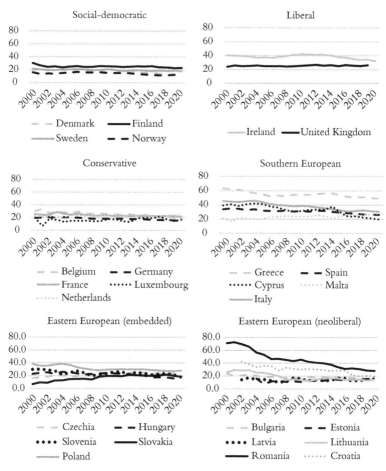

Source: Eurostat, 2021a.

country-specific figures (results not shown here), and is particularly pronounced in countries where overall levels of self-employment are high. In particular, own account workers can be regarded as potentially precarious employees. Findings from Eurofound (2017: 22), based on the European Working Conditions Survey (EWCS), also show that among the self-employed, older workers are overrepresented among the particularly 'vulnerable' self-employed, who mostly work alone, often have only one or few clients and chose self-employment mainly out of economic necessity. Yet, also among older workers, the category of self-employed also includes a sizeable number of successful entrepreneurs with their own employees (see Figure 5.11).

Figure 5.11: Incidence of own-account self-employment and self-employment with employees for men, aged 55–64, 2000–20

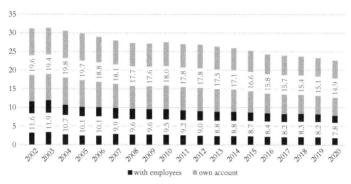

Source: Eurostat, 2021a.

Summary

Taken together, our analyses show that the late careers of older workers have been flexibilized only to a modest degree and that, in objective terms, their employment appears to be still relatively secure. Despite this overall observation, however, older workers may nonetheless face certain risks in contemporary labour markets:

- As compared to younger employees, older workers have a lower risk of becoming unemployed. As argued earlier, this may partly reflect their firm anchoring within the labour market, safeguarded by high levels of employment protection, but may also partly result from their option to alternatively exit into retirement in case of labour market hardships. However, once older employees drop into unemployment, they find it hard to re-enter employment and are at a higher risk of becoming long-term unemployed. Even though job loss is a rare event among older workers, its potential consequences appear to be severe.
- Fixed-term employment, which proved to be a major source of insecurity among the younger workforce, is much less common among older workers. It only appears to be of some importance where unemployment rates are high. Yet, even in these cases, its incidence among older workers remains well below that of younger workers.
- In contrast, part-time employment is found more often among the older workforce, particularly among older women. A closer investigation of its motives, however, reveals that it is often of voluntary nature, suggesting that it is often used to accommodate one's employment to individual circumstances rather than reflecting a forced transition into lower working hours. The latter is found only in countries within

strained labour markets, as the example of Southern Europe after the crisis has shown.

• Self-employment seems to play a more sizeable role among older workers. Among them, its incidence is considerably higher than among younger workers. Evidence from existing studies points to its ambivalent nature, as it can refer to both successful entrepreneurs with own employees but also to 'solo self-employed' working on their own account and often in more precarious conditions. Among older workers, the last form is more prevalent, even though there also exists a sizeable amount of older self-employed with their own employees.

• Our reconstruction of labour market data at the national level also revealed that there is a considerable variation in the flexibilization of employment forms among the older workforce across welfare regimes. Particularly in Southern European and Eastern European countries, which underwent notable economic crises in the 1990s and 2000s, (precarious) forms of atypical employment play a role and often have increased in importance during immediate crisis years. In such crises, unemployment rates among older workers also rose significantly and unemployment often became a long-term phenomenon. In contrast, in the employment-sustaining regimes, particularly among social-democratic countries, flexibilization has remained modest, and unemployment has remained low. If it occurs, the chances of re-entering employment are relatively favourable. The conservative countries appear to take an intermediate position: apart from high part-time rates among women, due to a persistent traditional model of gender roles, the incidence of atypical work forms is low among older workers, underlining the high level of employment protection that older (male) workers enjoy in these countries. At the same time, when employees fall out of employment, the same labour market barriers that tend to protect the employment 'insiders' appear to keep out older labour market 'outsiders'.

Subjectively perceived employment insecurity

In this section, we will investigate how these patterns relate to subjectively perceived employment insecurity. How far do older workers – who were earlier described as enjoying comparatively high levels of job security – perceive their employment to be at risk and how do they assess possible consequences of a job loss? To investigate these questions, we once more draw back to two indicators from the European Quality of Life Survey (EQLS) and apply them to the analysis of older workers.

We start with the previously used measure of cognitive job insecurity (see Chapter 2), that is, the question of how likely (older) employees perceive the risk of losing their jobs in the following six months. Table 5.3 displays the cumulated percentage of older workers who reported assessing this risk as being 'very likely' or 'rather likely' on a 5-point scale. Due to the restricted sample size available per wave of the EQLS, we consider older workers as those being aged between 50 and 64 years (instead of 55–64, as earlier).

As Table 5.3 shows, the share of older workers who fear a job loss within the next six months is comparatively low and remains mostly below that of younger employees (see Chapter 2). In most of the countries, less than 10 per cent of older workers expect to lose their job within the next half year. Yet, there are some notable exceptions: Eastern European countries, particularly those of the Baltic region, display high levels of job loss worries among its older workforce, amounting to almost a third of employees. Also among Central Eastern European (CEE) countries, values are initially high – ranging between 10 and 20 per cent respectively. For both groups it can be assumed that these pronounced worries are likely due to the transition shock of the 1990s that particularly pertained to older workers in the early transition years (see, for example, Täht and Saar, 2006; Bukodi and Róbert, 2006). Since then, figures appear to have declined, though with a certain 'rebound' after the financial crisis in 2008 (as reflected in figures for 2011). The 2008 crisis apparently also left its mark in Southern European countries, where job loss worries in the early to mid-2000s initially were low, but rose starkly after the crisis, particularly in Greece. More recent figures, however, suggest that figures nowadays are approaching pre-crisis levels.

In most other countries, safeguarded either by active employment policies (social-democratic countries) or strong employment protection (conservative countries), figures have remained at a lower level, hardly exceeding the 10 per cent level. Only in liberal countries, where labour markets are generally more vulnerable to cyclical variations, did job loss worries double throughout the crisis, but they returned to their low immediate level in the following years.

Aggregate figures provide little information and are at best implicit about the significance of atypical work forms for individual job loss worries. To investigate these in more detail, Table 5.4. presents results from a logistic regression to explain job loss worries, using data from the most recent EQLS wave from 2016. In three sequential models, different groups of factors are being introduced consecutively, the welfare regime (M1), individual level controls (that is, gender and education, differentiating between basic, upper secondary and tertiary education; M2), and the type of employment relationship (non-permanent[3] and part-time employment[4], M3).[5] Considering the hierarchical structure of the cross-national data, robust standard errors clustered by country again were estimated.

As M1 shows, welfare regime differences in 2016 are only of modest importance with only Eastern European countries (particularly the neoliberal group) and conservative countries displaying somewhat higher

Table 5.3: Job loss worry among older workers, aged 50–64, selected European countries, 2003–16

Regime	Country	2003 (%)	2007 (%)	2011 (%)	2016 (%)
Social-democratic	Denmark	7.3	6.9	11.0	5.1
	Finland	5.6	6.7	9.7	11.3
	Sweden	3.2	4.0	2.8	5.6
	Norway	na	2.2	na	na
Liberal	Ireland	2.8	5.2	16.9	5.8
	United Kingdom	4.4	8.7	14.6	7.2
Conservative	Austria	5.5	4.1	4.7	5.4
	Belgium	0.0	2.7	4.8	2.9
	Germany	10.7	3.7	2.6	4.6
	France	6.4	8.3	11.9	7.4
	Luxembourg	8.8	5.9	6.1	9.4
	Netherlands	2.3	3.5	5.6	3.6
Southern	Cyprus	7.2	11.3	28.3	12.6
	Greece	12.7	5.5	31.9	16.3
	Spain	5.6	5.3	18.5	8.3
	Italy	9.3	6.3	10.4	6.5
	Malta	8.3★	7.6	8.7	6.6
	Portugal	19.5	6.7	18.4	9.8
Eastern (embedded)	Czech Republic	17.6	12.1	26.1	12.9
	Poland	15.6	11.4	11.2	12.0
	Hungary	10.1	5.4	11.5	11.8
	Slovenia	12.5	9.6	8.3	9.6
	Slovakia	21.9	10.8	27.9	10.3
Eastern (neoliberal)	Bulgaria	47.1	22.8	24.2	7.1
	Croatia	na.	10.3	27.7	15.2
	Lithuania	31.1	18.8	21.0	19.6
	Estonia	30.9	13.4	17.8	16.0
	Latvia	35.2	19.2	15.9	18.5
	Romania	10.9	12.7	19.3	6.1

Note: question asked: 'How likely or unlikely do you think it is that you might lose your job in the next six months?', 5-point-scale, Table shows cumulated percentages for 'very likely'/ 'rather likely'.

Source: Eurofound, 2018 (own calculations; unweighted).

Table 5.4: Logistic regression to explain job loss worry among older workers, aged 50–64, 2016

	M1	M2	M3
Regime (ref.: social-democratic)			
Liberal	−0.009	−0.015	−0.033★
	(0.014)	(0.013)	(0.014)
Conservative	−0.035★	−0.042★	−0.041★
	(0.016)	(0.013)+	(0.013)
			+
Southern	0.014	−0.007	−0.020
	(0.021)	(0.020)	(0.017)
Eastern (embedded)	0.041★	0.028	0.029+
	(0.018)	(0.019)	(0.017)
Eastern (neoliberal)	0.083★★	0.090★★	0.090★★
	(0.027)	(0.030)	(0.028)
Socio-demographic controls			
Gender: female (ref.: male)		−0.024+	−0.025+
		(0.013)	(0.013)
Education: medium (ref.: low)		−0.049★★	−0.040★★
		(0.014)	(0.011)
Education: high (ref.: low)		−0.066★★	−0.054★★
		(0.013)	(0.013)
Type of employment			
Non-permanent (ref.: permanent)			0.153★★
			(0.025)
Part-time (ref.: full-time)			0.003
			(0.017)
Nagelkerke-R^2	0.033	0.051	0.096
N	2912	2912	2912

Note: significance levels: ★★<=0.01, ★ <=0.05, + <=0.10.

Source: Eurofound, 2018 (own calculations; unweighted). Average marginal effects. Robust standard errors, clustered by country in paratheses).

levels of job loss worries. This appears to be in line with the descriptive findings of lower levels of job loss worries in many countries. As could be expected, workers with medium or higher educational attainment worry less about a future loss of their job, likely because their higher human capital safeguards their professional position (M2). Women are slightly less worried about job loss, reflecting their higher lower market attachment and their frequent role as secondary earners, particularly among older generations. Notably, these patterns remain consistent even when simultaneously controlling for the type of job (M3). As expected, workers without a permanent contract clearly worry more about their future employment, given the limited duration of their current contract and potential labour market barriers for older employees. No statistically significant effect is found for part-time work. This may be explained by our previous finding that among older workers, part-time employment often reflects rather a voluntary choice and less a forced flexibilization of their employment contract. Overall, the explanatory power of the model is rather modest (Nagelkerke-R^2=0.096), suggesting that other factors need to be considered when explaining job loss risks.

In the previous analyses, we had looked at older worker's worries about losing their job. Another indicator from the EQLS informs us about the perceived likelihood of re-entering employment once becoming unemployed. This indicator of perceived insecurity in the labour market (see also Chapter 2) asks how likely employees perceive the chance of finding a job of similar salary when becoming unemployed. Table 5.5 first presents descriptive evidence for this indicator (fielded only in the last two EQLS waves 2011 and 2016). Results show that older workers are rather sceptical about their job prospects once becoming unemployed, given that in virtually all countries under study (except Sweden in 2016), only less than half of them expect to find a similar job. However, there are marked cross-country differences in the degree to which they expect this.

Highest expectations of a successful labour market entry for both time points are found in Scandinavian countries, where more than 40 per cent of respondents consider it likely to find a similar job. Similarly high rates are found in liberal countries in 2016, rising from somewhat lower values after the crisis (particularly in Ireland, where percentages have almost doubled since then). Both employment-sustaining regimes thus apparently foster the perceived likelihood of re-entering employment once becoming unemployed, even among older workers. Notably, state-based support through active employment policies seems to make this perception more 'crisis-prone' than the market-based maintenance in liberal countries which makes the perceived insecurity in the labour market more vulnerable to cyclical variations. The opposite picture is found in Southern European countries where across both time points, less than 20 per cent of respondents expect to find a similar job (with the sole exception of Malta where figures on re-employment chances in 2016 appeared to have recovered somewhat). As consistently lower percentages in 2011 suggest, this 'Southern European pessimism' may be due to the economic downturn throughout the economic crisis. Yet, the fact that 2016 figures still remain persistently lower than in other European countries indicates that older workers indeed also perceive the institutional rigidities of Southern European insider-outsider labour markets. Eastern European countries exhibit similar values around the

Table 5.5: Re-employment likelihood among older workers, aged 50–64, 2011–16

Regime	Country	Year	
		2011 (%)	2016 (%)
Social-democratic	Denmark	42.8	45.9
	Finland	40.7	40.9
	Sweden	42.3	59.5
Liberal	Ireland	15.7	41.0
	United Kingdom	39.0	46.0
Conservative	Austria	33.9	35.9
	Belgium	25.6	26.1
	Germany	23.7	30.6
	Francer	31.5	33.3
	Luxembourg	23.6	24.3
	Netherlands	25.5	27.2
Southern	Cyprus	15.8	7.0
	Greece	4.3	9.0
	Spain	13.5	16.4
	Italy	18.5	15.4
	Malta	6.7	26.1
	Portugal	12.8	19.9
Eastern (embedded)	Czech Republic	23.3	30.9
	Poland	19.6	30.1
	Hungary	20.7	37.0
	Slovenia	12.5	21.3
	Slovakia	25.2	20.9
Eastern (neoliberal)	Bulgaria	15.2	31.1
	Croatia	15.3	17.4
	Lithuania	19.3	37.4
	Estonia	25.0	34.2
	Latvia	17.3	30.4
	Romania	24.1	31.6

Note: question asked: 'How likely or unlikely is it that you will find a job of similar salary?', 5-point-scale, Table shows cumulated percentages for 'very likely'/'rather likely'.

Source: Eurofound, 2018 (own calculations; unweighted).

Table 5.6: Logistic regression to explain perceived re-employment chances among older workers, aged 50–64, 2016

	M1	M2	M3
Regime (ref.: social-democratic)			
Liberal	-0.032	-0.033	-0.049
	(0.054)	(0.054)	(0.055)
Conservative	-0.148★	-0.146★★	-0.148★★
	(0.046)	(0.047)	0.048)
Southern	-0.253★★	-0.251★★	-0.253★★
	(0.037)	(0.038)	(0.038=
Eastern (embedded)	-0.185★★	-0.180★★	-0.175★★
	(0.046)	(0.048)	(0.049)
Eastern (neoliberal)	-0.140★★	-0.135★	-0.130★
	(0.041)	(0.052)	(0.053)
Socio-demographic controls			
Gender: female (ref.: male)		-0.012	-0.021
		(0.022)	(0.023)
Education: medium (ref.: low)		-0.017	0.011
		(0.021)	(0.021)
Education: high (ref.: low)		0.013	0.022
		(0.025)	(0.025)
Type of employment			
Non-permanent (ref.: permanent)			0.072★
			(0.029)
Part-time (ref.: full-time)			0.031
			(0.026)
Nagelkerke R^2	0,058	0.059	0.064
N	2912	2912	2912

Note: significance levels: ★★<=0.01, ★ <=0.05.

Source: Eurofound, 2018 (own calculations; unweighted). Average marginal effects. Robust standard errors, clustered by country in parentheses).

crisis but have experienced a stronger recovery in perceived labour market chances up to 2016. Patterns in conservative countries are remarkable: even though a number of these countries have endured the crisis rather well, only around a third or less expect successful labour market re-entry. Apparently, it is also the insider-outsider labour market structure, caused by high levels of employment regulation, that suppresses further optimism of re-employment among older workers in these countries.

Table 5.6 again supplements the descriptive findings with a logistic regression analysis to additionally identify individual level drivers of perceived re-entry chances. Variables and model construction are identical to the previous analyses of job loss worries. Results first confirm the descriptive findings of pronounced regime differences between Scandinavian and liberal regimes, on the one hand, and conservative as well as Southern and Eastern European countries, on the other hand (M1). Notably, individual characteristics of older employees do not seem to strongly influence their perception of potential future re-employment. Neither for the two sexes nor for educational grades, significant differences are found (M2). For the type of job, only workers in non-permanent employment show a higher optimism of re-employment, possibly because of the expectation to find yet another (fixed-term) job that ranges with their current (lower) income than workers in (better paid) permanent employment would expect (M3). All in all, however, it seems to be mainly institutional features that affect older workers perceived labour market chances. The explanatory power of the model again is low, suggesting that other factors would need to be considered additionally.

Insecurity of old age income prospects

Older workers' late employment careers also need to be considered in relation to their future pension consequences. Will contributions made throughout their working life suffice to receive a decent pension once retired? Another EQLS indicator allows us to assess this question in more detail. Exclusively in the last EQLS wave in 2016, respondents were asked to assess whether they worry about not having adequate income in old age.

Figure 5.12 shows the percentage share of those who reported assessing this risk as being rather high (reflected in choosing a value between 6 and 10 on a 10-point scale, ranging from 1 = not worried at all to 10 = extremely worried). It is evident that there are considerable cross-national variations in the degree of old age income worries. In both Scandinavian and liberal countries, less than 50 per cent of employees report such worries. In contrast, more than half of older people in Southern European countries report such worries; in Greece (88.7 per cent) and Spain (82.2 per cent) particularly, the percentage is extraordinarily high. Clearly more than half of respondents are also worried in Eastern European countries while conservative countries reveal a heterogeneous picture, with few worries in Austria, the Netherlands and Luxembourg, and more pronounced worries in Belgium, France and Germany. In general, the differentiation between employment-oriented regimes and those with stronger insider-outsider labour markets – which we found in earlier analyses of job security and re-entry chances – also seems to be reflected in future pension prospects.

In a final regression analysis, we further investigate how far pension prospects are related to employment in atypical work forms. Indeed, earlier literature suggests such a link, highlighting that, for example, women's

Figure 5.12: Perceived worry about not having adequate income in old age of respondents aged 50–64 years, selected countries, 2016

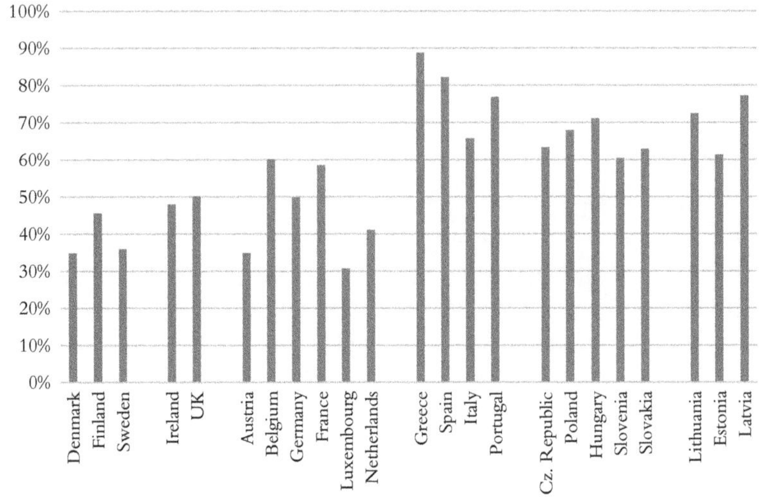

Source: Eurofound, 2018 (own calculations; unweighted).

employment in part-time jobs makes them more prone to lower pension entitlements and thus increases their old age poverty risks (Eurostat, 2019a: 112). Workers in temporary employment may be disadvantaged with regard to additional occupational pensions and also in the public system as they 'less often reach job tenure needed to benefit from the full protection' (OECD, 2019b: 73). Self-employed workers are often not fully covered in pension schemes and thus risk becoming poor in old age (Eurofound, 2017: 52, Höppner 2021). In order to investigate these effects, we construct a logistic regression model with the previously used explanatory variables (see the earlier section on 'Subjectively perceived employment insecurity'). In order to analyse how far those that express job loss worries or perceive their employment chances as being low are also more worried about their future, we also include dummies for the respective variables. Table 5.7 presents the results of our analysis.

The previously observed regime-specific patterns, particularly the very high level of old age income worries in Southern and Eastern European countries, are also reflected in the regression analysis (M1). Model M2 shows that individual characteristics strongly impact on job loss worries. As expected, it is particularly those with higher educational degrees who report lesser pension worries, likely due to their better income situation that increases their pension contributions. Women report higher income worries about old age than men. This may reflect the still persistent traditional gender model among the cohorts under study here, in which the male spouse is

Table 5.7: Logistic regression to explain old age income worries among older workers, aged 50–64, 2016

	M1	M2	M3	M4
Regime (ref.: social-democratic)				
Liberal	0.166**	0.158**	0.155**	0.155**
	(0.036)	(0.037)	(0.038)	(0.036)
Conservative	0.071	0.054	0.054	0.047
	(0.049)	(0.049)	(0.049)	(0.048)
Southern	0.303**	0.270**	0.264**	0.251**
	(0.032)	(0.037)	(0.037)	(0.036)
Eastern (embedded)	0.277**	0.252**	0.246**	0.234**
	(0.030)	(0.033)	80.037)	(0.033)
Eastern (neoliberal)	0.267**	0.258**	0.253**	0.240**
	(0.035)	(0.037)	(0.037)	(0.038)
Socio-demographic controls				
Gender: female (ref.: male)		0.047*	0.055*	0.056*
		(0.022)	(0.024)	(0.024)
Education: medium (ref.: low)		-0.087**	-0.083**	-0.080**
		(0.028)	(0.028)	(0.028)
Education: high (ref.: low)		-0.170**	-0.165**	-0.158**
		(0.031)	(0.030)	(0.031)
Type of employment				
Non-permanent (ref.: permanent)			0.075*	0.065+
			(0.036)	(0.036)
Part-time (ref.: full-time)			-0.038	-0.036
			(0.028)	(0.029)
Subjective (un)certainty				
Job loss worry				0.101**
				(0.032)
Likely to find new job				-0.059**
				(0.021)
Nagelkerke R²	0.100	0.121	0.124	0.133
N	2912	2912	2912	2912

Note: significance levels: **<=0.01, * <=0.05, + <=0.10.

Source: Eurofound, 2018 (own calculations; unweighted). Average marginal effects. Robust standard errors, clustered by country in paratheses).

primarily responsible for a household's earnings and female spouse often earns only a supplementary (part-time) income, reflected in their respective disadvantages in later pension savings. Fixed-term employees show higher levels of pension worries, likely due to their less continuous careers, lower income and lesser pension contributions. Finally, our results show that those concerned about the current security of their job are also those who worry about their later retirement income (M4). Current labour market insecurities thus seems to be closely related to future pension insecurities. This is further corroborated by the finding that it is also those who evaluate their future re-employment chances positively who are more hopeful about their old age income prospects. Another notable finding is that the effect of fixed-term employment remains marginally significant, even after controlling for job loss worries and re-entry prospects. Apparently, it is not only the (subjectively perceived) insecurity associated with these jobs that negatively affects future pension expectations, but also its structural disadvantages (such as lower pay, lesser pension contribution and so on).

Even though from an objective perspective, older workers' employment thus seems to have remained largely secure, those at the margins of employment – such as in fixed-term employment or with no regular contract and those with few qualifications – might find themselves in a precarious position, not only with regard to their current employment, but also regarding their future pension prospects. Considering the results we found for earlier generations, the magnitude of these problems may increase over time. Much more than older workers, younger workers today are being faced with precarious and insecure labour market positions such as fixed-term employment (see Chapter 2). Even though young people are aware of the increasing risks to saving early in their life course, they find it difficult to make such savings under the insecure employment conditions they are being faced with (Hofäcker et al, 2017, 2021). If the employment of these young people remains precarious, they will find it difficult to accumulate enough savings for a decent pension. Even when they find more secure employment in mid-career, they have often foregone important years early in their contribution histories. These trends, as well as the findings reported earlier in this chapter, emphasize that it is of utmost importance to politically address the pension consequences of insecure employment for today's older employees, but even more so for younger cohorts.

Conclusion

This book has analyzed the link between objective and subjective job insecurity along the life courses of individuals. While objective job insecurity had been investigated extensively in previous literature, subjective job insecurity had comparatively received lesser attention. In empirical terms, analyzing job insecurity poses a challenge, given that its nature is multidimensional and it is influenced by a complex set of factors at different levels, individual and collective. Earlier research has either looked on objective or subjective job insecurity separately. We addressed the two dimensions in their own specificity, but also analysed the interplay between objective and subjective factors. We could thus additionally highlight inconsistencies between the two dimensions and their relative incidence. Only in this way can we provide a complete picture of job insecurity across welfare states.

In this book, we have combined quantitative and qualitative data to investigate different aspects of objective and subjective insecurity and to link the two dimensions. The results show that the process that leads to the formation of subjective job insecurity is linked both to macro level factors, associated with the characteristics of the institutional context in which individuals live, and to micro level factors, linked to the demographic and socio-economic characteristics of the individuals which ultimately affect objective conditions and subjective perceptions. Among these features, the macro level of protection of the specific welfare state regime and the individual's perception of their situation with respect to their peers and the previous generation emerge as key drivers to a condition of job insecurity.

The book started with a definition of the field of analysis, providing an overview of existing definitions of objective and subjective employment insecurity (Chapter 1). Along with definitions, the chapter looked at the evolution of theoretical and empirical studies in the field, from the classics to more recent literature dealing with both the macro and micro level factors influencing objective and subjective job insecurity. Based on this overview we elaborated an analytic framework about how the two dimensions vary in relation to institutional characteristics at the macro level, but also how they vary in accordance with different individual characteristics, including age, education and gender.

The empirical chapters focused on the consequences of objective and subjective job insecurity at particular life stages of individuals. Chapter 2 focused on a comparison between young adults and adult workers, Chapter 3 dealt with the consequences of job insecurity on leaving the parental home as a key transition to adult life, Chapter 4 dealt with job insecurity for mid-career workers while Chapter 5 focused on older workers and the consequences of job insecurity in later stages of life.

In this chapter, we provide a summary of the main findings emerging both at macro and micro level.

Summary of key findings at the institutional (macro) level

The mutual interplay of welfare state protection and labour market flexibility in early career

As mentioned, the book focused on both macro and micro level factors that influence the objective and subjective perception of job insecurity. Starting with the former, the analyses presented in the book highlight two key institutional drivers of insecurity that impact on individuals' life: welfare state protection and labour market flexibility and their mutual combination (Tables 1.1 and 1.2). The comparative analyses of young and adult workers presented in Chapter 2 already highlighted that objective and subjective job insecurity do not always overlap. The analysis of the interrelationship between the objective and subjective dimensions of job insecurity, focusing on some 'inconsistent' profiles where security in one dimension was flanked with insecurity in the other dimension, instead provided a complex picture of the interplay between the two dimensions.

Scandinavian countries generally guarantee low levels of job insecurity and thereby should reduce the risk of individuals of falling into an inconsistent category. Indeed, if high levels of protection are universal and labour market policies actively promote labour market re-entry, overall levels of insecurity are expected to be low. At the same time, even people in objectively uncertain jobs will likely tend to feel secure. Indeed, in most of the analyses in this book, the overall level of insecurity perceived by workers of different ages was often lowest under the social-democratic regime. However, particularly when looking at the inconsistent profiles, this was verified to a lesser extent than initially expected. The number of permanent workers who feel insecure even if they have a secure job (negatively inconsistent group) is indeed lower in the Scandinavian cluster than in other welfare regime configurations. Yet, at the same time, there are no differences between Scandinavian and other countries concerning positive mismatches (high subjective job despite lower objective job security).

This surprising finding could be linked to recent welfare state reforms in Nordic countries through which the conditionality for access to social protection and unemployment benefits has increased (Hussain et al, 2012; Burroni, 2016). Furthermore, involuntary nonstandard work is very high in the Nordic countries, and there exists notable segmentation between local and immigrant workers (Friberg and Eldring, 2013). As a consequence, the perception of insecurity has likely increased for these workers, and only people inside the 'core' labour market still perceived themselves as protected.

The liberal Anglo-Saxon welfare regime had been described as similarly protective against subjective job insecurity, yet according to market-based mechanisms (Ebralidze, 2011). If levels of protection are low, but labour markets are highly flexible (as in countries with a liberal market economy), overall levels of subjective insecurity are also low. Given that job insecurity can be more easily overcome, even people in objectively uncertain jobs tend to feel secure. Our results confirm that in these countries, youth and young adult workers in permanent positions are comparatively protected from subjective job insecurity, compared to other systems. Notably, even adult employees with temporary contracts have higher chances of being 'confident' (namely, falling into the profile of positive mismatch) than their Scandinavian peers. It can be argued that the tradition of flexibility and high mobility in the labour market may contribute to such a result, as it makes job loss less consequential and allows for a quick labour market re-entry.

On the other side, the two other welfare state models, the Southern European and the Eastern European regime, were considered countries where the level of subjective job insecurity is very high mainly due to the presence of very strained or segmented labour market. Indeed, if labour markets are inflexible (as in the case of Southern European, Eastern European and conservative countries) or characterized by high unemployment (Eastern European and Southern European countries), then low protection translates directly into high levels of job insecurity. This applies even for those in objectively secure positions, who feel less secure than in other regimes (negatively inconsistent profiles). In a certain sense, nobody can feel permanently secure in these regimes. Our results show that this holds true particularly for workers in the Southern European cluster, who have a higher probability of being negatively inconsistent, indicating that workers perceive greater job insecurity even if working in permanent contracts. For employees with temporary contracts, the share of those feeling subjectively secure is comparable to that of their peers in social-democratic countries. Similarly, in Eastern European countries (both Baltic and Central Eastern European), both young and adult workers show a higher likelihood of being negatively mismatched, hence supporting the assumption that the neoliberal regulation of the labour market (widespread in post-socialist countries) while

Table 6.1: Summary of institutional macro level factors influencing job insecurity

	Institutional background		Patterns of insecurity			
	Welfare state protection	Labour market flexibility	Overall level of objective insecurity	Overall level of subjective insecurity	Positively inconsistent (objectively insecure, but subjectively secure)	Negatively inconsistent (objectively secure, but subjectively insecure)
Social-democratic	High	High, through active labour market policies	Low	Low	High	Moderate
Liberal	Low	High, through little regulation	High	Moderately low	High	Low
Conservative	High	Labour market segmentation	Moderate, but segmented	Moderate, but segmented	Low	Moderate, segmented
Southern	Low	Rigid labour markets	High	(Very) high	Low	(Very) high
Eastern	Low	Strained labour markets	High	High	Low	High

Source: own illustration.

labour market problems continue to prevail tends to increase the concern and feeling of insecurity of employees

According to previous research on objective insecurity, even if a decent level of labour protection is present, such as is the case in the conservative welfare regime, job insecurity is expected to be higher when labour markets and access to welfare benefits are segmented. In such a system, the labour market 'outsiders' in particular may feel insecure, while the 'insiders' are comparatively protected. The results showed that the conservative model seems to confirm a protective role for both insiders and outsiders: concerning the chances of exhibiting a negatively inconsistent profile (permanent workers feeling insecure), young and young adult workers in the Conservative cluster have a similar likelihood as compared to their Scandinavian and Anglo-Saxon peers Similarly, the conservative regime appears to be protective even for temporary workers: adult employees with temporary contracts have similar chances of being 'confident' (namely falling into the profile of positive mismatch) than their Scandinavian peers and in general, employees of all ages have higher chances of being confident than their peers in the Southern European countries.

Early career transitions: the significance of other institutional factors

The interplay between quantitative and qualitative data has shown that the degree of welfare state protection and labour market regulation is important, yet is not the only relevant institutional characteristic that influences patterns of job insecurity. In none of the countries investigated did quantitative data reveal a significant difference in the probability of exiting parental home between young people in temporary positions and those in permanent jobs (Chapter 2). Remarkably, there were also no substantial differences in the afore-mentioned probability with regard to individual characteristics within countries. The results suggest that what matters most for leaving the parental home is not the type of job, but rather the mere fact of having one: with the only exception of the Eastern European countries, unemployed individuals always have significantly lower chances of exiting the home of their family of origin.

However, the analyses focused only on the actual behaviour of young people, while the transition to autonomous living is a complex decision. There are additional factors (such as cultural factors, the idea of transition to adult life, availability of informal support, family protection, and so on) that can mediate these influences. In our book, this was demonstrated particularly when the relationship between both objective and subjective job insecurity and the decision to leave parental home and live autonomously from the family of origin was taken into consideration (Chapter 3). Various factors may be at work underneath, influencing these results, and influencing the time and the way in which young people do or do not leave parental home. Indeed, the subsequent qualitative analysis highlighted how social, cultural and institutional factors influence the relationship between job insecurity and housing autonomy in the countries under study. Key factors were the meaning of and the pressure on leaving the parental home, the protection offered by the institutional context, and the level of salaries associated with different types of contracts. Overall, qualitative results showed that, in a first group of countries, the individual self-perception of one's own labour market position affected decisions of leaving the parental home, though in different ways. While in Italy, Poland and Greece, it was connected with the objective level of job insecurity reflected in the type of job, young people in Ukraine and Bulgaria associated their feeling of insecurity more to the (low) income attached to the contract and not to the security of their jobs. In these countries it is easy to find a job, but wages are very low. In a second group of countries, including the UK and Estonia, it was a mix of reasons: not only having a secure job but having enough money that affected the decisions of leaving the parental home. Thirdly, Germany, and to a lesser extent Sweden, were cases where only the institutional context mediated the relationship between job insecurity and housing autonomy. In these cases, perceived job insecurity did not affect the decision to leave the parental home at all, thanks to housing and labour policies for young people that support this transition (such as, unemployment support while looking for a first job looking, rent facilities for young people, and so on).

Taken together, our findings to a certain extent challenge the applicability of classical welfare state typologies in explaining patterns of job insecurity: countries of similar welfare state regimes appear to offer different level of protection in term of subjective job insecurity for youth. In particular, the cluster of Eastern European countries appears to show similarities with the Southern European countries, while being significantly different from liberal or social-democratic countries.

The significance of national institutions in mid- and late career

The analyses in Chapters 4 and 5 have shown that, in contrast to early transitions in private and employment life, both mid-career and late career are characterized by relative stability in employment.

In mid-career, atypical work forms objectively are of relatively modest importance. Particularly for women around childbirth, part-time employment appears to play a significant role. Yet, how secure employment is perceived to be differs between institutional regimes. While in social-democratic countries, active labour market policies and generous welfare state transfers apparently promote low levels of job insecurity, the situation appears to be most critical in Southern European countries where male and female employees show higher job loss and re-employment worries. While the situation in Eastern European countries initially was similar, more recent trends show a decrease in objective labour market insecurities and a respective decline in job loss worries. Conservative countries once again show a pronounced insider-outsider structure when job loss worries are modest from a comparative perspective, yet, re-entry chances once losing employment are viewed more negatively in mid-career.

Finally, the book investigated what will be the long-term consequences of job insecurity along the life course and the perception of older workers' late employment careers in relation to their future retirement consequences (Chapter 5). Findings by and large replicate regime-specific patterns with regard to subjective insecurities and their repercussions for future old-age income prospects. Particularly in Southern and Eastern European countries, such worries are reported among half of the population or more. In contrast, less than half of respondents in both Scandinavian and liberal countries report worries about their old-age income. This is particularly true for those at the margins of employment – such as those in unstable employment or with few qualifications – both of which groups disproportionately report worries about their current employment, but also regarding their future pension prospects.

Putting the intergenerational trends in atypical employment together, this foreshadows critical developments for the future. Given that younger workers in particular are faced with such unstable employment (see Chapters 2 and 3), they will likely have future difficulties in accumulating sufficient pension savings. Even when they find more secure employment in mid-career, they may have foregone contributions to ensure a decent future pension. As argued in Chapter 5, future policies will need to address the pension consequences of insecure employment, particularly for younger cohorts.

Towards a summary of institutional influences

Taking together the results of the book, our results seem to suggest that nation-specific institutions continue to matter. This holds particularly for the overall level of subjective security which is comparatively lowest in social-democratic countries – where generous welfare states buffer the risks of uncertain employment – and liberal countries – where the consequences of labour market insecurity are minimized through a highly flexible labour market in which job loss is less consequential and re-entry is facilitated. Thus, countries of different regimes can offer the same level of feelings of security. Here the combination of labour market regulation and welfare state policies can produce similar effects on youth. Yet, this works only if low levels of protection are complemented with high labour market flexibility (liberal). If labour markets are inflexible (Southern Europe) or characterized by high unemployment (Eastern), then the risk that low protection translates directly into job insecurity is high. Even if there is protection, job insecurity can be high when labour markets and access to welfare benefits are segmented (conservative). Our results also showed that, while it is important to study the interplay between labour market and welfare state institutions, these institutions are embedded in cultural factors which need to be considered further.

Yet, our results also demonstrated that a schematic implementation of a welfare regime typology does not sufficiently address the complex interplay of objective and subjective insecurities. In particular, if we link the inconsistent profiles to the welfare regimes the results seem interesting. Focusing on these kind of profiles, allows us to say that the theories of welfare state regimes (Esping-Andersen, 1990; Ferrera, 1996; Blossfeld et al, 2005, 2011; Burroni et al, 2021) and 'varieties of capitalism' (Hall and Soskice, 2001) seem to explain only in part the perception of job insecurity today. One possible explanation may be that the 2008 financial and economic crisis may have changed the subjective perception of insecurity. Indeed, our results suggest that in all countries and across life-course phases, the economic crisis has led to a rise particularly in unemployment and thus also in subjectively perceived insecurity. Particularly in countries where the economic crisis was perceived most strongly – such as Southern and Eastern Europe – substantial increases in subjective employment insecurity were observed; these remained comparatively high, even after the decline of objective insecurities after the crisis. Yet, in addition to this cyclical effect, there may also be more general societal trends that have changed the perception of insecurity in the countries studied. Such trends may include phenomena such as deunionization, financialization of the economy, globalization, and the digital revolution (Kalleberg and Vallas, 2017), together with recent welfare state reforms. More research will be needed to explore this complex interplay of macro level factors in more detail.

Summary of key findings at the individual level

Our book has also deepened the analysis on individuals' characteristics and identified the major divides across which differences in terms of both objective and subjective job insecurity may be observable. In the following, we provide an overview of the major findings for each of the micro level characteristics identified.

Life phases

Objective and subjective insecurity differ between life phases. They are clearly highest in early career, but significantly decline across age groups. That is partly due to the fact that people tend to establish themselves in the labour market over time. It may, however, also reflect generational differences in the experience of career insecurity (younger cohorts experience more insecurity). Consistently, young people tend to show lower levels of job insecurity related to re-employment opportunities, compared to adult workers. Such optimism may also be due to lower expectations associated with entry jobs, which may not be seen to include the same benefits of jobs in further life stages. Given that individuals currently in unstable employment will become older over the next decades, subjective insecurity (and subjective perceptions) may spread further across age groups (that is, into those then making up the older group). This may also be the case for objective insecurity, given that those in uncertain work conditions in early career may lack material security in later life. Chapter 5 has discussed this with regard to pension savings.

Gender

Not all analyses allowed us to systematically differentiate by gender. Descriptively, the differences in perceived insecurity are rather modest (Chapter 4). However, our results suggest that objective insecurity (insecure jobs) more often translates into subjective insecurity for men (Chapters 3, 4 and 5). This may reflect the still persistent traditional gender model among the cohorts under study here and the persistent cultural expectations of men as major breadwinners of their household.

Human capital

A unique finding in all chapters was that low human capital increases both objective and subjective insecurity, but in some countries, such as Greece or Italy, high levels of education are less protective, according to the type of labour market. Even in the relatively stable life phases (mid-career, Chapter 4, and late career, Chapter 5) results underline the high significance of human capital in avoiding labour market risks. Those with higher education in particular are best able to avoid labour market insecurities and their negative spill-over effects on their quality of life. With regard to pensions, it is particularly those with higher educational degrees who report lesser pension worries, likely due to their better income situation that increases their pension contributions. In contrast, those with low levels of human capital see their disadvantages accumulate over the life course, and such inequalities will increasingly spread also into old age (Chapter 5).

Types of employment

One cannot speak of one type of 'insecure employment', as the analysis of inconsistent profiles demonstrated (Chapter 2). Perceived insecurity is highest among the unemployed (Chapter 2), followed by those on fixed-term contracts and then permanent contracts. However, particularly for the latter two (fixed term versus permanent), their effect depends on the objective insecurity (for example, in terms of wages) respectively the cultural perception associated with these work forms. This is nicely demonstrated in Chapter 3.

In contrast, for older workers, fixed-term employment significantly increases the worry about future pensions. Apparently, it is not only the (subjectively perceived) insecurity associated with these jobs that negatively affects such expectations, but also its structural disadvantages.

Over and above, part-time work is not uniquely viewed as being uncertain. For women, it can mean an opportunity of work-family reconciliation (Chapter 4) while for older workers it can be used as a bridge into retirement (Chapter 5). Thus, both groups do not necessarily regard this work as being uncertain. However, for men, this type of job may contradict their male breadwinner role, and thus it promotes job insecurity among them. (Chapter 4).

Policy implications

Our results also show that it is important to focus on both objective and subjective dimensions of employment (in)security. Their simultaneous consideration provides a more complete picture of employment patterns in modern societies and how they are being perceived by individuals. Our results show that not only the objective insecurity that new, atypical forms of employment entails is important, but also workers' subjective perceptions play an important role for their individual quality of life. Policy makers are thus well-advised to consider these in the future design of their policies.

Our results furthermore show that subjectively perceived insecurity does depend on objective working conditions, but that this link is not perfect. Even workers that are objectively in uncertain employment may feel subjectively safe. Vice versa, workers may feel insecure, even though their job conditions are objectively safe. This finding highlights that it is not necessarily the formal introduction of new work forms that creates insecurity, but the way in which such work forms are being regulated and how their consequences are being mediated. In countries, where being in atypical work is not considered as an existential threat, individual worries and their respective spill-over effects for the individual appear to be less pronounced. Our results suggest that that there are apparently two alternative institutional approaches to achieve this aim. One is active state support that buffers the consequences of atypical work through active labour market policies and generous public transfers. The other, alternative, solution is the guarantee of a flexible labour market in which job losses may occur but are often compensated through favourable re-entry chances into employment. The question of which of these solutions a country may opt for will not only depend on its general political orientation, but will also need to consider the broader institutional and cultural or normative context in which such policies are being embedded.

Our results also suggest that job insecurity depends largely on internal differences *within* each country rather than on perceived differences *between* countries. Individuals frequently compare themselves with other workers in the same country, not with workers in other countries, as the qualitative analyses especially showed; here it emerges that young generations tend to compare themselves more often with previous generations than with their peers in other European countries. If people are excluded from access to welfare benefits (as they are only provided to those in regular and permanent employment) or do not enjoy labour market protection in less regulated work forms, they may feel very insecure as compared to 'regular workers', even if their objective job insecurity is higher compared to people in countries with low institutional protection. Politically, this may mean that it is not the introduction of public support per se that is important, but rather that avoiding the formation of a group of disadvantaged 'outsiders' is central. Universal and inclusive, rather than group-specific or clientelist policies may be better able to achieve this aim. Our results have shown that particular attention in this respect needs to be paid to those at the margins, particularly those with lower education who may be in need of specific support programmes in order to achieve similar levels of security.

Finally, our results have also shown that job insecurity is a societal problem that spans across generations. Not least due to the greater impact on them of atypical employment, it is a key question for youth. Our results show the role that objective and subjective job (in)security plays for their autonomy. For them, having a job is a central question and more important than being financially buffered through financial benefits. To solve the situation for youth, active labour market policies should play a greater role than passive ones. Against this background, the EU initiative to provide a 'Job Guarantee' appears to be a move in the right direction. At the same time, our results also show that the focus should not be on youth and the early life course alone. Our results show that even though statistically, objective insecurity plays a lesser role for mid-career and older workers, subjective (in)security is still an important issue. This holds particularly for older workers, who fear deficits in their old age security when being faced with (objective or subjective) labour market insecurities. This problem will become even more important, given that future retirees (that is, today's youth), particularly those with lower educational or occupational resources, will look back on much more fragile and segmented careers than previous generations. Future pension policies will need to consider these changes in employment lives when reforming their pension systems. Policy makers thus will have to pay attention to future inequalities in building policies for better future social sustainability.

Notes

Chapter 2

[1]   Data for subjective job insecurity are available through the EQLS survey, whose latest available wave is that of 2016, therefore we are not able to observe any recent change associated with the COVID-19 pandemic.

Chapter 3

[1]   Germany is excluded from quantitative analyses since longitudinal data are only available for a limited number of years (waves EU-SILC18 and EU-SILC19) resulting in a very small number of observable exits, ultimately preventing robust analyses. Ukraine is also excluded from quantitative analysis because it is not available in the EU-SILC panel data.

[2]   These interviews had been collected during the Expect Project (Horizon 2020) 'Social exclusion of youth in Europe', coordinated by Marge Unt and Michael Gebel and founded by European Union's Horizon 2020 research and innovation programme under grant agreement No 649496. For other results of the project see Unt and alt, 2021.

Chapter 4

[1]   This age range was chosen to avoid potential overlaps with the subsequent analysis in Chapter 5 on older employees, which employs an age range of 50–64 years.

[2]   In line with previous descriptive analyses, variables were constructed to differentiate those perceiving their risk of job loss as being 'very likely' or 'rather likely' respectively those who find it 'very likely' or 'rather likely' to find a job of similar salary from all other respondents.

[3]   Note, however, that, given the comparatively small number of countries under consideration, the estimated models need to be treated with a certain care.

[4]   The respective questions referred to satisfaction with 'your current job', 'your present standard of living' and 'your family life'.

Chapter 5

[1]   Aggregate figures are hard to straightforwardly interpret, given that, for the age group under study, the general rise in women's employment rates over time (see also Chapter 5) and the early retirement trend of the 1980/980s overlap. The general retirement trends described for men can, however, broadly be generalised for women as well.

[2]   The only notable exception is Malta where involuntary part-time has remained low. The reason for this Maltese peculiarity may be that unemployment in Malta has remained comparatively low, both among older workers and the overall workforce. Women thus more often opt for part-time work as a way of increasing their flexibility in employment (Vella, 2008).

3   Non-permanent employment combines both fixed-term employment and employment without a contract.

4   In line with the classical ILO definition, part-time employment was classified as employment of 30 hours or less per week.

5   We do not consider self-employment in this and the following analysis, given that the logic of a 'job loss' or 're-employment' is not a reasonable concept for the self-employed.

References

Abbiati, G. (2012). Instabilità, Precarietà, Insicurezza: Cosa Si Intende Quando Si Parla di 'Insicurezza' del Lavoro? *Stato e Mercato*, no. 2/2012.

Allmendinger, J. (1989). Educational Systems and Labour Market Outcomes. *European Sociological Review*, 5(3), 231–50.

Anderson, C.J. and Pontusson, J. (2007). Workers, Worries and Welfare States: Social Protection and Job Insecurity in 15 OECD Countries. *European Journal of Political Research*, 46(2), 211–35.

Athanasiades, C., Deliyanni-Kouimtzi, V., Figgou, L., Flouli, A., and Sourvinou, M. (2017). *Young Adults In Insecure Labour Market Positions in Greece – The Results from a Qualitative Study* (WP No 22.; EXCEPT Working Papers). Tallinn University.

Azmat, G., Güell, M., and Manning, A. (2006). Gender Gaps in Unemployment Rates in OECD Countries. *Journal of Labor Economics*, 24(1), 1–37.

Balz, A. (2017). Cross-National Variations in the Security Gap: Perceived Job Insecurity among Temporary and Permanent Employees and Employment Protection Legislation. *European Sociological Review*, 33(5), 675–92.

Baranowska-Rataj A., Bertolini S., Ghislieri, C., Meo, A., Moiso V., Ricucci R., et al (2015). *Becoming Adult in Hard Times: Current and Future Issues on Job Insecurity and Autonomy*. Torino: Accademia University Press.

Barbera, F., Bertolini, S., Dancelli, M., and Ferragutti, P. (2007). Flessibilità del Lavoro, Trasmissione della Ricchezza e Investimenti sul Territorio. In M. Dancelli (ed) *Osservatorio del Nord Ovest. Rapporti focalizzati*. Carocci, 45–63.

Barbieri, P. (2011). Italy: No Country for Young Men (and Women): The Italian Way of Coping with Increasing Demands for Labour Market Flexibility and Rising Welfare Problems. In H.P. Blossfeld, S. Buchholz, D. Hofäcker, and K. Kolb (eds) *Globalized Labour Markets and Social Inequality in Europe*. London: Palgrave Macmillan, 108–145.

Barbieri, P. and Scherer, S. (2005). Le Conseguenze Sociali della Flessibilizzazione del Mercato del Lavoro in Italia. *Stato e Mercato*, 2, 291.

Barbieri, P. and Scherer, S. (2009). Labour Market Flexibilization and Its Consequences in Italy. *European Sociological Review*, 25(6), 677–92.

Beck, U. (1992) *Risk Society: Towards a New Modernity*. London: Sage Publications.

Bernardi, F. (2006). *Análisis de la Historia de Acontecimientos*. Madrid: Centro de Investigaciones Sociológicas.

Bertolini, S. (2012a). *Flessibilmente Giovani: Percorsi Lavorativi e Transizione alla Vita Adulta nel Nuovo Mercato del Lavoro*. Bologna: Il Mulino.

Bertolini, S. (2012b). La Relazione tra Flessibilizzazione del Mercato del Lavoro e Formazione della Famiglia: Come si Decide in Condizioni di In-certezza Lavorativa. In M. Naldini, C. Solera, and P.M. Torrioni (eds) *Corsi di Vita, Generazioni e Mutamento Sociale*. Bologna: Il Mulino.

Bertolini S. and Hofäcker D. (2023). *Studying the Situation of Youth in Europe: Bringing Together Methodologies for International Comparison*, COST Action CA17114, supported by COST (European Cooperation in Science and Technology). https://www.tlu.ee/sites/default/files/Young-In/WG4%20 Working%20Paper%20Bertolin%20Hofaecker%20(Final%20Version%20 1.03.23.)%20(1).pdf

Bertolini, S. and Goglio, V. (2019). Job Uncertainty and Leaving Parental Home in Italy. Longitudinal Analysis of the Effect of Labour Market Insecurity on Propensity to Leave the Parental Household among Youth. *International Journal of Sociology and Social Policy*, 39(7/8), 574–594.

Bertolini, S., Hofäcker, D., and Torrioni, P. (2018). Labour Market Flexibility and Home-Leaving in Different Welfare States: Does Labour Force and Contractual Status Matter? *Studies of Transition States and Societies*, 10(3), 28–50.

Bertolini, S., Bolzoni, M., Moiso, V., and Musumeci, R. (2018). *The Comparative Qualitative Research Methodology of the EXCEPT Project* (WP No 56; EXCEPT Working Papers). Tallinn University.

Bertolini, S., Musumeci, R., Athanassiades, C., Flouli, A., Deliyanni-Kouimtzi, V., Veneta Krasteva, M., et al (2021). Is Housing Autonomy Still a Step Towards Adulthood in Times of Job Insecurity? In M. Unt, M. Gebel, S. Bertolini, V. Deliyanni-Kouimtzi, and D. Hofaecker (eds) *Social Exclusion of Youth in Europe*. Bristol: Policy Press.

Betti, G., Bettio, F., Georgiadis, T., and Tinios, P. (2015). *Unequal Ageing in Europe: Women's Independence and Pensions*, New York: Palgrave Macmillan.

Bičáková, A. (2016). Gender Unemployment Gaps in the EU: Blame the Family. *IZA Journal of Labour Studies*, 5, 22.

Bicakova, A. and Kaliskova, K. (2021). Career-breaks and Maternal Employment in CEE Countries, *CERGE-EI Working Papers wp706*, The Center for Economic Research and Graduate Education - Economics Institute, Prague.

Bird, P., Campbell-Hall, V., Kakuma, R., and the MHaPP Research Programme Consortium (2013). Cross-national Qualitative Research: The Development and Application of an Analytic Framework in the Mental Health and Poverty Project. *International Journal of Social Research Methodology*, 16(4), 337–49.

Blossfeld, H.-P. and Hofmeister, H. (eds) (2006). *Globalization, Uncertainty and Women's Careers: An International Comparison.* Cheltenham and Northampton, MA: Edward: Elgar.

Blossfeld, H.-P. and Stockmann, R. (1999). The German Dual System in Comparative Perspective. *International Journal of Sociology,* 28(4), 3–28.

Blossfeld, H.-P., Buchholz, S. and Hofäcker, D. (2006). *Globalization, Uncertainty and Late Careers in Society.* London and New York: Routledge.

Blossfeld, H.-P., Buchholz, S., and Kurz, K. (eds) (2011). *Aging Populations, Globalization and the Labor Market.* Cheltenham and Northampton, MA: Edward Elgar.

Blossfeld, H.P., Hofäcker, D., and Bertolini S. (2011) *Youth on Globalised Labour Market. Rising Uncertainty and its Effects on Early Employment and Family lives in Europe.* Opladen: Barbara Budrich.

Blossfeld, H.-P., Mills, M., and Bernardi, F. (eds) (2006). *Globalization, Uncertainty and Men's Careers: An International Comparison.* Cheltenham and Northampton, MA: Edward: Elgar.

Blossfeld, H.-P., Buchholz, S., Hofäcker, D., and Bertolini, S. (2012). Selective Flexibilization and Deregulation of the Labor Market. The Answer of Continental and Southern Europe. *Stato e Mercato,* 3, 363–90.

Blossfeld, H.-P., Buchholz, S., Hofäcker, D., and Kolb, K. (eds) (2011). *Globalized Labour Markets and Social Inequality in Europe.* London: Palgrave Macmillan.

Blossfeld, H.-P., Klijzing, E., Mills, M., and Kurtz, K. (eds) (2005). *Globalization, Uncertainty and Youth in Society.* London and New York: Routledge.

Böckerman, P. (2004). Perception of Job Instability in Europe. *Social Indicators Research,* 67(3), 283–314.

Bohle, D. and Greskovits, B. (2012). *Capitalist Diversity on Europe's Periphery.* Ithaca, NY: Cornell University Press.

Booth, A.L. and van Ours, J.C. (2013). Part-time Jobs: What Women Want? *Journal of Population Economics,* 26, 263–83.

Box-Steffensmeier, J.M. and Jones, B.S. (2004). *Event History Modeling: A Guide for Social Scientists.* Cambridge: University Press.

Breen, R. (1997) Risk, Recommodification and Stratification. *Sociology,* 32(3), 473–89.

Buchholz, S. (2008). *Die Flexibilisierung des Erwerbsverlaufs: Eine Analyse von Einstiegs- und Ausstiegsprozessen in Ost- und Westdeutschland.* Wiesbaden: VS Verlag für Sozialwissenschaften.

Buchholz, S., Hofäcker, D., Mills, M., Blossfeld, H.-P., Kurz, K., and Hofmeister, H. (2009) Life Courses in the Globalization Process: The Development of Social Inequalities in Modern Societies. *European Sociological Review,* 25(1), 53–71.

Bukodi, E. and Róbert, E. (2006) Late Careers and Career Exits in Hungary. In H.-P. Blossfeld, S. Buchholz, and D. Hofäcker (eds) *Globalization, Uncertainty and Late Careers in Society*. London and New York: Routledge, 323–351.

Burroni, L. (2016). *Capitalismi a Confronto: Istituzioni e Regolazione dell'Economia nei Paesi Europei*. Bologna: Il Mulino.

Burroni, L., Pavolini, E., and Regini, M. (eds) (2021). *Mediterranean Capitalism Revisited: One Model, Different Trajectories*. Ithaca, NY: Cornell University Press.

Chung, H. and Mau, S. (2014). Subjective Insecurity and the Role of Institutions. *Journal of European Social Policy*, 24(4), 303–18.

Chung, H. and van Oorschot, W. (2010). Employment Insecurity of European Individuals during the Financial Crisis: A Multi-level Approach. *Working Papers on the Reconciliation of Work and Welfare in Europe*. University of Edinburgh, REC-WP 14/2010. https://nbn-resolving.org/urn:nbn:de:0168-ssoar-197964

Chung, H. and van Oorschot, W. (2011). Institutions versus Market Forces: Explaining the Employment Insecurity of European Individuals during (the Beginning of) the Financial Crisis. *Journal of European Social Policy*, 21(4), 287–301.

Cipollone, A., Patacchini, E. and Vallanti, G. (2014). Female Labour Market Participation in Europe: Novel Evidence on Trends and Shaping Factors. *IZA Journal of Labor Studies*, 3, 18.

Clark, A. and Postel-Vinay, F. (2009). Job Security and Job Protection. *Oxford Economic Papers*, 61(2), 207–39.

Delsen, L. (1990). Part-time Early Retirement in Europe. *The Geneva Papers on Risk and Insurance: Issues and Practice*, 15(2), 139–57.

Denia, A. and Guilló, M.D. (2019). The Gender Gap in Involuntary Part-time Employment: The Case of Spain. *International Journal of Business and Social Science*, 12(10), 169–82.

De Witte, H. (2010). Job Insecurity and Psychological Well-being: Review of the Literature and Exploration of Some Unresolved Issues. *European Journal of Work and Organizational Psychology*, 8(2), 155–77.

Di Mauro, C. and Musumeci, R. (2011). Linking Risk Aversion and Type of Employment. *The Journal of Socio-Economics*, 40(5), 490–5.

Dixon, J.C., Fullerton, A.S., and Robertson, D.L. (2013). Cross-national Differences in Workers' Perceived Job, Labour Market, and Employment Insecurity in Europe: Empirical Tests and Theoretical Extensions. *European Sociological Review*, 29(5), 1053–67.

Doeringer, P.B. (1990). Economic Security, Labor Market Flexibility, and Bridges to Retirement. In P.B. Doeringer (ed) *Bridges to Retirement*. Ithaca, NY: Cornell University IRL Press, 3–22.

Ebbinghaus, B. (2006). *Reforming Early Retirement in Europe, Japan and the USA*. Oxford: Oxford University Press.

Ebbinghaus, B. and Hofäcker, D. (2013). Reversing Early Retirement in Advanced Welfare Economies: A Paradigm Shift to Overcome Push and Pull Factors. *Comparative Population Studies*, 38(4), 807–40.

Ebralidze, E. (2011). Labor Market Regulation and Perceived Job Insecurities in the Early Career – Do Danish Employees Worry Less? In H.-P. Blossfeld, D. Hofäcker, and S. Bertolini (eds) *Youth on Globalized Labour Markets*. Opladen: Barbara Budrich, 93–118.

Erlinghagen, M. (2008). Self-perceived Job Insecurity and Social Context: A Multi-level Analysis of 17 European Countries. *European Sociological Review*, 24(2), 183–97.

Esping-Andersen, G. (1990). *The Three Worlds of Welfare Capitalism*. Princeton: Princeton University Press.

Esping-Andersen, G. (1999). *Social Foundations of Postindustrial Societies*. Oxford: Oxford University Press.

Eurofound (2012). *European Quality of Life Survey (EQLS)*. https://www.eurofound.europa.eu/surveys/european-quality-of-life-surveys/european-quality-of-life-survey-2016

Eurofound [European Foundation for the Improvement of Living and Working Conditions] (2014). *Mapping Youth Transitions in Europe*. Luxembourg: Publications Office of the European Union.

Eurofound [European Foundation for the Improvement of Living and Working Conditions] (2016). *The Gender Employment Gap: Challenges and Solutions*. Luxembourg: Publications Office of the European Union.

Eurofound [European Foundation for the Improvement of Living and Working Conditions] (2017). *Exploring Self-employment in the European Union*. Luxembourg: Publications Office of the European Union.

Eurofound [European Foundation for the Improvement of Living and Working Conditions] (2018). *European Quality of Life Survey Integrated Data File, 2003–2016* [data collection] (3rd edition). UK Data Service. SN: 7348.

Eurostat (2008). Employment Gender Gap in the EU is Narrowing: Labour Market Trends 2000–2007, *Statistics in Focus*, 99/2008. Luxembourg: Office for Official Publications of the European Communities.

Eurostat (2012). *EU Statistics on Income and Living Conditions (EU-SILC)*.

Eurostat (2019a). *Ageing Europe: Looking at the Lives of Older People in Europe – 2019 Edition*. Luxembourg: Publications Office of the European Union.

Eurostat (2019b). *EU Statistics on Income and Living Conditions. (EU-SILC)*.

Eurostat (2019c). *How Do Women and Men Use Their Time? Statistics Explained*. https://ec.europa.eu/eurostatstatistics-explained/index.php?title=How_do_women_and_men_use_their_time_-_statistics&oldid=463738#Overview

Eurostat (2020). *The Life of Women and Men in Europe – A Statistical Portrait.* https://ec.europa.eu/eurostat/cache/infographs/womenmen_2020/index.html?lang=en

Eurostat (2021a). *Self-employment by Sex, Age and Citizenship.* https://appsso.eurostat.ec.europa.eu/nui/show.do?dataset=lfsa_esgan&lang=en

Eurostat (2021b). *Youth Long-term Unemployment Rate (12 Months or Longer) by Sex and Age.* https://ec.europa.eu/eurostat/databrowser/view/yth_empl_120/default/table?lang=en

Eurostat (2021c). *Unemployment Rate, by Age Group.* https://ec.europa.eu/eurostat/databrowser/view/une_rt_a/default/table?lang=en

Eurostat (2021d). *Share of Young Temporary Employees, by Age Group.* https://ec.europa.eu/euros tat/data browser/view/yth_empl_050/default/table?lang=en

Fenger, H.J.M. (2007). Welfare Regimes in Central and Eastern Europe: Incorporating Post-Communist Countries in a Welfare Regime Typology. *Contemporary Issues and Ideas in Social Sciences*, 3(2), 1–30.

Ferragina, E. (2019). Does Family Policy Influence Women's Employment? Reviewing the Evidence in the Field. *Political Studies Review*, 17(1), 65–80.

Ferrera, M. (1996). The 'Southern Model' of Welfare in Social Europe. *Journal of European Social Policy*, 6(1), 17–37.

Filandri, M. and Bertolini S. (2016). Young People and Home Ownership in Europe. *International Journal of Housing Policy*, 16(2): 144–64.

Finch, J. (1989). *Family Obligations and Social Change.* Oxford: Polity Press.

Finch, J. (2007). Displaying Families. *Sociology*, 41(1): 65–81.

Flynn, M. and Li, Y. (2016). Employment and Retirement of Older Workers in the UK. In D. Hofäcker, M. Hess, and S. König (eds) *Delaying Retirement: Progress and Challenges of Active Ageing in Europe, the United States and Japan.* London: Palgrave Macmillan, 221–40.

Folkman, S. and Lazarus, R.S. (1985). If It Changes It Must Be a Process: Study of Emotion and Coping during Three Stages of a College Examination. *Journal of Personality and Social Psychology*, 48(1), 150–70.

Friberg, J.H. and Eldring, L. (2013). *Labour Migrants from Central and Eastern Europe in the Nordic Countries: Patterns of Migration, Working Conditions and Recruitment Practices.* Copenhagen: Nordic Council of Ministers.

Friedman, D., Hechter, M., and Kanazawa, S. (1994). A Theory of the Value of Children. *Demography*, 31(3), 375–401.

Fullerton, A.S. and Wallace, M. (2007). Traversing the Flexible Turn: US Workers' Perceptions of Job Security, 1977–2002. *Social Science Research*, 36(1), 201–21.

Fullerton, A.S., Dixon, J.C., and McCollum, D.B. (2020). The Institutionalization of Part-time Work: Cross-national Differences in the Relationship between Part-time Work and Perceived Insecurity. *Social Science Research*, 87 (March): 102402.

Gallie, D. (2017). The Quality of Work in a Changing Labour Market. *Social Policy & Administration*, 51(2), 226–43.

Gallie, D., Felstead, A., Green, F., and Inanc, H. (2016). The Hidden Face of Job Insecurity. *Work, Employment and Society*, 31(1), 36–53.

Gash, V. (2008). Bridge or Trap? To What Extent Do Temporary Workers Make More Transitions to Unemployment than to the Standard Employment Contract, *European Sociological Review*, 24(5), 651–68.

Gauthier, A.H., Emery, T., and Bartova, A. (2016). The Labour Market Intentions and Behaviour of Stay-at-home Mothers in Western and Eastern Europe. *Advances in Life Course Research*, (30), 1–15.

Gebel, M. and Giesecke, J. (2016). Does Deregulation Help? The Impact of Employment Protection Reforms on Youths' Unemployment and Temporary Employment Risks in Europe. *European Sociological Review*, 32(4), 486–500.

Giersch, H. (1985). Eurosclerosis, Kieler Diskussionsbeiträge, No. 112, Institut für Weltwirtschaft (IfW), Kiel.

Green, F. (2009). Job Insecurity, Employability, Unemployment and Well-Being. *Studies in Economics*, 0918. School of Economics, University of Kent.

Greenhalgh, L. and Rosenblatt, Z. (1984). Job Insecurity: Toward Conceptual Clarity. *The Academy of Management Review*, 9(3), 438–48.

Grimaldi, A., Ghislieri, C., and Montalbano, G. (2009). Faire Face aux Problèmes de Travail: Un Questionnaire Italien. *L'Orientation Scolaire et Professionnelle*, 38(11), 97–111.

Grönlund, A., Halldén, K., and Magnusson, C. (2017). A Scandinavian Success Story? Women's Labour Market Outcomes in Denmark, Finland, Norway and Sweden. *Acta Sociologica*, 60(2), 97–119.

Gruber, J. and Wise, D. (1999). *Social Security and Retirement around the World*. Chicago: Chicago University Press.

Gruber, J. and Wise, D. (2004). *Social Security Programs and Retirement around the World: Micro-estimation*. Chicago: Chicago University Press.

Guillemard, A.-M. (1991). Die Destandardisierung des Lebenslaufs in den Europäischen Wohlfahrtsstaaten. *Zeitschrift für Sozialreform*, 37(2); 620–39.

Hall, P.A. and Soskice, D. (2001). *Varieties of Capitalism: The Institutional Foundations of Comparative Advantage*. Oxford: Oxford University Press.

Hantrais, L. (2009). *International Comparative Research: Theory, Methods and Practice*. Basingstoke and New York: Palgrave Macmillan.

Hatfield, I. (2015). *Self-employment in Europe*. London: Institute for Public Policy Research (IPPR). http://www.ippr.org/publications/self-employment-in-europe

Hess, M. (2018). Expected and Preferred Retirement Age in Germany. *Zeitschrift für Gerontologie und Geriatrie*, 51(1), 98–104.

Hipp, L. (2016). Insecure Times? Workers' Perceived Job and Labor Market Security in 23 OECD Countries. *Social Science Research*, 60 (November), 1–14.

Hofäcker, D. (2006). Women's Employment in Times of Globalization: A Comparative Overview. In H.-P. Blossfeld and H. Hofmeister (eds) *Globalization, Uncertainty and Women's Careers. An International Comparison.* Cheltenham and Northampton, MA: Edward Elgar, 32–58.

Hofäcker, D. (2010). *Older Workers in a Globalizing World: An International Comparison of Retirement and Late-Career Patterns in Western Industrialized Countries.* Cheltenham and Northampton, MA: Edward Elgar.

Hofäcker, D. and Blossfeld, H.-P. (2011). Globalization, Uncertainty and its Effects on Early Family and Employment Lives: An Introduction. In H.-P. Blossfeld, D. Hofäcker, and S. Bertolini (eds) *Youth on Globalised Labour Market: Rising Uncertainty and Its Effects on Early Employment and Family Lives in Europe.* Opladen: Barbara Budrich, 9–38.

Hofäcker, D., Hess, M., and König, S. (2016). *Delaying Retirement: Progress and Challenges of Active Ageing in Europe, the United States and Japan.* London: Palgrave Macmillan.

Hofäcker, D., Hess, M., and König, S. (2019). Wandel von Ruhestandsübergängen im Politischen Paradigmenwechsel Europas. *Zeitschrift für Gerontologie und Geriatrie*, 52(Supplement 1), 40–51.

Hofäcker, D., Neumann-Schmidt, I., and Braun, S. (2018). *Objective and Subjective Measures of Poverty. A Pan-European Comparison of Patterns and Determinants.* SSM Seminar on Multidimensional Poverty, Brussels.

Hofäcker, D., Schadow, S., and Kletzing, J. (eds) (2017). Long-term Socio-economic Consequences of Insecure Labour Market Positions, *EXCEPT Working Papers*, WP No 16. Tallinn: Tallinn University.

Hofäcker, D., Schadow, S., and Kletzing, J. (2021). Syntheses of Long-term Socio-economic Consequences of Insecure Labour Market Positions for Youth in Europe. In M. Unt, M. Gebel, S. Bertolini, V. Deliyanni- Kouimtzi, and D. Hofäcker (eds) *Social Exclusion of Youth in Europe: The Multifaceted Consequences of Labour Market Insecurity.* Bristol: Policy Press, 340–60.

Hofäcker, D., Stoilova, R., and Riebling, J.R. (2013). The Gendered Division of Paid and Unpaid Work in Different Institutional Regimes: Comparing West Germany, East Germany and Bulgaria. *European Sociological Review*, 29(2), 192–209.

Höppner, J. (2021). How Does Self-employment Affect Pension Income? A Comparative Analysis of European Welfare States. *Social Policy & Administration*, 55(5), 921–39.

Horemans, J. and Marx, I. (2017). Poverty and Material Deprivation among the Self-Employed in Europe: An Exploration of a Relatively Uncharted Landscape, *IZA Discussion Papers* No. 11007. Bonn: IZA – Institute of Labor Economics.

Horemans, J., Marx, I., and Nolan, B. (2016). Hanging In, But Only Just: Part-time Employment and In-work Poverty Throughout the Crisis. *IZA Journal of Labor Studies*, 5(5).

Hussain, A., Kangas, O., and Kvist, J. (2012). Welfare State Institutions, Unemployment and Poverty: Comparative Analysis of Unemployment Benefits and Labour Market Participation in 15 European Union Countries. In J. Kvist, J. Fritzel, B. Hvinden, and O. Kangas (eds) *Changing Social Equality: The Nordic Welfare Model in the 21st Century*. Bristol: Policy Press, 119–42.

Inanc, H. (2012). Labour Market Insecurity and Family Relations in the United Kingdom. PhD, University of Oxford.

ISSP Research Group (2017). International Social Survey Programme: Work Orientations IV – ISSP 2015. GESIS Data Archive, Cologne. ZA6770 Data file Version 2.1.0. https://doi.org/10.4232/1.12848

Jansen, M. (2011). Employment Insecurity and Its Repercussions on Family Formation: A Theoretical Framework. In H.-P. Blossfeld, D. Hofäcker, and S. Bertolini (eds) *Youth on Globalised Labour Markets: Rising Uncertainty and Its Effects on Early Employment and Family Lives in Europe*. Opladen: Barbara Budrich, 9–38.

Kalleberg, A.L. (2018). *Precarious Lives: Job Insecurity and Well-Being in Rich Democracies*. Cambridge and Medford, MA: Polity Press.

Kalleberg, A.L. and Vallas, S.P. (eds) (2017). *Precarious Work*. Bingley: Emerald Publishing.

Karamessini, M., Symeonaki, M., Parsanoglou, D., and Stamatopoulou, G. (2019). Mapping Early Job Insecurity Impacts of the Crisis in Europe. In B. Hvinden, C. Hyggen, M.A Schoyen, and T. Sirovátka (eds) *Youth Unemployment and Job Insecurity in Europe: Problems, Risk Factors and Policies*. Cheltenham, UK and Northampton, MA: Edward Elgar, 24–44.

Kiersztyn, A. (2017). Non-standard Employment and Subjective Insecurity: How Can We Capture Job Precarity Using Survey Data? In A.L. Kalleberg and S.P. Vallas (eds) *Precarious Work*. Bingley: Emerald Publishing, 91–122.

Klijzing, E. (2005). Globalization and the Early Life Course. In H.P. Blossfeld, E. Klijzing, M. Mills, and K. Kurz (eds) *Globalization, Uncertainty and Youth in Society: The Losers in a Globalizing World*. London and New York: Routledge, 25–49.

Kohli, M. (1985). Die Institutionalisierung des Lebenslaufs: Historische Befunde und Theoretische Argumente. *Kölner Zeitschrift für Soziologie und Sozialpsychologie*, 37(1), 1–29.

Kohli, M., Rein, M., Guillemard, A.-M., and van Gunsteren, H. (1991). *Time for Retirement: Comparative Studies of Early Exit from the Labor Force*, Cambridge and New York: Cambridge University Press.

Krasteva, V., Jeliazkova, M., and Draganov, D. (2018). *Young Adults in Insecure Labour Market Positions in Bulgaria – The Results from a Qualitative Study* (WP No. 20; EXCEPT Working Papers). Tallinn University.

Kubicki, P., Stasiowski, J., and Włodarczyk, Z. (2017). *Young Adults in Insecure Labour Market Positions in Poland – The Results from a Qualitative Study* (WP No 21; EXCEPT Working Papers). Tallinn University.

Kuroki, M. (2012). The Deregulation of Temporary Employment and Workers' Perceptions of Job Insecurity. *Industrial and Labor Relations Review*, 65(3), 560–77.

Lambert, S.J., Henly, J.R., and Kim, J. (2019). Precarious Work Schedules as a Source of Economic Insecurity and Institutional Distrust. *RSF: The Russell Sage Foundation Journal of the Social Sciences*, 5(4), 218.

Lazarus, R.S. and Folkman, S. (1987). Transactional Theory and Research on Emotions and Coping. *European Journal of Personality*, 1(3), 141–69.

Leeper, T.J. (2018). *Interpreting Regression Results using Average Marginal Effects with R's Margins*. https://cran.r-project.org/web/packages/margins/vignettes/TechnicalDetails.pdf

Lewandowski, P., Góra, M., and Lis, M. (2017). Temporary Employment Boom in Poland – A job quality vs. Quantity Tradeoff? Working paper. Warsaw: IBS Institute for Structural Research.

Lindbeck, A. and Snower, D.J. (1988). *The Insider-Outsider Theory of Employment and Unemployment*. Cambridge MA: MIT Press.

Lippke, S. Strack, J., and Staudinger, U.M. (2015). Erwerbstätigkeitsprofile von 55- bis 70-Jährigen. In N.F. Schneider, A. Mergenthaler, U.M. Staudinger, and I. Sackreuther (eds) *Mittendrin? Lebenspläne und Potentiale älterer Menschen beim Übergang in den Ruhestand, Beiträge zur Bevölkerungswissenschaft 47*. Opladen: Barbara Budrich, 67–94.

Livingston, S. and Hasebrink, U. (2010). Designing a European Project on Child Internet Safety: Reflections on Comparative Research in Practice. In L. Weibull (ed) *Nordicom*. Gothenburg: University of Gothenburg, 135–48.

Lobodzinska, B. (1996). Women's Employment or Return to 'Family Values' in Central-Eastern Europe. *Journal of Comparative Family Studies*, 27(3), 519–44.

Lübke, C. and Erlinghagen, M. (2014). Self-Perceived Job Insecurity across Europe over Time: Does Changing Context Matter? *Journal of European Social Policy*, 24(4), 319–36.

Lück, D. (2006). Cross-national Comparison of Gender Role Attitudes and Their Impact on Women's Life Courses. In H.-P. Blossfeld and H. Hofmeister (eds) *Globalization, Uncertainty and Women's Careers. An International Comparison*. Cheltenham and Northampton, MA: Edward Elgar, 405–32.

Ma, T. (2010). Attitudes toward Female Labor Force Participation in Eastern and Western Europe. *Journal of the Washington Institute of China Studies*, 4(4), 35–47.

Maestripieri, L. and León, M. (2019). So Close, So Far? Part-time Employment and Its Effects on Gender Equality in Italy and Spain. In H. Nicolaisen, H.C. Kavli, and R. Steen Jensen (eds) *Dualization of Part-time Work. The Development of Labour Market Insiders and Outsiders*. Bristol: Policy Press, 55–83.

Mayer, K.U. and Schoepflin, U. (1989). The State and the Life Course. *Annual Review of Sociology*, 15, 187–209.

Mills, M. (2011). *Introducing Survival and Event History Analysis*. Los Angeles: SAGE.

Mills, M.C., Blossfeld, H.P., and Klijzing, E. (2005). Becoming an Adult in Uncertain Times: A 14-country Comparison of the Losers of Globalization. In H.P. Blossfeld, E. Klijzing, M. Mills, and K. Kurz (eds) *Globalization, Uncertainty and Youth in Society*. London and New York: Routledge, 393–411.

Mückenberger, U. (1985). Die Krise des Normalarbeitsverhältnisses. *Zeitschrift für Sozialreform*, 7, 8, 415 ff., 457 ff.

Naldini, M. (2003). *The Family in the Mediterranean Welfare States*. London and Portland, ORPortland: Frank Cass.

Naldini, M., Pavolini, E., and Solera, C. (2016). Female Employment and Elderly Care: The Role of Care Policies and Culture in 21 European Countries. *Work, Employment & Society*, 30(4), 607–30.

Näswall, K. and De Witte, H. (2003). Who Feels Insecure in Europe? Predicting Job Insecurity from Background Variables. *Economic and Industrial Democracy*, 24(2), 189–215.

Nazio, T. (2008). *Cohabitation, Family and Society*. New York and London: Routledge.

Nazio, T. and Blossfeld, H.-P. (2003). The Diffusion of Cohabitation among Young Women in West Germany, East Germany and Italy. *European Journal of Population/Revue Européenne de Démographie*, 19(1), 47–82.

Neumann, I., Braun, S., and Hofäcker, D. (2018). Explaining the Differences Between Objective and Subjective Poverty: A Pan-European Perspective. In P. Boyadjieva, M. Kanoushev, and M.J. Ivanov (eds) *Inequalities and Social (Dis)integration: In Search of Togetherness*. Sofia: Iztok Zapad, 255–74.

OECD (1997). The Definition of Part-time Work for the Purpose of International Comparisons. *Labour Market and Social Policy*. Occasional Paper No. 22, Paris: OECD.

OECD (2002). Taking the Measure of Temporary Employment. In *OECD Employment Outlook 2002*. Paris: OECD, 127–85.

OECD (2010). How Good is Part-time Work? *OECD Employment Outlook 2010: Moving Beyond the Jobs Crisis*. Paris: OECD, 211–66.

OECD (2012). Gender Equality in Employment. *Closing the Gender Gap: Act Now*. Paris: OECD, 149–269.

OECD (2014). Non-regular Employment, Job Security and the Labour Market Divide. *OECD Employment Outlook 2014*. Paris: OECD, 141–209.

OECD (2019a). *Part-time and Partly Equal: Gender and Work in the Netherlands.* Paris: OECD.

OECD (2019b). *Pensions at a Glance 2019: OECD and G20 Indicators.* Paris: OECD.

OECD (2020) Recent Trends in Employment Protection Legislation. *OECD Employment Outlook 2020: Worker Security and the COVID-19 Crisis.* Paris: OECD.

OECD (2021a). *OECD Labour Force Statistics.* https://stats.oecd.org/

OECD (2021b). *OECD Family Data Base.* https://www.oecd.org/els/fam ily/database.htm

OECD (2021c). *Youth Not in Employment, Education or Training (NEET).* Paris: OECD.

OECD (2021d) *Pensions at a Glance 2021: OECD and G20 Indicators.* Paris: OECD.

Oppenheimer, V.K. (1994). Women's Rising Employment and the Future of the Family in Industrial Societies. *Population and Development Review,* 20(2), 293–342.

Ostner, I. and Lewis, J. (1995). Gender and the Evolution of European Social Policies. In S. Leibfried and P. Pierson (eds) *European Social Policy: Between Fragmentation and Integration.* Washington: The Brookings Institution, 159–93.

Petrogiannis, K. (2011). Conceptions of the Transition to Adulthood in a Sample of Greek Higher Education Students. *International Journal of Psychology,* 11(1), 121–37.

Pfau-Effinger, B. (2012). Women's Employment in Institutional and Cultural Context. *International Journal of Sociology and Social Policy,* 32(9), 530–43.

Pfau-Effinger, B. and Smidt, M. (2011). Differences in Women's Employment Patterns and Family Policies: Eastern and Western Germany. *Community, Work & Family,* 14(2), 217–32.

Quilgars, D., Elsinga, M., Jones, A., Toussaint, J., Ruonavaara, H., and Naumanen, P. (2009). Inside Qualitative, Cross-national Research: Making Methods Transparent in a EU Housing Study. *International Journal of Social Research Methodology,* 12(1), 19–31.

Regini, M. (2000). *Modelli di Capitalismo: Le Risposte Europee alla Sfida della Globalizzazione.* Rome: Laterza.

Reiska, E., Roosmaa, E. L., Oras, K., and Taru, M. (2018). *Young Adults in Insecure Labour Market Positions in Estonia: the Results From a Qualitative Study* (WP No 23; EXCEPT Working Papers). Tallinn University.

Reyneri E. (2017). *Introduzione alla sociologia del mercato del lavoro.* Bologna: Il Mulino.

Richter, A. (2011). *Job Insecurity and Its Consequences: Investigating Moderators, Mediators and Gender.* Department of Psychology, Stockholm University. http://urn.kb.se/resolve?urn=urn:nbn:se:su:diva-63877

Rokicka, M., Kłobuszewska, M., Palczyńska, M., Shapoval, N., and Stasiowski, J. (2015). *Composition and Cumulative Disadvantage of Youth across Europe* (WP No.1; EXCEPT Working Papers). Tallinn University.

Rubenson, K. (2006). The Nordic Model of Lifelong Learning. *Compare: A Journal of Comparative and International Education*, 36(3), 327–41.

Saint-Paul, G. (1996). Exploring the Political Economy of Labour Market Institutions. *Economic Policy*, 23, 265–315.

Salladarré, F., Hlaimi, B., and Wolff, F.C. (2007). Decomposing Gender Differences in Temporary Contracts. *Working Papers*, hal-00174821.

Scherer, S. (2004). Stepping-Stones or Traps? The Consequences of Labour Market Entry Positions on Future Careers in West Germany, Great Britain and Italy. *Work, Employment & Society*,18(2), 369–94.

Schlee, C. (2018). *Youth Employment Policies in Germany* (WP No 52; EXCEPT Working Papers). Tallinn University.

Small, M.L. (2011). How to Conduct a Mixed Methods Study: Recent Trends in a Rapidly Growing Literature. *Annual Review of Sociology*, 37(1), 57–86.

Solera, C. (2009). *Women In and Out of Paid Work: Changes across Generations in Italy and Britain*. Bristol: Policy Press.

Sologub, I., Nikolaieva, O., and Vakhitova, H. (2018). *Youth Employment Policies in Ukraine* (WP No 24; EXCEPT Working Papers). Tallinn University.

Stiemke, P. and Heß, M. (2020). Der Zusammenhang zwischen Bildung und der Freiwilligkeit von Erwerbsaustritten. *WSI Mitteilungen*, 73(4), 238–46.

Strandh, M. and Baranowska-Rataj, A. (2018). *Youth Employment Policies in Sweden* (WP No. 50; EXCEPT Working Papers). Tallinn University.

Sverke, M., Hellgren, J., and Näswall, K. (2002). No Security: A Meta-Analysis and Review of Job Insecurity and Its Consequences. *Journal of Occupational Health Psychology*, 7(3), 242–64.

Täht, K. and Saar, E. (2006) Late Careers and Career Exits in Estonia. In H.-P. Blossfeld, S. Buchholz, and D. Hofäcker (eds) *Globalization, Uncertainty and Late Careers in Society*, London and New York: Routledge, 301–22.

Tavora, I. (2012). The Southern European Social Model: Familialism and the High Rates of Female Employment in Portugal. *Journal of European Social Policy*, 22(1), 63–76.

Unt, M., Gebel, M., Bertolini, S., Deliyanni-Kouimtzis, V., and Hofaecker, D. (eds) (2021). *Social Exclusion of Youth in Europe, The Multifaceted Consequences of Labour Market Insecurity*. Bristol: Policy Press.

Vella, L. (2008). Part-time Employment and Social Legislation in Malta. *Bank of Valletta Review*, (38), 29–46.

Visser, J. (2002). The First Part-time Economy in the World: A Model to be Followed? *Journal of European Social Policy*, 12(1), 23–42.

Weisstanner, D. and Armingeon, K. (2021). Redistributive Preferences: Why Actual Income is Ultimately More Important than Perceived Income. *Journal of European Social Policy*. 32(2).

Yoon, Y. (2018). *Youth Employment Policies in United Kingdom* (WP No. 51; EXCEPT Working Papers). Tallinn University.

Index

References to figures are in *italics*; tables are in **bold**